Lecture Notes in Artificial Intelligence   7217

Subseries of Lecture Notes in Computer Science

Louise Dennis   Olivier Boissier
Rafael H. Bordini (Eds.)

Programming
Multi-Agent Systems

9th International Workshop, ProMAS 2011
Taipei, Taiwan, May 3, 2011
Revised Selected Papers

 Springer

Series Editors

Randy Goebel, University of Alberta, Edmonton, Canada
Jörg Siekmann, University of Saarland, Saarbrücken, Germany
Wolfgang Wahlster, DFKI and University of Saarland, Saarbrücken, Germany

Volume Editors

Louise Dennis
University of Liverpool, Department of Computer Science
Ashton Building, Ashton Street
Liverpool, L69 3BX, UK
E-mail: l.a.dennis@liverpool.ac.uk

Olivier Boissier
ENS Mines Saint-Etienne
158 Cours Fauriel
42023, Saint-Etienne, France
E-mail: olivier.boissier@emse.fr

Rafael H. Bordini
PUCRS, Faculty of Informatics (FACIN)
Av. Ipiranga 6681
90619-900 Porto Alegre, RS, Brazil
E-mail: r.bordini@pucrs.br

ISSN 0302-9743   e-ISSN 1611-3349
ISBN 978-3-642-31914-3   e-ISBN 978-3-642-31915-0
DOI 10.1007/978-3-642-31915-0
Springer Heidelberg Dordrecht London New York

Library of Congress Control Number: 2012941921

CR Subject Classification (1998): I.2.11, D.2.4, D.3, D.1, I.2, D.2.1, D.2

LNCS Sublibrary: SL 7 – Artificial Intelligence

Typesetting: Camera-ready by author, data conversion by Scientific Publishing Services, Chennai, India

Printed on acid-free paper

Springer is part of Springer Science+Business Media (www.springer.com)

Preface

These are the proceedings of the International Workshop on Programming Multi-Agent Systems (ProMAS 2011), the ninth of a series of workshops that is aimed at discussion and providing an overview of current state-of-the-art technology for programming multi-agent systems.

The aim of the ProMAS workshop series is to bring together leading researchers from both academia and industry to discuss the design of programming languages and tools to implement multi-agent systems (MAS), as well as to discuss current issues of state-of-the-art technology for programming multi-agent systems, especially when used for the development of industrial-strength applications. In particular, the workshops promote the discussion and exchange of ideas concerning the concepts, properties, requirements, and principles that are an important part of programming technologies for MAS.

Topics include, but are not limited to, programming languages for multi-agent systems; theoretical and practical aspects of multi-agent programming; semantics for multi-agent programming languages; algorithms, techniques, or protocols for multi-agent issues (e.g., coordination, cooperation, negotiation); implementation of social and organizational aspects of multi-agent systems; implementing the environment of multi-agent systems; computational methods for specification and verification of multi-agent systems; and generic tools and infrastructures for multi-agent programming.

The ProMAS workshop is a well-established part of the agents community, having been held in conjunction with the influential AAMAS conference on autonomous agents and multi-agent systems in Melbourne (2003), New York (2004), Utrecht (2005), Hakodate (2006), Honolulu (2007), Estoril (2008), Budapest (2009) and Toronto (2010). The ninth edition was, once again, an AAMAS workshop and was held on May 3 in Taipei, Taiwan. ProMAS 2011 received 12 submissions. These were reviewed by members of the Program Committee and ten papers were accepted for presentation. Of these ten papers, eight appear in this proceedings volume.

In addition to the regular papers presented at the workshop, Pablo Noriega (IIIA-CSIC, Spain) gave an invited talk on programming social intelligence, based on joint work with Michael Luck, Mark d'Inverno, Juan-Antonio Rodríguez-Aguilar and Carles Sierra. The social aspects of multi-agent systems and their application to social simulation are major areas of research and are important areas of cross-fertilizations between the fields.

As in previous editions, the themes addressed in the accepted papers included in this volume range from technical topics such as model checking agent systems to conceptual issues such as the relationship between goals and commitments. We used for the proceedings a structure closely related to the paper sessions as they were held during the workshop, as follows.

Foundations of Agent Programming Languages

The paper by Khan and Lespérance examines the issue of plan selection in BDI agent programming languages. In particular, it examines the issue of selecting plans, in situations where there may be multiple concurrent intentions, in such a way that a selected plan is inconsistent with none of the intentions. This seeks to widen the criteria taken into account during plan selection which, typically, only considers a single intention.

Telang et al. seek to draw a distinction between the concept of goals, commonly used in BDI style languages, and the concept of commitments, which explicitly reference the way one agent relates to another. They present an operational semantics which handles both of these concepts in a way that takes explicit account of inter-agent cooperation.

Multi-Agent Oriented Programming

The paper by Toledo et al. presents a multi-agent application dedicated to knowledge management, built using a new platform, *JaCaMo*, which integrates the various dimensions for creating a multi-agent system: a programming language for individual agents, an organizational language for programming the coordination between the agents, and the environment within which the agents operate. That platform represents an important step toward a properly unified approach to the programming of multi-agent systems as it accounts for the multiple aspects of such systems.

Píbil et al. take an entirely pragmatic approach, presenting the experience of a programmer unfamiliar with BDI-style languages in using the *Jason* implementation of AgentSpeak to construct a non-trivial multi-agent system. This case study raises a number of pragmatic issues ranging from tool support to semantic underpinnings that hinder a novice in using such languages.

The paper by Ranathunga et al. examines expectations as an umbrella concept for organizational ideas such as norms, commitments, and contracts. They describe the semantics for and implementation of expectation monitoring into the Jason interpreter for AgentSpeak which allows agents to monitor their expectations locally rather than relying on global monitoring at the organizational level. This also allows programmers to describe naturally, at the agent level, how they should react to fulfillments and violations of their expectations.

Model Checking

Köster and Lohmann look at the issue of abstraction in agent model checking. This is an important area in creating efficient model checkers for multi-agent systems. Their technique is based on collapsing an agent's state with handcrafted equivalence relations.

The paper by Mohammed and Furbach treats the verification problem for multi-agent systems as one of reachability analysis. They present a logic which can express both the qualitative and quantitative properties of interest in such systems and show how this logic can be modelled in a constraint satisfaction system.

Lastly, Jongmans et al. take a look at state-space reduction techniques used in model checkers for imperative systems and consider their applicability in model checkers designed for BDI style multi-agent systems, specifically a custom model checker for the GOAL language. They develop a generic framework for applying reduction algorithms to agent-based model checkers with particular emphasis on modelling the techniques of partial-order reduction and program slicing.

Multi-Agent Programming Contest

The Multi-Agent Programming Contest (MAPC) has been an important event in the research scenario on multi-agent oriented programming. It has helped some of the best-known platforms for multi-agent programming to be much improved based on practical experience with non-trivial problems, and has also helped attract the interest of young people to do research on multi-agent programming. We are delighted that the organizers of the 2011 edition of the Multi-Agent Programming Contest, the 7th in the series that started in 2005, chose the proceedings of ProMAS 2011 to publish their selected papers. The 2011 edition of MAPC was organized by Tristan Behrens, Jürgen Dix, Michael Köster, Federico Schlesinger (all from Clausthal University of Technology) and Jomi Hübner (from the Federal University of Santa Catarina).

In the first MAPC paper, Tristan Behrens, Michael Köster, Federico Schlesinger, Jürgen Dix, and Jomi F. Hübner discuss MAPC 2011 itself. Each paper that follows presents one of the competing teams. Marc Dekker et al. present the winning team, HactarV2, from Delft University of Technology. Mikko Etienne, Steen Vester, and Jørgen Villadsen present the Python-DTU team, from the Technical University of Denmark. Dominic Carr et al. presented the Bogtrotters team from University College Dublin. Lastly, Sahar Mirzayi, Vahid Nateghi, and Fatemeh Eskandari present the Simurgh team from Arak University.

We would like to thank all the authors, the invited speaker, the Program Committee members, and all those who attended ProMAS 2011 in Taipei for their invaluable contributions to the success of ProMAS 2011 and indeed their continued support to ProMAS over the last decade. Special thanks to Springer who have published the proceedings of ProMAS since its very first edition.

February 2012

Louise A. Dennis
Olivier Boissier
Rafael H. Bordini

Organization

The 9th International Workshop on Programming Multi-Agent Systems (ProMAS-2011) took place with the 10th International Conference on Autonomous Agents and Multi-Agent Systems in Taipei, on May 3, 2011.

ProMAS Steering Committee

Rafael H. Bordini	FACIN–PUCRS, Brazil
Mehdi Dastani	Utrecht University, The Netherlands
Jürgen Dix	Clausthal University of Technology, Germany
Amal El Fallah Seghrouchni	Univesity of Paris VI, France

ProMAS-2011 Organizing Committee

Olivier Boissier	Ecole des Mines de St Etienne, France
Rafael H. Bordini	FACIN–PUCRS, Brazil
Louise A. Dennis	University of Liverpool, UK

Program Committee

Matteo Baldoni	University of Turin, Italy
Juan Botia	Universidad de Murcia, Spain
Lars Braubach	University of Hamburg, Germany
Rem Collier	University College Dublin, Ireland
Ian Dickinson	Epimorphics Ltd., UK
Marc Esteva	IIIA-CSIC, Spain
Michael Fisher	University of Liverpool, UK
Jorge Gomez-Sanz	Computense University of Madrid, Spain
Vladimir Gorodetsky	IIAS, Russia
Dominic Greenwood	Whitestein Technologies AG, Switzerland
James Harland	RMIT University, Australia
Koen Hindriks	TU Delft, The Netherlands
Benjamin Hirsch	Technical University of Berlin, Germany
Jomi Hübner	Federal University of Santa Catarina, Brazil
João Leite	New University of Liston, Portugal
Brian Logan	University of Nottingham, UK
Viviana Mascardi	University of Genova, Italy
Philippe Mathieu	University of Lille, France
John-Jules Meyer	Utrecht University, The Netherlands
Jörg Müller	TU Clausthal, Germany
Andrea Omicini	University of Bologna, Italy

Agostino Poggi	University of Parma, Italy
Alexander Pokahr	University of Hamburg, Germany
Alessandro Ricci	University of Bologna, Italy
Birna van Riemsdijk	TU Deflt, The Netherlands
Ralph Ronnquist	Intendico Pty. Ltd., Australia
Ichiro Satoh	National Institute of Informatics, Japan
Michael Ignaz Schumacher	HES-SO, Switzerland
Munindar Singh	NCSU, USA
Tran Cao Son	New Mexico State University, USA
Patrick Taillibert	Thales Aerospace Division, France
Paolo Torroni	University of Bologna, Italy
Jørgen Villadsen	DTU Informatics, Denmark
Gerhard Weiss	University of Maastricht, The Netherlands
Michael Winikoff	University of Otago, New Zealand
Neil Yorke-Smith	American University of Beirut and SRI

Additional Reviewers

Marco Lützenberger	TU Berlin, Germany
Elisa Marengo	University of Turin, Italy

Table of Contents

Part IV: Multi-Agent Programming Contest

Part I

Foundations of Agent Programming Languages

Logical Foundations for a Rational BDI Agent Programming Language (Extended Version)[*]

Shakil M. Khan and Yves Lespérance

Department of Computer Science and Engineering,
York University, Toronto, ON, Canada
{skhan,lesperan}@cse.yorku.ca

Abstract. To provide efficiency, current BDI agent programming languages with declarative goals only support a limited form of rationality – they ignore other concurrent intentions of the agent when selecting plans, and as a consequence, the selected plans may be inconsistent with these intentions. In this paper, we develop logical foundations for a rational BDI agent programming framework with prioritized declarative goals that addresses this deficiency. We ensure that the agent's chosen declarative goals and adopted plans are consistent with each other and with the agent's knowledge. We show how agents specified in our language satisfy some key rationality requirements.

1 Introduction

This paper contributes to the foundations of Belief-Desire-Intention agent programming languages/frameworks (BDI APLs), such as PRS [10], AgentSpeak [19], etc. Recently, there has been much work on incorporating *declarative goals* in these APLs [7,28,21,5,27,22]. In addition to defining a set of plans that can be executed to try to achieve a goal, these programming languages also incorporate goals as declarative descriptions of the states of the world which are sought. A typical BDI APL with declarative goals (APLwDG) uses a user-specified hierarchical plan library Π containing abstract plans, a procedural goal-base Γ containing a set of plans that the agent is committed to execute, and a declarative goal-base Δ that has goals that the agent is committed to achieve. In response to events in the environment and to goals in Δ, in each cycle the agent interleaves selecting plans from Π, adopting them to Γ, and executing actions in Γ. The execution of some of these actions can in turn trigger the adoption of other declarative goals. This process is repeated until all the goals in Δ are successfully achieved. The role of these declarative goals in an APLwDG is essentially for monitoring goal achievement and performing recovery when a plan has failed by decoupling plan failure/success from that of goal. Since these declarative goals capture the reason for executing plans, they are necessary to perform rational deliberation, and react in a rational way to changes in goals that result from communication, e.g. requests.

While current APLwDGs have evolved over the past few years — e.g. some of them handle restricted forms of temporally extended goals [8] — to keep them tractable

---

[*] This paper is an extended version of [16] and is also a revised version of [14].

L.A. Dennis, O. Boissier, and R.H. Bordini (Eds.): ProMAS 2011, LNCS 7217, pp. 3–21, 2012.

and practical, they sacrifice some principles of rationality. In particular, while select-ing plans to achieve a declarative goal, they ignore other concurrent intentions of the agent. As a consequence, the selected plan may be inconsistent with the agent's other intentions. Thus the execution of such an intended plan can render other contemporary intentions impossible to bring about. Also, these APLwDGs typically rely on syntactic formalizations of declarative goals, subgoals, and their dynamics, whose properties are often not well understood.

Apart from this, there has been work that focuses on maintaining consistency of a set of concurrent intentions. For example, Clement et al. [3,4] argue that agents should be able to reason about abstract HTN plans and their interactions before they are fully refined. They propose a method for deriving summary information (i.e. external pre-conditions and effects) of abstract plans and discuss how this information can be used to coordinate the interactions of plans at different levels of abstractions. Thangarajah et al. [26] use such summary information to detect and resolve conflicts between goals at run time. Horty and Pollack [9] propose a decision theoretic approach to compute the utility of adopting new (non-hierarchical) plans, given a set of already adopted plans. While some of these approaches can be integrated in APLs (e.g. [26]), they leave out many aspects of rationality (e.g. they do not say what the agent should do if external interference makes two of her intentions permanently incompatible), and do not deal with declarative goals.

In this paper, we develop a logical framework for a rational BDI APL with prior-itized declarative goals called Simple Rational APL (SR-APL, henceforth), that ad-dresses these deficiencies of previous APLwDGs. Our framework combines ideas from the situation calculus-based Golog family of APLs (e.g. [6]), our expressive semantic formalization of prioritized goals, subgoals, and their dynamics [13,15], and work on BDI APLs. We ensure that the agent's chosen declarative goals and adopted plans are consistent with each other and with the agent's knowledge. In doing this, we must ad-dress two fundamental questions about rational agency: (1) *What does it mean for a BDI agent to be committed to concurrently execute a set of plans next while keeping the option of further commitments to other plans open, in a way that does not allow pro-crastination?* (2) *How to ensure consistency between an agent's adopted declarative goals and adopted plans, given that some of the latter might be abstract, i.e. might be only partially instantiated in the sense that they include subgoals for which the agent has not yet adopted a (concrete) plan?* We show how agents specified in our framework satisfy some key rationality requirements. Our framework tries to bridge the gap be-tween agent theories and practical APLs by providing a model and specification of an idealized BDI agent whose behavior is closer to what a rational agent does. As such, it allows one to understand how compromises made during the development of a practical APLwDG affect the agent's rationality.

The paper is organized as follows: in the next section, we discuss a motivating ex-ample. In Sections 3 and 4, we outline our formal BDI framework. In Section 5, we specify the semantics of SR-APL. In Section 6, we show that in the absence of exter-nal interference, our agent behaves in ways that satisfy some key rationality principles. Then in Section 7, we summarize our results and discuss possible future work.

2   A Motivating Example

Consider a blocks world domain, where each block is one of four possible colors: blue, yellow, green, and red. There is only a stacking action $stack(b, b')$: b can be stacked on b' in state s if $b \neq b'$, both b and b' are *clear* in s, and b is *on the table* in s. There are no unstacking actions, so the agent cannot use a block to build two different towers at different times. Assume that there are four blocks, B_B, B_Y, B_G, and B_R, one of each color. the agent knows the *color of* these blocks, and knows that initially all the blocks are on the table and are clear. Now assume that the agent has the following two goals: (1) to eventually have a 2 blocks tower that has a green block on top and a non-yellow block underneath, and (2) to have a 2 blocks tower with a blue block on top and a non-red block underneath; thus $\Delta = \{\lozenge \mathrm{Twr}_Y^G, \lozenge \mathrm{Twr}_R^B\}$, where $\mathrm{Twr}_{C_2}^{C_1} \doteq \exists b, b'. \, \mathrm{OnTbl}(b') \wedge \mathrm{On}(b, b') \wedge \neg C_2(b') \wedge C_1(b)$. Suppose our agent's plan library Π has two rules:

$$\lozenge \mathrm{Twr}_Y^G : [\mathrm{OnTbl}(b) \wedge \mathrm{OnTbl}(b') \wedge b \neq b' \wedge \mathrm{Clear}(b)$$
$$\wedge \, \mathrm{Clear}(b') \wedge \neg Y(b) \wedge G(b')] \leftarrow stack(b', b),$$
$$\lozenge \mathrm{Twr}_R^B : [\mathrm{OnTbl}(b) \wedge \mathrm{OnTbl}(b') \wedge b \neq b' \wedge \mathrm{Clear}(b)$$
$$\wedge \, \mathrm{Clear}(b') \wedge \neg R(b) \wedge B(b')] \leftarrow stack(b', b).$$

That is, if the agent has the goal to have a green and non-yellow tower and knows about a green block b' and a distinct non-yellow block b that are both clear and are on the table, then she should adopt the plan of stacking b' on b, and similarly for the goal of having a blue and non-red tower.

Now, consider a typical APLwDG, that (without considering the overall consistency of the agent's intentions) simply select plans from Π for the agent's goals in Δ and eventually executes them in an attempt to achieve her goals. We claim that such an APL is not always sound and rational. For instance, according to this plan library, one way of building a green non-yellow (and a blue non-red) tower is to construct a green-blue (a blue-green, respectively) tower. While these two plans are individually consistent, they are inconsistent with each other, since the agent has only one block of each color. Thus a rational agent should not adopt these two plans. However, it can be shown that the following would be a legal trace for our blocks world domain in such an APL:

$$\langle \{\}, \Delta \rangle \Rightarrow \langle \{\sigma_1\}, \Delta \rangle \Rightarrow \langle \{\sigma_1, \sigma_2\}, \Delta \rangle \Rightarrow \langle \{\sigma_2\}, \{\lozenge \mathrm{Twr}_Y^G\} \rangle.$$

The agent first moves to configuration $\langle \{\sigma_1\}, \Delta \rangle$ by adopting the plan $\sigma_1 = stack(B_B, B_G)$ in response to $\lozenge \mathrm{Twr}_R^B$, then to $\langle \{\sigma_1, \sigma_2\}, \Delta \rangle$ by adopting $\sigma_2 = stack(B_G, B_B)$ to handle $\lozenge \mathrm{Twr}_Y^G$, and then to $\langle \{\sigma_2\}, \{\lozenge \mathrm{Twr}_Y^G\} \rangle$ by executing the intended action σ_1. At this point, the agent is stuck and cannot complete successfully. Thus, in such an APL, not only is the agent allowed to adopt two inconsistent plans, but the execution of one of these plans makes other concurrent goals impossible (e.g. the execution of $stack(B_B, B_G)$ makes $\lozenge \mathrm{Twr}_Y^G$ impossible to achieve).

The problem arises in part because actions are not reversible in this domain; there is no action for moving a block back to the table or for unstacking it. This is common in real world domains, for instance, most tasks with deadlines or resources, e.g. doing some errands before noon, a robot delivering mail without running out of battery power, etc. While such irrational behavior could in principle be avoided by using appropriate conditions in the antecedent of the plan-selection rules (e.g. by stating that the agent should only adopt a given plan if she does not have certain other goals), this puts an excessive burden on the agent programmer. Ideally, such reasoning about goals should be delegated to the agent.

3   Preliminaries

Our base framework for modeling goal change is the situation calculus as formalized in [17,20]. In this framework, a possible state of the domain is represented by a situation. There is a set of initial situations corresponding to the ways the agent believes the domain might be initially, i.e. situations in which no actions have yet occurred. Init(s) means that s is an initial situation. The actual initial state is represented by a special constant S_0. There is a distinguished binary function symbol do where $do(a, s)$ denotes the successor situation to s resulting from performing the action a. Thus the situations can be viewed as a set of trees, where the root of each tree is an initial situation and the arcs represent actions. Relations (and functions) whose truth values vary from situation to situation, are called relational (functional, respectively) fluents, and are denoted by predicate (function, respectively) symbols taking a situation term as their last argument. There is a special predicate Poss(a, s) used to state that action a is executable in situation s. Finally, the function symbol Agent(a) denotes the agent of action a.

We use a theory $\mathcal{D}$ that includes the following set of axioms:[1] (1) action precondition axioms, one per action a characterizing Poss(a, s), (2) successor state axioms (SSA), one per fluent, that succinctly encode both effect and frame axioms and specify exactly when the fluent changes [20], (3) initial state axioms describing what is true initially including the mental states of the agents, (4) axioms identifying the agent of actions, one per action a characterizing Agent(a), (5) unique name axioms for actions, and (6) domain-independent foundational axioms describing the structure of situations [17].

Following [23], we model knowledge using a possible worlds account adapted to the situation calculus. $K(s', s)$ is used to denote that in situation s, the agent thinks that she could be in situation s'. Using K, the knowledge of an agent is defined as: Know(Φ, s) $\doteq \forall s'. K(s', s) \supset \Phi(s')$, i.e. the agent knows Φ in s if Φ holds in all of her K-accessible situations in s. K is constrained to be reflexive, transitive, and Euclidean in the initial situation to capture the fact that agents' knowledge is true, and that agents have positive and negative introspection. The dynamics of knowledge is specified by providing a SSA for K that supports knowledge expansion as a result of sensing actions [23] and some *informing* communicative actions [12]. As shown in [23], the constraints on K continue to hold after any sequence of actions since they are preserved by the SSA for K. We also assume that the agent is aware of all actions.

To support modeling temporally extended goals, we introduced a new sort of *paths* along with an axiomatization for paths in [13]. A path is essentially an infinite sequence

---

[1] We will be quantifying over formulae, and thus assume $\mathcal{D}$ includes axioms for encoding of formulae as first order terms, as in [25]. We will also be using lists of programs, and assume that $\mathcal{D}$ includes an axiomatization of lists.

of situations, where each situation along the path can be reached by performing some *executable* action in the preceding situation. We use (possibly sub/super-scripted) variables p to denote paths. There is a predicate OnPath(p, s), meaning that the situation s is on path p. Also, Starts(p, s) means that s is the starting situation of path p. A path p starts with s iff s is the earliest situation on p.

We use $\Phi(s), \Psi(s), \cdots$, etc. to denote *state formulae* in the context of knowledge (and $\phi(p), \psi(p), \cdots$, etc. for *path formulae* in that of goals), each of which has a free situation variable s (path variable p, respectively). s (and p) will be bound by the context where the formula $\Phi(s)$ (and $\phi(p)$, respectively) appears. Where the intended meaning is clear, we sometimes suppress the situation variable (path variable) from $\Phi, \Psi, \cdots$, etc. ($\phi, \psi, \cdots$, etc. respectively). Also, we often use now to refer to a placeholder constant that stands for the current situation.

We will use some useful constructs that are defined in [13]. A state formula Φ *eventually holds* over the path p if Φ holds in some situation that is on p, i.e.: $\Diamond \Phi(p) \doteq \exists s'.\ \text{OnPath}(p, s') \wedge \Phi(s')$. Secondly, Suffix$(p', p, s)$ means that path p' is a suffix of another path p w.r.t. a situation s; Suffix(p', p, s) holds iff s is on p, and p' is the sub-path of p that starts with s. Finally, SameHist(s_1, s_2) means that the situations s_1 and s_2 share the same history of actions, but perhaps starting from different initial situations.

4   Formalization of Prioritized Goals

In [13], we proposed a logical framework for modeling *prioritized goals* and their dynamics. Our formalization here is based on [13], but modified as specified in the last paragraph of this section. In our framework in [13], an agent can have multiple *goals* or *desires* at different priority levels, possibly inconsistent with each other. We specify how these goals evolve when actions/events occur and the agent's knowledge changes. We define the agent's *chosen goals* or *intentions*, i.e. the goals that the agent is actively pursuing, in terms of this goal hierarchy. In that framework, agents constantly optimize their chosen goals. To this end, we keep all prioritized goals in the goal-base unless they are explicitly dropped. At every step, we compute an optimal set of chosen goals given the hierarchy of prioritized goals, preferring higher priority goals, such that chosen goals are consistent with each other and with the agent's knowledge. Thus at any given time, some goals in the hierarchy are *active*, i.e. chosen, while others are *inactive*. Some of these inactive goals may later become active (e.g. if a higher priority active goal that is currently blocking an inactive goal becomes impossible or is dropped) and trigger the inactivation of other currently active (lower priority) goals.

Goal Semantics. As in [13], we specify the agent's prioritized goals or *p-goals* using accessibility relation/fluent G. A path p is G-accessible at priority level n in situation s if all the goals of the agent at level n are satisfied over this path and if it starts with a situation that has the same action history as s. The latter requirement ensures that the agent's G-accessible paths are compatible with the actions that have been performed so far. We say that an agent has the p-goal that ϕ at level n in situation s (i.e. PGoal(ϕ, n, s)) iff ϕ holds over all paths that are G-accessible at n in s. A smaller n represents higher priority, and the highest priority level is 0. Thus as in [13], we assume that the set of p-goals are totally ordered according to priority. Note that, in this framework one can evaluate goals over infinite paths and thus can handle arbitrary temporally extended goals; hence, unlike some other situation calculus based accounts where goal formulae are evaluated w.r.t. finite paths (e.g. [24]), in this framework one can handle, for example, unbounded maintenance goals.

As in [13], we allow the agent to have infinitely many p-goals. However in many cases, the modeler will want to specify a finite set of initial p-goals. When a finite number of p-goals is assumed, we can use the functional fluent $NPGoals(s)$ to represent the number of prioritized goals that the agent has in situation s. The modeler/programmer will usually provide some specification of the agent's initial p-goals at the various priority levels, using some *initial goal axioms*. For instance, the initial prioritized goals for our blocks world example with domain theory $\mathcal{D}_{BW}$ can be specified as follows:

$$\text{(a) Init}(s) \supset ((G(p, 0, s) \equiv \exists s'. \text{ Starts}(p, s') \wedge \text{Init}(s') \wedge \Diamond \text{Twr}_Y^G)$$
$$\wedge (G(p, 1, s) \equiv \exists s'. \text{ Starts}(p, s') \wedge \text{Init}(s') \wedge \Diamond \text{Twr}_R^B)),$$
$$\text{(b) } \forall n, p, s. \text{ Init}(s) \wedge n \geq 2 \supset (G(p, n, s) \equiv \exists s'. \text{ Starts}(p, s') \wedge \text{Init}(s')).$$

(a) specifies the p-goals of the agent in the initial situations (we assume that the goal $\Diamond \text{Twr}_Y^G$ has higher priority than $\Diamond \text{Twr}_R^B$); (b) makes $G(p, n, s)$ true for every path p that starts with an initial situation for $n \geq 2$. Thus at these levels, the agent has the trivial p-goal that she be in an initial situation.

An agent's chosen goals must be realistic. To filter out the paths that are known to be impossible from G, we define *realistic* p-goal accessible paths: p is G_R-accessible at level n in s if it is G-accessible at n in s and if it starts with a situation that is K-accessible in s. In our framework, an agent has the *realistic p-goal* that ϕ at level n in situation s (i.e. RPGoal(ϕ, n, s)) iff ϕ holds over all G_R-accessible paths at n in s.

We define chosen goals or *c-goals* using realistic p-goals. Note that an agent's realistic p-goals at various priority levels can be viewed as candidates for her c-goals. Given the set of realistic p-goals, in each situation the agent's c-goals are specified to be those that are in the maximal consistent set of higher priority realistic p-goals. We define this iteratively starting with a set that contains the highest priority realistic p-goal accessible paths, i.e. G_R-accessible paths at level 0. At each iteration we obtain the intersection of this set with the set of next highest priority G_R-accessible paths. If the intersection is not empty, a new chosen set of p-goal accessible paths (and p-goals defined by these paths) at level i is obtained. We call a p-goal chosen by this process an *active* p-goal. If on the other hand the intersection is empty, then it must be the case that the p-goal represented by this level is either in conflict with another active higher priority p-goal/a combination of two or more active higher priority p-goals, or is known to be impossible. In that case, that p-goal is ignored (i.e. marked as *inactive*), and the chosen set of p-goal accessible paths at level i is the same as at level $i - 1$. To get the prioritized intersection of the set of G_R-accessible paths up to level n, the process is repeated until $i = n$ is reached. $G_\cap(p, n, s)$ is used to denote that in situation s, path p is in the prioritized intersection of G_R-accessible paths up to level n. We say that a path p is $G_\cap$-accessible in situation s, i.e. $G_\cap(p, s)$, if $G_\cap(p, n, s)$ holds for all levels n. Finally, we say that an agent has the c-goal that ϕ in situation s (i.e. CGoal(ϕ, s)) if ϕ holds over all $G_\cap$-accessible paths in

s. We can show that initially our blocks world agent has the p-goals/c-goals that $\Diamond\mathrm{Twr}_Y^G$ and $\Diamond\mathrm{Twr}_R^B$, i.e.: $\mathcal{D}_{BW} \models \forall s.\ \mathrm{Init}(s) \supset \mathrm{CGoal}(\Diamond\mathrm{Twr}_Y^G \wedge \Diamond\mathrm{Twr}_R^B, s)$.

To get positive and negative introspection of goals, we impose two inter-attitudinal constraints on the K and G-accessibility relations in the initial situations. We have shown that these constraints then continue to hold after any sequence of actions since they are preserved by the SSAs for K and G. See [11] for details.

Goal Dynamics. An agent's goals change when her knowledge changes as a result of the occurrence of an action (including exogenous events), or when she adopts or drops a goal. There are two special actions, for *adopting a p-goal ϕ at some level n* and *dropping a p-goal ϕ*, $adopt(\phi, n)$ and $drop(\phi)$, and a third action for *adopting a subgoal ψ relative to a supergoal ϕ*, $adoptRT(\psi, \phi)$.

The dynamics of p-goals are specified using a SSA for G as follows (the agent's c-goals are automatically updated when her p-goals change). Firstly, to handle the occurrence of a non-adopt/drop action a, all p-goals are progressed to reflect the fact that this action has occurred. Secondly, to handle adoption of a p-goal ϕ at level m, a new formula containing the p-goal is added to the agent's goal hierarchy at m. To be precise, in addition to progressing all p-goals at all levels, a new level containing the p-goal that ϕ is inserted at m and all current levels with priority greater or equal to m are pushed one level down the hierarchy. Finally, to handle the dropping of a p-goal ϕ, the levels that imply the dropped goal in the agent's goal hierarchy are replaced by the trivial formula that the history of actions in the current situation has occurred, and thus the agent no longer has the p-goal that ϕ. See [13] for details.

Handling Subgoals. We also handle subgoal adoption and model the dependencies between goals and the subgoals and plans adopted to achieve them. The latter is important since subgoals and plans adopted to bring about a goal should be dropped when the parent goal becomes impossible, or is dropped. We handle this as follows: adopting a subgoal ψ relative to a parent goal ϕ adds a new p-goal that contains *both this subgoal and this parent goal*, i.e. $\psi \wedge \phi$. This ensures that when the parent goal is dropped, the subgoal is also dropped, since when we drop the parent goal ϕ, all the p-goals at all G-accessibility levels that imply ϕ including $\psi \wedge \phi$ are also dropped. Note that the parent goal ϕ could be a p-goal at multiple levels. We assume that the subgoal ψ is always adopted w.r.t. the *highest priority supergoal level*, i.e. the highest priority level where ϕ holds. Also, the subgoal ψ is always adopted at the level immediately below the supergoal ϕ's level. The reason for doing this is that since ψ is a means to the end ϕ, they should have similar priorities. ψ is said to be a subgoal of ϕ in situation s (i.e. $\mathrm{SubGoal}(\psi, \phi, s)$) iff there is a G-accessibility level n in s such that ϕ is a p-goal at n while ψ is not, and for all G-accessibility levels in s where ψ is a p-goal, ϕ is also a p-goal. See [15,11] for details of our formalization of subgoals.

Prioritized Goals for Committed Agents. The formalization of prioritized goal dynamics in [13] ensures that the agent always tries to optimize her chosen goals. She will abandon a c-goal ϕ if an opportunity to commit to a higher priority but inconsistent with ϕ goal arises. As such, our account in [13] displays an idealized form of rationality. This is in contrast to Bratman's [1] practical rationality that takes into consideration the resource-boundedness of real world agents. According to Bratman, intentions limit the agent's reasoning as they serve as a *filter for adopting new intentions*. However, the agent is allowed to override this filter in some cases, e.g. when adopting ϕ increases her utility considerably. The framework in [13] can be viewed as a theory of intention where the filter override mechanism is always triggered.

Note that, in that framework, the agent's c-goals are very dynamic. For instance, as mentioned earlier, a currently inactive p-goal ϕ may become active at some later time, e.g. if a higher priority active c-goal that is currently blocking ϕ (as it is inconsistent with ϕ) becomes impossible. This also means that another currently active c-goal ψ may as a result become inactive, not because ψ has become impossible, was achieved, or was dropped, but due to the fact that ψ has lower priority than and is inconsistent with the newly activated goal ϕ (see [13] for a concrete example).

Such very dynamic c-goals/intentions are problematic as a foundation for an APL, as the agent spends a lot of effort in "recomputing" her intentions and plans to achieve them, and her behavior becomes hard to predict for the programmer. To avoid this, here we use a modified version of our formalization in [13] that eliminates the filter override mechanism altogether so that agents' p-goals/desires are dropped as soon as they become inactive. We can do this with the following simple changes: (1) we require that initially the agent knows that her p-goals are all possible and consistent with each other, (2) we don't allow the agent to adopt p-goals that are inconsistent with her current c-goals/intentions, and (3) we modify the SSA for G so that the agent's p-goals are dropped when they become impossible or inconsistent with other higher priority c-goals. In the resulting "committed agent" framework, an agent's p-goals are much more dynamic than in the original framework. On the other hand, her c-goals are now much more persistent, and are simply the consequential closure of her desires, as these must now all be consistent with each other and with the agent's knowledge. The resulting model of goals is somewhat simplistic, but is sufficient in an APL context.

5 Agent Programming with Prioritized Goals

Our proposed framework SR-APL combines elements from BDI APLs such as AgentSpeak [19] and from the ConGolog APL [6], which is defined on top of the situation calculus. In addition, to facilitate monitoring of goal achievement and performing plan failure recovery, we incorporate declarative goals in SR-APL. To specify the operational semantics of plans in SR-APL, we will use a subset of the ConGolog APL. This subset includes programming constructs such as primitive actions a, wait/test actions $\Phi?$, sequence of actions $\delta_1; \delta_2$, nondeterministic choice of arguments $\pi v.\ \delta$, nondeterministic iteration δ^*, and concurrent execution of programs $\delta_1 \| \delta_2$, to mention a few. Also, as in ConGolog, we will use Trans(σ, s, σ', s') to say that program σ in situation s can make a single step to reach situation s' with the program σ' remaining, and Final(σ, s) to mean that the program σ may legally terminate in situation s. Finally, Do(σ, s, s') means that there is a terminating execution of program σ that starts in s and ends in s'.

Components of SR-APL. First of all, we have a *set of axioms/theory* $\mathcal{D}$ specifying actions that can be done, the initial knowledge and (both declarative and procedural) goals of the agent, and their dynamics, as discussed in Section 3 and 4. Moreover, we also have a *plan library* Π with rules of the form $\phi : \Psi \leftarrow \sigma$, where ϕ is a goal formula, Ψ is a knowledge formula, and σ is a plan; a rule $\phi : \Psi \leftarrow \sigma$ means that if the agent has the c-goal that ϕ and knows that Ψ, then she should consider adopting the plan that σ. The *plan language* for σ is a simplified version of ConGolog and includes the empty program nil, primitive actions, waiting for a condition, sequences, and the special action for subgoal adoption, $adoptRT(\Diamond\Phi, \sigma)$; here $\Diamond\Phi$ is a subgoal to be adopted and σ is the plan relative to which it is adopted.[2] While our account of goal change is expressive enough to handle arbitrary temporally extended goals, here we focus on achievement goals and procedural goals exclusively. We believe that extending our framework to support maintenance goals should be straightforward, since maintenance goals behave like additional constraints on the agent behavior in contrast to achievement goals for which the agent needs to plan for.

Semantics of SR-APL. An SR-APL agent can work on multiple goals at the same time. Thus at any time, an agent might be committed to several plans that she will execute in an interleaved fashion. We use our situation calculus domain theory $\mathcal{D}$ to model *both adopted declarative goals and plans.* Initially $\mathcal{D}$ only contains declarative goals. As specified by the SSA for G, $\mathcal{D}$ is updated by adding plans or other declarative goals to the agent's goal hierarchy when a transition rule (see below) makes the agent perform an *adopt* or *adoptRT* action. We ensure that an agent's declarative goals and adopted plans are consistent with each other and with the agent's knowledge. In our semantics, we specify this by ensuring that there is at least one possible course of actions (i.e. a path) known to the agent, and if she were to follow this path, she would end up realizing all of her declarative goals and executing all of her procedural goals.

One way of specifying an agent's commitment to execute a plan σ next in $\mathcal{D}$ is to say that she has the intention that $\text{Starts}(s) \land \exists s'.\, \text{OnPath}(s') \land \text{Do}(\sigma, s, s')$, i.e. that each of her intention-accessible paths p is such that it starts with some situation s, it has the situation s' on it, and s' can be reached from s by executing σ. However, this does not allow for the interleaved execution of several plans, since Do requires that σ be executed before any other actions/plans.

A better alternative is to represent the procedural goal as $\text{Starts}(s) \land \exists s'.\, \text{OnPath}(s') \land \text{DoAL}(\sigma, s, s')$, which says that the agent has the intention to execute *at least* the program σ next, and possibly more. $\text{DoAL}(\sigma, s, s')$ holds if there is an execution of program σ, possibly interleaved with other actions by the agent herself, that starts in situation s and ends in s', which we define as:[3]

$$\text{DoAL}(\sigma, s, s') \doteq \text{Do}(\sigma \| (\pi a.\, \text{Agent}(a) = agt?; a)^*, s, s').$$

---

[2] We use the ConGolog APL here because it has a situation calculus-based semantics that is well specified and compatible with our agent theory. We could have used any APL with these characteristics.

[3] Note that, while our theory supports exogenous actions performed by other agents, we assume that all actions in the plans of agt that specify her behavior must be performed by agt herself.

However, a new problem with this approach is that it allows the agent to *procrastinate* in the execution of the intended plans in $\mathcal{D}$. For instance, suppose that the agent has the p-goal at priority level n_1 to execute the program σ_1 and at level n_2 to execute σ_2 next. Then, according to our definition of DoAL, the agent has the intention at level n_1 to execute σ_1 and at level n_2 to execute σ_2, possibly concurrently with other actions next, since we use DoAL to specify those goals. The "other actions" at level n_1 (n_2, respectively) are meant to be actions from the plan σ_2 (σ_1, respectively). However, nothing requires that the additional actions that the agent might execute are indeed from $\sigma_2(\sigma_1$, respectively), and thus this allows her to perform actions that are unnecessary as long as they do not perturb the execution of σ_1 and σ_2.

To deal with this, we include an additional component, a *procedural intention-base* Γ, to an SR-APL agent. Γ is a list of plans that the agent is currently actively pursuing. To avoid procrastination, we will require that any action that the agent actually performs comes from Γ (as specified in the transition rule A_{step} below). In the following, we will use $\Gamma^{\|}$ to denote the concurrent composition of the programs in Γ:[4]

$$\Gamma^{\|} \doteq \textbf{if } (\Gamma = [\text{nil}]) \textbf{ then } \text{nil } \textbf{else } \text{First}(\Gamma)\|(\text{Rest}(\Gamma))^{\|}.$$

In SR-APL, a *program configuration* $\langle \sigma, s \rangle$ is a tuple consisting of a program σ and a ground situation s. An *agent configuration* on the other hand is a tuple $\langle \Gamma, s \rangle$ that consists of a list of plans Γ and a ground situation s. The initial agent configuration is $\langle[\text{nil}], S_0\rangle$. Although strictly speaking an agent configuration includes the knowledge and the goals of the agent, these can be obtained from the (fixed) theory $\mathcal{D}$ and the situation in the configuration.

The semantics of SR-APL are defined by a two-tier transition system. *Program-level transition rules* specify how a program written in our plan language may evolve. On top of this, we use *agent-level transition rules* to specify how an SR-APL agent may evolve. Our program-level transition rules are simply a subset of the ConGolog transition rules. We use $\langle \sigma, s \rangle \rightarrow \langle \sigma', s' \rangle$ as an abbreviation for $\text{Trans}(\sigma, s, \sigma', s')$.

Agent-Level Transition Rules. These transition rules are given in Table 1 and are similar to those of a typical BDI APL.[5] First of all, we have a rule A_{sel} for *selecting and adopting a plan* using the plan library Π for some realistic p-goal $\Diamond\Phi$. It states that if: (a) there is a rule in the plan library Π which says that the agent should adopt an instance of the plan σ if she has $\Diamond\Phi$ as her p-goal and knows that some instance of Ψ, (b) $\Diamond\Phi$ is a realistic p-goal with priority n in s for which the agent hasn't yet adopted any subgoal, (c) the agent knows in s that Ψ', (d) θ unifies Ψ and Ψ', and (e) the agent does not intend not to adopt $\text{DoAL}(\sigma\theta)$ w.r.t. $\Diamond\Phi$ next, then she can adopt the plan $\sigma\theta$, adding $\text{DoAL}(\sigma\theta)$ as a subgoal of $\Diamond\Phi$ to her goals in the theory $\mathcal{D}$, and adding $\sigma\theta$ to Γ (here $\text{Handled}(\phi, s)$ is defined as $\exists\psi. \text{SubGoal}(\psi, \phi, s)$).

---

[4] We will use various standard list operations, e.g. First (representing the first item of a list), Rest (representing the sublist that contains all but the first item of a list), Cons (for constructing a new list from an item and a list), Member (for checking membership of an item within a list), Remove (for removing all instances of a given item from a list), Replace (for replacing a given item with another item in a list), etc.

[5] We use $\text{CGoal}(\exists s'. \text{DoAL}(\sigma, now, s'), s)$ or simply $\text{CGoal}(\text{DoAL}(\sigma), s)$ as a shorthand for $\text{CGoal}(\exists s'. \text{Starts}(now) \land \text{OnPath}(s') \land \text{DoAL}(\sigma, now, s'), s)$.

We can show that if an agent does not have the c-goal in s not to adopt a subgoal ψ w.r.t. a supergoal ϕ, then she does not have the c-goal that $\neg\psi$ next in s, i.e.:

Table 1. Agent Transition Rules

(A_{sel})	$\dfrac{\begin{array}{c}\text{Member}(\Diamond\Phi : \Psi \leftarrow \sigma, \Pi),\ \ \mathcal{D} \models \text{RPGoal}(\Diamond\Phi, n, s),\\ \mathcal{D} \models \neg\text{Handled}(\Diamond\Phi, s) \wedge \text{Know}(\Psi', s),\ \ \text{mgu}(\Psi, \Psi') = \theta,\\ \mathcal{D} \models \neg\text{CGoal}(\neg\exists s'.\, \text{Do}(adoptRT(\text{DoAL}(\sigma\theta), \Diamond\Phi), now, s'), s)\end{array}}{\langle \Gamma, s\rangle \Rightarrow \langle\text{Cons}(\sigma\theta, \Gamma), do(adoptRT(\text{DoAL}(\sigma\theta), \Diamond\Phi), s)\rangle}$
(A_{step})	$\dfrac{\begin{array}{c}\text{Member}(\sigma, \Gamma),\ \ \mathcal{D} \models \text{RPGoal}(\text{DoAL}(\sigma), n, s),\\ \mathcal{D} \models \langle\sigma, s\rangle \rightarrow \langle\sigma', do(a, s)\rangle \wedge \neg\text{CGoal}(\neg\exists s'.\, \text{Do}(a, now, s'), s)\end{array}}{\langle\Gamma, s\rangle \Rightarrow \langle\text{Replace}(\sigma, \sigma', \Gamma), do(a, s)\rangle}$
(A_{exo})	$\dfrac{\mathcal{D} \models \text{Exo}(a) \wedge \text{Poss}(a, s)}{\langle\Gamma, s\rangle \Rightarrow \langle\Gamma, do(a, s)\rangle}$
(A_{clean})	$\dfrac{\text{Member}(\sigma, \Gamma),\ \ \mathcal{D} \models \neg\exists n.\, \text{RPGoal}(\text{DoAL}(\sigma), n, s)}{\langle\Gamma, s\rangle \Rightarrow \langle\text{Remove}(\sigma, \Gamma), s\rangle}$
(A_{rep})	$\dfrac{\begin{array}{c}\mathcal{D} \models \neg\exists s'.\, \langle\Gamma^{\|}, s\rangle \rightarrow \langle\Gamma', s'\rangle,\ \ \mathcal{D} \models \neg\text{Final}(\Gamma^{\|}, s),\\ \text{For all } \sigma \text{ s.t. Member}(\sigma, \Gamma) \text{ we have:}\\ \mathcal{D} \models \exists n.\, \text{RPGoal}(\text{DoAL}(\sigma), n, s) \wedge \text{Handled}(\text{DoAL}(\sigma), s),\\ \mathcal{D} \models \neg\text{CGoal}(\neg\exists s'.\, \text{Do}(adopt(\text{Do}(\overrightarrow{a}), NPGoals(s)), now, s'), s),\\ \mathcal{D} \models \text{Agent}(\overrightarrow{a}) = agt \wedge \text{Do}(\overrightarrow{a}, s, s') \wedge \langle\Gamma^{\|}, s'\rangle \rightarrow \langle\Gamma', s''\rangle\end{array}}{\langle\Gamma, s\rangle \Rightarrow \langle\text{Cons}(\overrightarrow{a}, \Gamma), do(adopt(\text{Do}(\overrightarrow{a}), NPGoals(s)), s)\rangle}$

Theorem 1

$\mathcal{D} \models \neg\text{CGoal}(\neg\exists s'.\, \text{Do}(adoptRT(\psi, \phi), now, s'), s) \supset$

$\qquad \neg\text{CGoal}(\neg\exists s', p'.\, \text{Starts}(s') \wedge \text{Suffix}(p', do(adoptRT(\psi, \phi), s')) \wedge \psi(p'), s).$

Theorem 1 and condition (e) above imply that the agent does not have the c-goal not to execute $\sigma\theta$ concurrently with $\Gamma^{\|}$ and possibly other actions next, i.e.:

$$(i).\ \neg\text{CGoal}(\neg\exists s', s''.\, \text{Do}(adoptRT(\text{DoAL}(\sigma\theta), \Diamond\Phi), now, s')$$
$$\wedge\, \text{DoAL}(\sigma\theta \| \Gamma^{\|}, s', s''), s).$$

Moreover, it can be shown that in our framework, an agent acquires the c-goal that ψ after she adopts it as a subgoal of ϕ in s, provided that she has the realistic goal at some level n in s that ϕ, and that she does not have the c-goal in s that $\neg\psi$ next, i.e.:

Theorem 2

$\mathcal{D} \models \exists n.\, \text{RPGoal}(\phi, n, s) \wedge$

$\qquad \neg\text{CGoal}(\neg\exists s', p'.\, \text{Starts}(s') \wedge \text{Suffix}(p', do(adoptRT(\psi, \phi), s')) \wedge \psi(p'), s)$

$\qquad \supset \text{CGoal}(\psi, do(adoptRT(\psi, \phi), s)).$

From (b), (i), and Theorem 2, we have that:

$$(ii). \ \text{CGoal}(\exists s'. \ \text{DoAL}(\sigma\theta \parallel \Gamma^{\parallel}, now, s'), do(adoptRT(\text{DoAL}(\sigma\theta), \Diamond\Phi), s)).$$

(i) ensures that the adopted subgoal $\sigma\theta$ is consistent with $\Gamma^{\parallel}$ in the sense that they can be executed concurrently, possibly along with other actions in s. (ii) confirms that $\sigma\theta$ is indeed intended after the $adoptRT$ action has happened.

Note that this notion of consistency is a weak one, since it does not guarantee that there is an execution of the program $(\sigma\theta \parallel \Gamma^{\parallel})$ after the $adoptRT$ action happens, but rather ensures that the program $\text{DoAL}(\sigma\theta \parallel \Gamma^{\parallel})$ is executable. In other words, $\sigma\theta$ and the programs in Γ *alone* might not be concurrently executable, and additional actions might be required. We'll come back to this issue later.

Secondly, we have a transition rule A_{step} for single stepping the agent program by *executing an intended action* from Γ. It says that if: (a) a program σ in Γ can make a program-level transition in s by performing a primitive action a with program σ' remaining in $do(a, s)$ afterwards, (b) $\text{DoAL}(\sigma)$ is a realistic p-goal with priority n in s, and (c) the transition is consistent with the agent's goals in the sense that she does not have the c-goal not to execute a in s, then the agent can execute a, and Γ and s can be updated accordingly.

Once again we have a weak consistency requirement in condition (c) above. Ideally, we would have added to (c) that the agent can continue from $do(a, s)$ in the sense that she does not have the c-goal not to execute the remaining program σ' concurrently with the other programs in Γ in $do(a, s)$, i.e. that $\mathcal{D} \models \neg\text{CGoal}(\neg\exists s'. \ \text{Do}(a; (\sigma' \parallel \Gamma^{\parallel}), now, s'), s)$. However, note that Γ may not be complete in the sense that it may include plans that have actions that trigger the adoption of subgoals, for which the execution of $\Gamma^{\parallel}$ waits; but Γ does not have any adopted plans yet that can achieve these subgoals. Thus $\Gamma^{\parallel}$ by itself might currently have no complete execution, and will only become completely executable when all such subgoals have been fully expanded.

For example, consider a new agent for our blocks world domain who has a goal to eventually build a 3 blocks tower, i.e. $\Diamond 3\text{Tower}$, where $3\text{Tower} \doteq \exists b, b', b''. \ \text{OnTbl}(b) \wedge \text{On}(b', b) \wedge \text{On}(b'', b')$. Also, in addition to the above rules, her plan library Π includes the following rule:

$$\Diamond 3\text{Tower} : [\text{OnTbl}(b) \wedge \text{OnTbl}(b') \wedge \text{OnTbl}(b'') \wedge b \neq b' \wedge$$
$$\text{Clear}(b) \wedge \text{Clear}(b') \wedge \text{Clear}(b'') \wedge \neg Y(b') \wedge G(b') \wedge Y(b'')] \leftarrow \sigma_1,$$
$$\text{where } \sigma_1 = adoptRT(\Diamond \text{Twr}_Y^G, \text{DoAL}(\sigma_2)); \sigma_2, \text{ and } \sigma_2 = \text{Twr}_Y^G?; stack(b'', b').$$

This says that, if the agent knows about a non-yellow block b, a distinct green block b', and a yellow block b'' that are all clear and on the table, then her goal of building a 3 blocks tower can be fulfilled by adopting the plan that involves adopting the subgoal to eventually build a green non-yellow tower, waiting for the achievement of this subgoal, and then stacking b'' on b'. Suppose that in response to $\Diamond 3\text{Tower}$, the agent adopted σ_1 as above as a subgoal of this goal using the A_{sel} rule, and thus σ_1 is added to Γ. In the next few steps, she will step through the adopted plan σ_1, executing one action at a time in an attempt to achieve her goal that $\Diamond 3\text{Tower}$. Note that, in SR-APL, the hierarchical decomposition of a subgoal, e.g. σ_1 above, is a two step process. In the first step, in response to the execution (via A_{step}) of the $adoptRT(\lozenge Twr_Y^G, DoAL(\sigma_2))$ action in her plan σ_1 in Γ, the agent adopts $\lozenge Twr_Y^G$ as a subgoal of executing the remaining program σ_2, possibly along with other actions, i.e. w.r.t. $DoAL(\sigma_2)$. Then in the second step, she uses the A_{sel} rule to select and adopt a plan for the subgoal $\lozenge Twr_Y^G$. We assume that the subgoal $\lozenge Twr_Y^G$ must always be achieved before the supergoal. To do this, we suspend the execution of the supergoal by waiting for the achievement of the subgoal. This can be specified by the programmer by having the supergoal σ_2 start with the wait action Twr_Y^G? that waits for the subgoal to complete. But this means that σ_2 (and thus σ_1) by itself, i.e. without the DoAL construct, might not have a complete execution as it might get blocked when it reaches Twr_Y^G?. Moreover, since σ_2 is a member of Γ, $\Gamma^{\parallel}$ will have a complete execution only when all the subgoals in Γ have been fully expanded. Thus to deal with this, we use a weak consistency check that does not perform full lookahead over $\Gamma^{\parallel}$. However, our semantics ensures that any action a performed by the agent must not make the concurrent execution of all the adopted plans of the agent possibly with other actions impossible, i.e. it must be consistent with $DoAL(\Gamma^{\parallel})$, since A_{step} requires that doing a must be consistent with all her DoAL procedural goals (and other concurrent declarative goals) in her goal hierarchy, i.e. that $\mathcal{D} \models \neg CGoal(\neg\exists s'. Do(a, now, s'), s)$.

Thirdly, we have a rule A_{exo} for *accommodating exogenous actions*, i.e. actions occurring in the agent's environment that are not under her control. When such an action a occurs in s, the agent must update her p-goals by progressing the situation component of her configuration to $do(a, s)$.

Fourthly, we use the A_{clean} rule for *dropping adopted plans from the procedural goal-base Γ that are no longer intended in the theory $\mathcal{D}$*. It says that if there is a program σ in Γ, and executing σ possibly along with other actions is no longer a realistic p-goal, then σ should be dropped from Γ. This might be required when the occurrence of an exogenous action forces the agent to drop a plan by making it impossible to execute or inconsistent with her higher priority realistic p-goals. Recall that our theory automatically drops such plans from the agent's goal-hierarchy specified by $\mathcal{D}$.

Finally, we have a rule A_{rep} for *repairing an agent's plans in case she gets stuck*, i.e. when for all programs σ in Γ, the agent has the realistic p-goal that $DoAL(\sigma)$ at some level n (and thus all of these $DoAL(\sigma)$ are still individually executable and collectively consistent), but together they are not concurrently executable without some non-σ actions in the sense that $\Gamma^{\parallel}$ has no program-level transition in s. This could happen as a result of an exogenous action or as a side effect of our weak consistency check, as discussed below. The A_{rep} rule says that if: (a) $\Gamma^{\parallel}$ does not have a program level transition in s (which ensures that A_{step} can't be applied), (b) $\Gamma^{\parallel}$ is not considered to be completed in s, (c) every program in Γ is currently a realistic p-goal that has been handled (which ensures that A_{clean} and A_{sel} can't be applied), (d) there is a sequence of actions $\vec{a}$ that the agent does not intend not to execute next, and (e) $\vec{a}$ repairs Γ in the sense that there is a program level transition of $\Gamma^{\parallel}$ after $\vec{a}$ has been executed in s, then in an attempt to repair Γ, the agent should adopt $\vec{a}$ at the lowest priority level (i.e. at $NPGoals(s)$).

Why do we need this rule? One reason is because the agent could get stuck due to the occurrence of an exogenous action e, e.g. when e makes the preconditions of a plan

σ in Γ false; note that, DoAL(σ) might still be executable after the occurrence of e, e.g. if there is an action sequence $\overrightarrow{r}$ (encoded by the DoAL construct) that can be used to restore the preconditions of σ.

Another reason repair may be needed is that we use partial lookahead when executing actions via A_{step}. For example, assume a domain with actions a, b, and r, all of which are initially possible. The execution of b makes the preconditions of a false, while that of r restores them. Our agent has two adopted plans, DoAL(a) and DoAL(b) in the theory $\mathcal{D}$, and $\Gamma = [a, b]$. Note that $b; a$ is not a valid execution of $\Gamma^{\|}$, since the execution of b invalidates the preconditions of a. But $b; r; a$ is indeed a valid execution of (DoAL(a) $\wedge$ DoAL(b)). Since we only do partial consistency checking, our semantics allows the agent to perform b as the first action.[6] That is, to execute b using the A_{step} transition rule, we only need to ensure that b has a program-level transition in s and that this transition is consistent with the agent's goals in $\mathcal{D}$, i.e. with DoAL(a) and DoAL(b), both of which hold. After the execution of b, the agent will get stuck, as there is no action in the progression of Γ that she can perform. To deal with this, we include the repair rule that makes the agent plan for and commit to a sequence of actions that can be used to repair Γ, which for our example is r. Note that, we could have avoided the need for repairing plans in this case by strengthening the conditions of the A_{step} rule to do full lookahead by expanding all subgoals in Γ. However, this requires modeling the plan selection/goal decomposition process as part of the consistency check, which we leave for future work. We could have also relied on plan failure recovery techniques [28]. Finally, our repair rule does a form of conformant planning; more sophisticated forms of planning such as synthesizing conditional plans that include sensing actions could also be performed.

When the agent has complete information, there must be a repair plan available to the agent (whose actions can be performed by the agent herself) if her goals are consistent. In our framework, since the SSA for G drops all inconsistent goals/plans, the agent's p-goals are always consistent, and thus if complete information is assumed, it is always possible to repair the remaining plans. Consider our previous example: if the agent has DoAL(a) and DoAL(b) as her realistic p-goals, $\Gamma = [a, b]$, and if she has the c-goal not to execute an action from $\Gamma^{\|}$ (i.e. CGoal($\neg\exists s'. \langle \Gamma^{\|}, now \rangle \rightarrow \langle \Gamma', s' \rangle, s$)), then it must be the case that she does not have the c-goal not to execute $\Gamma^{\|}$ along with other actions (e.g. r), i.e. $\neg$CGoal($\neg\exists s'.$ DoAL($a\|b, now, s'$), s). Otherwise, one of DoAL(a) or DoAL(b) would have been dropped by the SSA for G as an agent's p-goals are always consistent with each other. Thus there must be a plan $\overrightarrow{a}$ that can repair Γ. Since the agent has complete information, this plan must work in all her epistemic alternatives (our repair rule does a form of conformant planning). Also, since by definition, the agent of the "other actions" in the DoAL construct is the agent herself, this means that she is also the agent of $\overrightarrow{a}$. If on the other hand the agent has only incomplete information, then a repair plan may need to perform sensing actions and branch on the results. We leave this kind of conditional planning for future work.

Also, note that this rule allows the agent to procrastinate in the sense that in addition to the plan that actually repairs Γ, she is allowed to adopt and execute actions that are

---

[6] Note that this does not mean that A_{step} allows the agent to perform an action that makes one of her goals impossible, e.g. to execute b when such a repair action r is not available.

unnecessary. This could be avoided by constraining the repair plan $\vec{a}$, e.g. by requiring it to be the shortest or the least costly plan etc. We leave this for future work.

In our operational semantics, we want to ensure that the procedural goals in Γ are consistent with those in the theory $\mathcal{D}$ before expansion of a subgoal/execution of an action occurs; so we assume that the A_{clean} rule has higher priority than A_{sel} and A_{step}. We can do this by adding appropriate preconditions to the antecedent of the latter, which we leave out for brevity.

To summarize, in SR-APL we formalize both declarative goals and plans uniformly in the same goal hierarchy specified by $\mathcal{D}$. We maintain the consistency of adopted declarative and procedural goals by ensuring that there is at least one path known to the agent over which all of her adopted declarative goals hold and that includes the concurrent execution of all of her adopted plans, possibly along with other actions. Whenever the agent's goals/plans become inconsistent due to some external interference, the successor state axiom for G in $\mathcal{D}$ will drop some of the adopted goals/plans if necessary, respecting their priority, and consistency of the goal-base is automatically restored. We also have a procedural goal-base Γ containing the adopted plans in $\mathcal{D}$, whose sole purpose is to ensure that the agent does not procrastinate w.r.t. her adopted plans. The set of transition rules of SR-APL allows an SR-APL agent to select, adopt, and execute plans from the plan library and thus serves as SR-APL's practical reasoning component. While adopting plans and executing actions, we use a weak consistency check, and thus avoid searching over the entire plan-space while ensuring consistency. SR-APL also includes a repair rule that can be used to repair plans if the agent gets stuck (a) as a result of our weak consistency check (and lack of lookahead in plan selection), (b) due to external interferences, or (c) due to the existence of an adopted declarative goal for which there is no plan specified in the plan library.

Let us now define some useful notions of program execution in SR-APL. A *labeled execution trace* $\mathcal{T}$ *relative to a theory* $\mathcal{D}$ is a (possibly infinite) sequence of configurations $\langle \Gamma_0, s_0 \rangle \overset{l_0}{\Rightarrow} \langle \Gamma_1, s_1 \rangle \overset{l_1}{\Rightarrow} \langle \Gamma_2, s_2 \rangle \overset{l_2}{\Rightarrow} \langle \Gamma_3, s_3 \rangle \overset{l_3}{\Rightarrow} \cdots$, s.t. $\Gamma_0 = [\text{nil}]$, $s_0 = S_0$ is the actual initial configuration, and for all $\langle \Gamma_i, s_i \rangle$, the agent level transition rule l_i can be used to obtain $\langle \Gamma_{i+1}, s_{i+1} \rangle$. Here l_i is one of A_{sel}, A_{step}, A_{exo}, A_{clean}, and A_{rep}, and in the absence of exogenous actions, l_i can be one of A_{sel}, A_{step}, A_{clean}, and A_{rep}. We sometimes suppress these labels. A *complete trace* $\mathcal{T}$ *relative to a theory* $\mathcal{D}$ is a finite labeled execution trace relative to $\mathcal{D}$, $\langle \Gamma_0, s_0 \rangle \overset{l_0}{\Rightarrow} \cdots \overset{l_{n-1}}{\Rightarrow} \langle \Gamma_n, s_n \rangle$, s.t. $\langle \Gamma_n, s_n \rangle$ does not have an agent level transition, i.e. $\langle \Gamma_n, s_n \rangle \not\Rightarrow$.

For our blocks world example, we can show that our SR-APL agent for this domain will not adopt inconsistent plans as seen in Section 2 and will in fact achieve all her goals. Note that, when arbitrary exogenous actions can occur, even the best laid plans can fail. Here we only consider the case of where exogenous actions are absent. We model this using the following axiom, which we call $NoExo$: $\forall a. \neg exo(a)$. Given this, we can show that:

Proposition 1. (a). *There exists a complete trace* $\mathcal{T}$ *relative to* $\mathcal{D}_{BW} \cup \{NoExo\}$ *for our blocks world program.* (b). *For all such complete traces* $\mathcal{T} = \langle \Gamma_0, s_0 \rangle \Rightarrow$ $\langle \Gamma_1, s_1 \rangle \Rightarrow \cdots \Rightarrow \langle \Gamma_n, s_n \rangle$, *we have:* $\mathcal{D}_{BW} \cup \{NoExo\} \models \text{Final}(\Gamma_n^{\parallel}, s_n) \wedge \text{Twr}_Y^G(s_n) \wedge$ $\text{Twr}_R^B(s_n)$. (c). *There are no infinite traces relative to* $\mathcal{D}_{BW} \cup \{NoExo\}$.

Thus when exogenous actions cannot occur, any execution of our SR-APL blocks world agent achieves all her goals.

6   Rationality of SR-APL Agents

We next prove some rationality properties that are satisfied by SR-APL agents. We only consider the case when exogenous actions do not occur. We could have considered exogenous actions, but in that case we would have to complicate the framework further, e.g. by assuming a fair environment that gives a chance to the agent to perform actions. Moreover, it is not obvious what rational behavior means in such contexts.

First of all, in each situation, for all domains $\mathcal{D}$ that are part of an SR-APL agent, the knowledge and c-goals/intentions as specified by $\mathcal{D}$ must be consistent:[7]

Theorem 3   (Consistency of Knowledge and CGoals)

$$\mathcal{D} \models \forall s. \ \neg Know(false, s) \wedge \neg CGoal(false, s).$$

We can also show that the procedural goals in Γ and the declarative and procedural goals in the theory $\mathcal{D} \cup \{NoExo\}$ remain consistent. Let's say that *the procedural goals in Γ are consistent with those in the theory $\mathcal{D}$ in situation s in a configuration* $\langle \Gamma, s \rangle$ iff for all σ s.t. $Member(\sigma, \Gamma)$, we have $\mathcal{D} \models CGoal(DoAL(\sigma), s)$. Also, define $\mathcal{D}_{Exo} \doteq \mathcal{D} \cup \{NoExo\}$. We have that:

Theorem 4   (Consistency of Γ and $\mathcal{D}_{\overline{Exo}}$). *If $\mathcal{T} = \langle \Gamma_0, s_0 \rangle \Rightarrow \langle \Gamma_1, s_1 \rangle \Rightarrow \cdots \Rightarrow \langle \Gamma_n, s_n \rangle$ is a complete trace of an SR-APL agent w.r.t. a theory $\mathcal{D}_{\overline{Exo}}$, then for all i s.t. $0 \leq i < n$, we have:*
(a). If $s_{i+1} = do(a, s_i)$ for some a, then the procedural goals in Γ_i are consistent with those in the theory $\mathcal{D}_{\overline{Exo}}$ in s_i,
(b). If $s_i = s_{i+1}$, then there exists j s.t. $0 < i < j \leq n$ and the goals in Γ_j are consistent with those in the theory $\mathcal{D}_{\overline{Exo}}$ in s_j,
(c). The procedural goals in Γ_n are consistent with those in the theory $\mathcal{D}_{\overline{Exo}}$ in s_n.

(a) and (c) are self-explanatory. (b) shows that whenever there is some procedural goal in Γ_i that is not a goal w.r.t. the theory $\mathcal{D}_{\overline{Exo}}$, the A_{clean} rule will remove it from Γ_i, and eventually consistency is restored.[8] It follows from Theorem 4 that in all configurations $\langle \Gamma, s \rangle$ where the plans in Γ are consistent with those in the theory $\mathcal{D}_{\overline{Exo}}$ in s, the agent intends to execute the programs in Γ concurrently starting in s, possibly with other actions, i.e. $\mathcal{D}_{\overline{Exo}} \models CGoal(\exists s'. \ DoAL(\Gamma^{\|}, now, s'), s)$.

Finally, our agents evolve in a rational way:

Theorem 5   (Rationality of Actions in a Trace). *If $\mathcal{T} = \langle \Gamma_0, s_0 \rangle \overset{l_0}{\Rightarrow} \langle \Gamma_1, s_1 \rangle \overset{l_1}{\Rightarrow} \cdots \overset{l_{n-1}}{\Rightarrow} \langle \Gamma_n, s_n \rangle$ is a trace of an SR-APL agent relative to a theory $\mathcal{D}_{\overline{Exo}}$, then for all i s.t. $0 < i \leq n$ and $s_i = do(a, s_{i-1})$, we have:*

---

[7] This follows independently from the underlying agent theory.
[8] Recall that applications of A_{clean} do not change the situation.

(a). $\mathcal{D}_{E\bar{x}o} \models \neg \text{CGoal}(\neg \exists s'. \text{Do}(a, now, s'), s_{i-1})$.

(b). *If* $l_{i-1} = A_{step}$ *then there exist* σ, σ' *s.t.* $\text{Member}(\sigma, \Gamma_{i-1})$ *and*

$\mathcal{D}_{E\bar{x}o} \models \langle \sigma, s_{i-1} \rangle \rightarrow \langle \sigma', do(a, s_{i-1}) \rangle \wedge \text{CGoal}(\exists s'. \text{DoAL}(a, now, s'), s_{i-1})$.

(c). $\mathcal{D}_{E\bar{x}o} \models \forall \phi, \psi, n. \; a = adoptRT(\psi, \phi) \vee a = adopt(\psi, n) \supset$

$\neg \text{CGoal}(\neg \exists s', p'. \text{Starts}(s') \wedge \text{Suffix}(p', do(a, s')) \wedge \psi(p'), s_{i-1})$.

This states that SR-APL is sound in the sense that any trace produced by the APL semantics is consistent with the agent's chosen goals. To be precise, (a) if an SR-APL agent performs the action a in situation s_{i-1}, then it must be the case that she does not have the intention not to execute a next in s_{i-1}. Moreover, (b) if a is performed via A_{step}, then a, which must have come from the procedural goal-base Γ, is indeed intended in s_{i-1} in the sense that she has the intention to execute a possibly along with some other actions next. Finally, (c) if a is the action of adopting a subgoal ψ w.r.t. a supergoal ϕ or that of adopting a goal ψ at some level n, then the agent does not have the c-goal in s_{i-1} not to bring about ψ next.

7   Discussion and Conclusion

Based on a "committed agent" variant of our rich theory of prioritized goal/subgoal dynamics [13], we have developed a specification of an APL framework that handles prioritized goals and maintains the consistency of adopted declarative and procedural goals. We also showed that an agent specified in this language satisfies some strong rationality properties. While doing this, we addressed some fundamental questions about rational agency. We model an agent's concurrent commitments by incorporating the DoAL construct in her adopted plans, which allows her to be open towards future commitments to plans, using a procedural goal-base Γ to prevent procrastination. We formalized a weak notion of consistency between goals and plans that does not require the agent to expand all adopted goals while checking for consistency.

While SR-APL agents rely on a user-specified plan library, they can achieve a goal even if such plans are not specified. Indeed the A_{rep} rule can be used as a first principles planner for goals that can be achieved using sequential plans. Thus, given a goal $\Diamond \Phi$, all the programmer needs to do to trigger the planner is to add a plan of the form $(\Diamond \Phi : true \leftarrow \Phi?)$ to the plan library Π. Since the program $\Phi?$ is neither executable nor final, it will eventually trigger the A_{rep} rule, which will make the agent adopt a sequence of actions to achieve Φ.

Here, we focused on developing an expressive agent programming framework that yields a rational/robust agent without worrying about tractability. Thus our framework is a specification and model of an ideal APL rather than a practical APL. In the future, we would like to investigate restricted versions of SR-APL that are practical, with an understanding of how they compromise rationality. We think this can be done. For instance if we assume a finite domain, then reasoning with the underlying theory should be decidable. We could adapt techniques from partial order planning such as summary information/causal links to support consistency maintenance. We could also simply find a global linear plan and cache it, using summary information to revise it when necessary.

There are some controller synthesis techniques that can deal with temporally extended goals [18,2].

Also, it would be desirable to study a version where the agent fully expands an abstract plan and checks its executability before adopting it. Finally, while our underlying agent theory supports arbitrary temporally extended goals, in SR-APL we only consider achievement goals. We would like to relax this in the future.

References

1. Bratman, M.E.: Intentions, Plans, and Practical Reason. Harvard University Press, Cambridge (1987)
2. Calvanese, D., De Giacomo, G., Vardi, M.Y.: Reasoning about Actions and Planning in LTL Action Theories. In: Proc. KR 2002, pp. 593–602 (2002)
3. Clement, B.J., Durfee, E.H.: Theory for Coordinating Concurrent Hierarchical Planning Agents Using Summary Information. In: Proc. AAAI 1999, pp. 495–502 (1999)
4. Clement, B.J., Durfee, E.H., Barrett, A.C.: Abstract Reasoning for Planning and Coordination. J. of Artificial Intelligence Research 28, 453–515 (2007)
5. Dastani, M.: 2APL: A Practical Agent Programming Language. J. of AAMAS 16(3), 214–248 (2008)
6. De Giacomo, G., Lespérance, Y., Levesque, H.J.: ConGolog, a Concurrent Programming Language Based on the Situation Calculus. Artificial Intelligence 121, 109–169 (2000)
7. Hindriks, K.V., de Boer, F.S., van der Hoek, W., Meyer, J.-J.C.: Agent Programming with Declarative Goals. In: Castelfranchi, C., Lespérance, Y. (eds.) ATAL 2000. LNCS (LNAI), vol. 1986, pp. 228–243. Springer, Heidelberg (2001)
8. Hindriks, K.V., van der Hoek, W., van Riemsdijk, M.B.: Agent Programming with Temporally Extended Goals. In: Proc. AAMAS 2009, pp. 137–144 (2009)
9. Horty, J.F., Pollack, M.E.: Evaluating New Options in the Context of Existing Plans. Artificial Intelligence 127, 199–220 (2001)
10. Ingrand, F.F., Georgeff, M.P., Rao, A.S.: An Architecture for Real-Time Reasoning and System Control. IEEE Expert 7(6), 34–44 (1992)
11. Khan, S.M.: Rational Agents : Prioritized Goals, Goal Dynamics, and Agent Programming Languages with Declarative Goals (in preparation). Ph.D. thesis, York University, Canada (2011)
12. Khan, S.M., Lespérance, Y.: ECASL: A Model of Rational Agency for Communicating Agents. In: Proc. AAMAS 2005, pp. 762–769 (2005)
13. Khan, S.M., Lespérance, Y.: A Logical Framework for Prioritized Goal Change. In: Proc. AAMAS 2010, pp. 283–290 (2010)
14. Khan, S.M., Lespérance, Y.: Towards a Rational Agent Programming Language with Prioritized Goals. In: Working Notes of DALT VIII, pp. 18–33 (2010)
15. Khan, S.M., Lespérance, Y.: Prioritized Goals and Subgoals in a Logical Account of Goal Change – A Preliminary Report. In: Baldoni, M., Bentahar, J., van Riemsdijk, M.B., Lloyd, J. (eds.) DALT 2009. LNCS (LNAI), vol. 5948, pp. 119–136. Springer, Heidelberg (2010)
16. Khan, S.M., Lespérance, Y.: SR-APL: A Model for a Programming Language for Rational BDI Agents with Prioritized Goals (Extended Abstract). In: Proc. AAMAS 2011, pp. 1251–1252 (2011)
17. Levesque, H.J., Pirri, F., Reiter, R.: Foundations for a Calculus of Situations. Electronic Transactions of AI (ETAI) 2(3-4), 159–178 (1998)
18. Pistore, M., Traverso, P.: Planning as Model Checking for Extended Goals in Non-Deterministic Domains. In: Proc. IJCAI 2001, pp. 479–484 (2001)

19. Rao, A.S.: AgentSpeak(L): BDI Agents Speak Out in a Logical Computable Language. In: Van de Velde, W., Perram, J.W. (eds.) MAAMAW 1996. LNCS (LNAI), vol. 1038, pp. 42–55. Springer, Heidelberg (1996)
20. Reiter, R.: Knowledge in Action. Logical Foundations for Specifying and Implementing Dynamical Systems. MIT Press (2001)
21. Sardiña, S., de Silva, L., Padgham, L.: Hierarchical Planning in BDI Agent Programming Languages: A Formal Approach. In: Proc. AAMAS 2006, pp. 1001–1008 (2006)
22. Sardiña, S., Padgham, L.: A BDI Agent Programming Language with Failure Recovery, Declarative Goals, and Planning. J. of AAMAS 23(1), 18–70 (2011)
23. Scherl, R., Levesque, H.J.: Knowledge, Action, and the Frame Problem. Artificial Intelligence 144(1-2), 1–39 (2003)
24. Shapiro, S., Brewka, G.: Dynamic Interactions Between Goals and Beliefs. In: Proc. IJCAI 2007, pp. 2625–2630 (2007)
25. Shapiro, S., Lespérance, Y., Levesque, H.J.: Goal Change in the Situation Calculus. J. of Logic and Computation 17(5), 983–1018 (2007)
26. Thangarajah, J., Padgham, L., Winikoff, M.: Detecting and Avoiding Interference between Goals in Intelligent Agents. In: Proc. IJCAI 2003, pp. 721–726 (2003)
27. van Riemsdijk, M.B., Dastani, M., Meyer, J.-J.C.: Goals in Conflict: Semantic Foundations of Goals in Agent Programming. J. of AAMAS 18(3), 471–500 (2009)
28. Winikoff, M., Padgham, L., Harland, J., Thangarajah, J.: Declarative and Procedural Goals in Intelligent Agent Systems. In: Proc. KR 2002, pp. 470–481 (2002)

Relating Goal and Commitment Semantics

Pankaj R. Telang[1,2], Munindar P. Singh[2], and Neil Yorke-Smith[3,4]

[1] Cisco Systems Inc., Research Triangle Park, NC 27709, USA
prtelang@ncsu.edu
[2] North Carolina State University, Raleigh, NC 27695-8206, USA
singh@ncsu.edu
[3] Olayan School of Business, American University of Beirut, Lebanon
[4] SRI International, Menlo Park, CA 94025, USA
nysmith@aub.edu.lb

Abstract. Whereas commitments capture how an agent relates with another agent, (private) goals describe states of the world that an agent is motivated to bring about. Researchers have observed that goals and commitments are complementary, but have not yet developed a combined operational semantics for them. This paper makes steps towards such a semantics by relating the respective lifecycles of goals and commitments. We study how the the concepts cohere for one agent and how they engender cooperation between agents. We illustrate our approach via a real-world scenario in the domain of aerospace aftermarket services. We state how our semantics yields important desirable properties, including convergence of the configurations of cooperating agents, thereby delineating some theoretically well-founded yet practical modes of cooperation in a multiagent system.

1 Introduction and Motivation

Whereas the study of goals is a long-standing theme in AI, the last several years have seen the motivation and elaboration of a theory of (social) commitments. The concepts of goals and commitments are intuitively complementary. A commitment describes how an agent relates with another agent, while a goal describes a state of the world that an agent is motivated to bring about. A commitment carries deontic force in terms of what an agent would bring about for another agent, while a goal describes an agent's proattitude toward some condition.

Researchers have begun tying these two concepts together. We go beyond existing works by developing a formal, modular approach that accomplishes the following. First, it characterizes the lifecycles and more generally the operational semantics of the two concepts. Second, it characterizes the interplay between goals and commitments. Third, this approach distinguishes the purely semantic aspects of their lifecycles from the pragmatic aspects of how a cooperative agent may reason. Fourth, it shows that certain desirable properties can be guaranteed for agents who respect selected rules of cooperation. These properties include *convergence*: the agents achieve a level of consistency internally (between the

L.A. Dennis, O. Boissier, and R.H. Bordini (Eds.): ProMAS 2011, LNCS 7217, pp. 22–37, 2012.

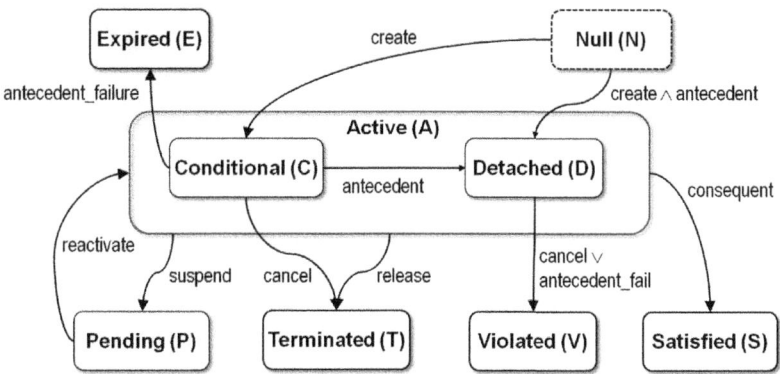

Fig. 1. Commitment lifecycle as a state transition diagram

states of their goals and commitments) and externally (between the states of their commitments relevant to each other).

We begin in Sect. 2 by introducing the concepts of commitment and goals, and for each presenting their lifecycle as a state transition diagram. Sect. 3 presents our combined operational semantics, which is based on guarded rules. We distinguish between two types of rules: mandatory structural rules which reflect the lifecycle of goals and commitments, and practical rules that an agent may choose to follow in order to achieve certain desirable properties. In Sect. 4 we state convergence properties for agents that adopt both types of rules. Sect. 5 illustrates on a real-world scenario, and Sect. 6 places our work in context.

2   Background: Commitments and Goals

Commitments. A *commitment* expresses a social relationship between two agents. Specifically, a commitment C(DEBTOR, CREDITOR, antecedent, consequent) denotes that the DEBTOR commits to the CREDITOR to bringing about the consequent if the antecedent begins to hold [10]. Fig. 1 shows the lifecycle of a commitment simplified from Telang and Singh [12] (below, we disregard timeouts, and commitment delegation or assignment). A labeled rectangle represents a commitment state, and a directed edge represents a transition, labeled with the corresponding action or event.

A commitment can be in one of the following states: Null (before it is created), Conditional (when it is initially created), Expired (when its antecedent remains forever false, while it was still Conditional), Satisfied (when its consequent is brought about while it was Active regardless of its antecedent), Violated (when its antecedent has been true but its consequent will forever be false, or it is canceled when Detached), Terminated (when canceled while Conditional or released while Active), or Pending (when suspended while Active). Active has two substates: Conditional (when its antecedent is false) and Detached (when its antecedent has held) A debtor may create, cancel, suspend, or reactivate a commitment; a creditor may release a debtor from a commitment.

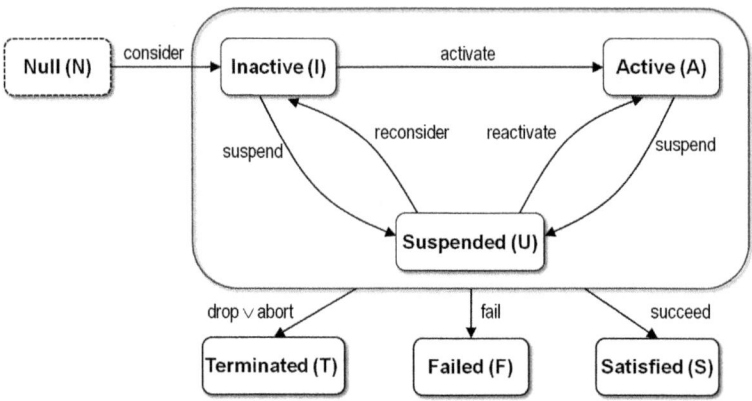

Fig. 2. Simplified lifecycle of an achievement goal as a state transition diagram

Goals. An agent's desires represent a proattitudes on part of the agent; an agent may concurrently hold mutually inconsistent desires. By contrast, goals are at least consistent desires: we take a rational agent to believe that its goals are mutually consistent. An agent's intentions are adopted or activated goals.

A *goal* $G = \mathsf{G}(x, p, r, q, s, f)$ of an agent x has a *precondition* (or context) p that must be true before G can become Active and an intention can be adopted to achieve it, a *in-condition* r that is true once G is Active until its achievement, and a *post-condition* (or effect) q that becomes true if G is successfully achieved [17]. The *success condition* s defines the success of G, and the *failure condition* f defines its failure. A goal G is successful iff s becomes true prior to f: that is, the truth of s entails the satisfaction of G only if f does not intervene. Often, the post-condition q and the success condition s coincide, but they need not. As for commitments, the success or failure of a goal depends only on the truth or falsity of the various conditions, not on which agent brings them about.

Fig. 2 simplifies Thangarajah et al.'s [14] lifecycle of an achievement goal (we do not consider maintenance goals). A goal can be in one of the following states: Null, Inactive (renamed from Pending to avoid conflict with commitments), Active, Suspended, Satisfied, Terminated, or Failed. The last three collectively are *terminal states*: once a goal enters any of them, it stays there forever. The semantic rules will link the the definition of a goal G and its states.

Before its creation, a candidate goal is in state Null; once considered by an agent (its "goal holder"), it commences as Inactive, in contrast to commitments which are created in state Active. Upon activation, the goal becomes Active; the agent may pursue its satisfaction by attempting to achieve s. If s is achieved, the goal moves to Satisfied. At any point, if the failure condition of the goal becomes true, the goal moves to Failed. At any point, the goal may enter Suspended, from which it may eventually return to an Inactive or Active state. Lastly, at any point the agent may drop or abort the goal, thereby moving it to the Terminated state.

3   Proposed Operational Semantics

Whereas a goal is specific to an agent (but see Sect. 6), a commitment involves a pair of agents. On the one hand, an agent may create commitments towards other agents in order to achieve its goals. On the other hand, an agent may consider goals in order to fulfill its commitments to other agents.

Chopra et al. [3] formalize a semantic relationship between commitments and goals. They write goals in either or both of the antecedent or consequent of a commitment, i.e., $C(x, y, g_1, g_2)$, where antecedent (g_1) and consequent (g_2) are objective conditions (success conditions of one or more goals), not goals. For example, a car insurer may commit to a repair garage to paying if the latter performs a repair: $C(\text{INSURER}, \text{REPAIRER}, \text{car\_repaired}, \text{payment\_made})$. Here, car_repaired is the success condition of the insurer's goal. The insurer may consider a goal with success condition of payment_made to satisfy the commitment.

3.1   Formal Semantics

We consider the *configuration* of an agent x as the tuple $S_x = \langle \mathcal{B}, \mathcal{G}, \mathcal{C} \rangle$ where $\mathcal{B}$ is its set of beliefs, $\mathcal{G}$ its set of goals, and $\mathcal{C}$ its set of commitments. Conceptually, an agent's configuration relates to both its cognitive and its social state: it incorporates its beliefs and goals as well as its commitments. Where necessary, we index sets or states by agent; for brevity, we omit the parts of the configuration that are clear. We adopt a standard propositional logic.

- $\mathcal{B}$ is the set of x's beliefs about the current snapshot of the world, and include beliefs about itself and other agents. Each snapshot is itself atemporal.
- $\mathcal{C}$ is a set of commitments, of the form $C(x, y, s, u)$, where x and y are agents and s and u are logical conditions. We use a superscript from Fig. 1 to denote the state of a commitment.
- $\mathcal{G}$ is a set of goals adopted by x, of the form $G(x, p, r, q, s, f)$. $\mathcal{G}$ includes goals that are Inactive. Since the goals in G are adopted, we take it that they are mutually consistent [17]. Superscripts from Fig. 2 denote goal states.

We capture the operational semantics of reasoning about goals and commitments via guarded rules in which S_i are configurations:

$$\frac{guard}{S_1 \longrightarrow S_2} \tag{1}$$

$S_i.\mathcal{B}$, $S_i.\mathcal{G}$, and $S_i.\mathcal{C}$ are the appropriate components of S_i. $S_i \longrightarrow S_j$ is a transition. In most settings, we can specify a family of transitions as an action. For example, for a commitment C, suspend(C) refers to the set of transitions $S_i \longrightarrow S_j$ where $C \in S_i.\mathcal{C}$ and suspend(C) $\in S_j.\mathcal{C}$. For actions a and b, $a \wedge b$ indicates that both must be performed.

The same guard may enable multiple transitions $S_i \longrightarrow S_j$ with the same S_i, indicating choice (of the agent involved). For example, intuitively, if a commitment corresponding to a goal expires, an agent could either (i) establish an alternative commitment or (ii) drop the goal. The resulting rules have the same guards, but specify different transitions.

We assume that rational agents seek to achieve their Active goals. That is, an agent at least believes that it has some means to achieve the success condition s of a goal it intends. Either the agent can adopt a plan whose success will achieve s, or it can seek to persuade another agent to bring about the condition s.

3.2   Structural Rules

We distinguish between two types of rules. *Structural* rules specify the progression of a commitment or a goal per their respective lifecycles. Each action that an agent can perform on a goal or a commitment derives a rule of this form. The guard of such a rule is an objective fact. For example, if f holds, a goal whose failure condition is f would be considered as having Failed. Rules such as these capture the hard integrity requirements represented by the lifecycles of goals and commitments. In our particular setting, such rules are both complete and deterministic, in that there is exactly one target state for each potential transition. The state diagrams in Fig. 1 and 2 correspond to the structural rules. The rules are straightforward to derive; we write one rule out in full below, and omit the remainder for reasons of space. We also do not write the standard lifting rule that relates transitions on single commitment/goal to transitions on sets.

A conceptual relationship is established between a goal and a commitment when they reference each other's objective conditions. Even when related in such a manner, however, the goal and the commitment independently progress in accordance with their respective lifecycles. For example, consider a goal $G = G(x, p, r, q, s, f)$ of agent x. To satisfy this goal, x may create a commitment $C(x, y, s, u)$. That is, agent x may commit to agent y to bring about u if y brings about s. When y brings about s, C detaches, and G is satisfied. We describe the progression of x's configuration as a structural rule:

$$\frac{\mathcal{B}_x \models s}{\langle G^A, C^A \rangle \longrightarrow \langle G^S, C^D \rangle} \tag{2}$$

where the superscripts denote commitment and goal states from Figs. 1 and 2. Some rules apply in multiple states, indicated via superscripts such as $C^{E \vee T}$.

3.3   Practical Rules

Practical (reasoning) rules capture not necessary integrity requirements, but rather patterns of pragmatic reasoning that agents may or may not adopt under different circumstances. The guard of such a rule is usually the antecedent or consequent of a commitment or the success or failure condition of a goal. The outcome of such a rule can be expressed as an action or an event from the applicable lifecycle diagram, which effectively summarizes a family of transitions from configurations to configurations. For example, an agent having an Active goal may decide to create a commitment as an offer to another agent, in order to persuade the second agent to help achieve its goal. Or, an agent may decide to create a goal to service a commitment.

Such practical rules may be neither complete nor deterministic, in that an agent may find itself at a loss as to how to proceed or may find itself with multiple options. Such nondeterminism corresponds naturally to a future-branching temporal model: each agent's multiplicity of options leads to many possible progressions of its configuration and of the configurations of its peers. The convergence results we show below indicate that our formulated set of rules are complete (i.e., sufficient) in a useful technical sense.

Note that the practical rules are merely options that an agent has available when it adopts these rules as patterns of reasoning—as illustrated in our earlier example of two possible agent actions when a commitment expires. An agent may refine on these rules to always select from among a narrower set of the available options, for example, through other reasoning about its preferences and utilities. Our approach supports such metareasoning capability in principle, but we defer a careful investigation of it to future research.

It is helpful to group the practical rules into two cases.

Case I: From Goals to Commitments. Here, an agent creates a commitment to satisfy its goal. Consider an agent x having a goal $G = \mathsf{G}(x, p, r, q, s, f)$, and a commitment from x to y: $C = \mathsf{C}(x, y, s, u)$. Notice that s occurs as the success condition of G and the antecedent of C. This case presumes that x lacks (or prefers not to exercise) the capability to bring about s, but can bring about u, and that y can bring about s. Thus x uses C as a means to achieve G (x's *end goal*). Agent x's (goal holder) practical reasoning rules are as follows.

Note that we do not assume that commitments are symmetric. That is, in general, an agent may have a commitment to another agent without the latter having a converse commitment to the former agent.

Recall that superscripts indicate the state of a goal or commitment; for a goal G, the Suspended state is indicated by G^U. The guard is a pattern-matching expression. For example, $\langle G^A \rangle$ matches all configurations in which G is Active, regardless of other goals and commitments.

– ENTICE: If G is active and C is null, x creates an offer (C) to another agent.

$$\frac{\langle G^A, C^N \rangle}{\mathsf{create}(C)} \ \text{ENTICE} \tag{3}$$

Motivation: (Only) by creating the commitment can the agent satisfy its goal.

– SUSPEND OFFER: If G is suspended, then x suspends C.

$$\frac{\langle G^U, C^A \rangle}{\mathsf{suspend}(C)} \ \text{SUSPEND OFFER} \tag{4}$$

Motivation: The agent may employ its resources in other tasks instead of working on the commitment.

– REVIVE: If G is active, and C is pending, then x reactivates C.

$$\frac{\langle G^A, C^P \rangle}{\mathsf{reactivate}(C)} \ \text{REVIVE} \tag{5}$$

Motivation: An active commitment is needed by the agent to satisfy its goal.

– WITHDRAW OFFER: If G fails or is terminated, then x cancels C.

$$\frac{\langle G^{T \vee F}, C^A \rangle}{\mathsf{cancel}(C)} \ \text{WITHDRAW OFFER} \tag{6}$$

Motivation: The commitment is of no utility once the end goal for which it is created no longer exists.

– REVIVE TO WITHDRAW: If G fails or is terminated and C is pending, then x reactivates C.

$$\frac{\langle G^{T \vee F}, C^P \rangle}{\mathsf{reactivate}(C)} \ \text{REVIVE TO WITHDRAW} \tag{7}$$

Motivation: If the goal fails or is terminated, and the commitment is pending, then the agent reactivates the commitment, and later cancels the commitment by the virtue of WITHDRAW OFFER. As per the commitment lifecycle from Fig. 1, an agent needs to reactivate a commitment before cancelling it.

– NEGOTIATE: If C terminates or expires, and G is active or suspended, then x creates another commitment C' to satisfy its goal.

$$\frac{\langle G^{A \vee U}, C^{E \vee T} \rangle}{\mathsf{create}(C')} \ \text{NEGOTIATE} \tag{8}$$

Motivation: The agent persists with its goal by trying alternative ways to induce other agents to cooperate.

– ABANDON END GOAL: If C terminates or expires, then x gives up on G.

$$\frac{\langle G^{A \vee U}, C^{E \vee T} \rangle}{\mathsf{drop}(G)} \ \text{ABANDON END GOAL} \tag{9}$$

Motivation: The agent may decide no longer to persist with its end goal. Note that an agent may also employ a structural rule to drop a goal without any condition.

It is necessary only that the rules cover *possible* combinations of goal and commitment states. For example, the $\langle G^A, C^V \rangle$ state is not possible since C can violate only after G satisfies; hence no rule is required.

Case II: From Commitments to Goals. Here, an agent creates a goal to bring about its part (consequent if debtor, antecedent if creditor) in a commitment.

Consider commitment $C = \mathsf{C}(x, y, s, u)$ and goals $G_1 = \mathsf{G}(x, p, r, q, u, f)$ and $G_2 = \mathsf{G}(y, p', r', q', s, f')$. The practical reasoning rules for agent x are as follows.

– DELIVER: If G_1 is null and C is detached, then x considers and activates goal G_1 to bring about C's consequent.

$$\frac{\langle G_1^N, C^D \rangle}{\text{consider}(G_1) \wedge \text{activate}(G_1)} \text{ DELIVER} \tag{10}$$

DELIVER': If G_1 is inactive and C is detached, then x activates goal G_1 to bring about C's consequent.

$$\frac{\langle G_1^I, C^D \rangle}{\text{activate}(G_1)} \text{ DELIVER'} \tag{11}$$

Motivation: The agent is honest in that it activates a goal that would lead to discharging its commitment.

– BACK BURNER: If G_1 is active and C is pending, then x suspends G_1.

$$\frac{\langle G_1^A, C^P \rangle}{\text{suspend}(G_1)} \text{ BACK BURNER} \tag{12}$$

Motivation: By suspending the goal, the agent may employ its resources to work on other goals.

– FRONT BURNER: If G_1 is suspended and C is detached, then x reactivates G_1.

$$\frac{\langle G_1^U, C^D \rangle}{\text{reactivate}(G_1)} \text{ FRONT BURNER} \tag{13}$$

Motivation: An active goal is necessary for the agent to bring about its part in the commitment.

– ABANDON MEANS GOAL: If G_1 is active and C terminates (y releases x from C) or violates (x cancels C), then x drops G_1.

$$\frac{\langle G_1^A, C^{T \vee V} \rangle}{\text{drop}(G_1)} \text{ ABANDON MEANS GOAL} \tag{14}$$

Motivation: The goal is not needed since the commitment for which it is created no longer exists.

– PERSIST: If G_1 fails or terminates and C is detached, then x activates goal G_1' identical to G_1.

$$\frac{\langle G_1^{T \vee F}, C^D \rangle}{\text{consider}(G_1') \wedge \text{activate}(G_1')} \text{ PERSIST} \tag{15}$$

Motivation: The agent persists in pursuing its part in the commitment.

– GIVE UP': If G_1 fails or terminates and C is detached, then x cancels C.

$$\frac{\langle G_1^{T \vee F}, C^D \rangle}{\text{cancel}(C)} \text{ GIVE UP} \tag{16}$$

Motivation: x gives up pursuing its commitment by cancelling or releasing it.

Many of the practical reasoning rules for agent y are similar to x's.

- DETACH: If G_2 is null and C is conditional, then y considers and activates goal G_2 to bring about C's antecedent.

$$\frac{\langle G_2^N, C^C \rangle}{\mathsf{consider}(G_2) \wedge \mathsf{activate}(G_2)} \text{ DETACH} \tag{17}$$

DETACH$'$: If G_2 is inactive and C is conditional, then y activates goal G_2 to bring about C's antecedent.

$$\frac{\langle G_2^I, C^C \rangle}{\mathsf{activate}(G_2)} \text{ DETACH'} \tag{18}$$

Motivation: The creditor brings about the antecedent hoping to influence the debtor to discharge the commitment.

- BACK BURNER: If G_2 is active and C is pending, then y suspends G_2.

$$\frac{\langle G_2^A, C^P \rangle}{\mathsf{suspend}(G_2)} \text{ BACK BURNER} \tag{19}$$

Motivation: By suspending the goal, the agent may employ its resources to work on other goals.

- FRONT BURNER: If G_2 is suspended and C is conditional, y reactivates G_2.

$$\frac{\langle G_2^U, C^C \rangle}{\mathsf{reactivate}(G_2)} \text{ FRONT BURNER} \tag{20}$$

Motivation: An active goal is necessary for the agent to bring about its part in the commitment.

- ABANDON MEANS GOAL: If G_2 is active and C expires or terminates (either x cancels, or y releases x from C), then y drops G_2.

$$\frac{\langle G_2^A, C^{E \vee T} \rangle}{\mathsf{drop}(G_2)} \text{ ABANDON MEANS GOAL} \tag{21}$$

Motivation: The goal is not needed since the commitment for which it is created no longer exists.

- PERSIST: If G_2 fails or terminates and C is conditional, then y activates goal G_2' identical to G_2.

$$\frac{\langle G_2^{T \vee F}, C^C \rangle}{\mathsf{consider}(G_2') \wedge \mathsf{activate}(G_2')} \text{ PERSIST} \tag{22}$$

Motivation: The agent persists in pursuing its part (either antecedent or consequent) in the commitment.

- GIVE UP: If G_2 fails or terminates and C is conditional, y releases x from C.

$$\frac{\langle G_2^{T \vee F}, C^C \rangle}{\mathsf{release}(C)} \text{ GIVE UP} \tag{23}$$

Motivation: y gives up pursuing its commitment by cancelling or releasing it.

4   Convergence Properties

We would like to be assured that a coherent world state will be reached, no matter how the agents decide to act, provided that they act according to the rules we have given. We conjuecture that the practical rules are sufficient for an agent to reach a coherent state, as stated in the following set of propositions.

Informally, in a *coherent* state, corresponding goals and commitments align.

Definition 1. *Let $G = \mathsf{G}(x,p,r,q,s,f)$ be a goal and $C = \mathsf{C}(x,y,s,u)$ a commitment. Then we say that any configuration that satisfies $\langle G^A, C^A \rangle$, $\langle G^U, C^P \rangle$, $\langle G^{T \vee F}, C^{E \vee T \vee V} \rangle$, or $\langle G^S, C^S \rangle$ is a coherent state of G and C.*

We have rules that can recreate goals and commitments (namely, PERSIST and NEGOTIATE). These rules could cause endless cycles; therefore we introduce:

Definition 2. *A* progressive rule *is any practical rule other than* PERSIST *and* NEGOTIATE. *The latter two rules we call* nonprogressive.

Propositions 1 and 2 capture the intuition of coherence of a single agent's configuration. All possible agent executions eventually lead to one of the coherent states if the agent obeys our proposed practical rules. They relate to the situations of Case I and Case II respectively.

Proposition 1. *Suppose $G = \mathsf{G}(x,p,r,q,s,f)$ and $C = \mathsf{C}(x,y,s,u)$. Then there is a finite sequence of progressive rules interleaving finitely many occurrences of nonprogressive rules that leads to a coherent state of G and C.*   □

Proposition 2. *Suppose $C = \mathsf{C}(x,y,s,u)$ and $G = \mathsf{G}(x,p,r,q,u,f)$. Then there is a finite sequence of progressive rules interleaving finitely many occurrences of nonprogressive rules that leads to a coherent state of G and C.*   □

Proposition 3 applies to the configurations of two agents related by a commitment. If the agents obey our proposed practical rules, then the state of the debtor's means goal follows the state of the creditor's end goal.

Proposition 3. (Goal convergence across agents) *Suppose $G_1 = \mathsf{G}(x, p_1, r_1, q_1, s, f_1)$ and $G_2 = \mathsf{G}(y, p_2, r_2, q_2, s, f_2)$ are goals, and $C = \mathsf{C}(x,y,s,u)$ is a commitment. Then there is a finite sequence of rules drawn from the practical rules that leads to G_2's state equaling G_1's state.*   □

The formal proof of these propositions is part of our current work [13].

5   Illustrative Application

We illustrate the value of integrated reasoning over commitments and goals with a real-world scenario, drawn from European Union CONTRACT project [15] in the domain of aerospace aftermarket services.

Fig. 3 shows a high-level process flow of aerospace aftermarket services. The participants are an airline operator, an aircraft engine manufacturer, and a parts

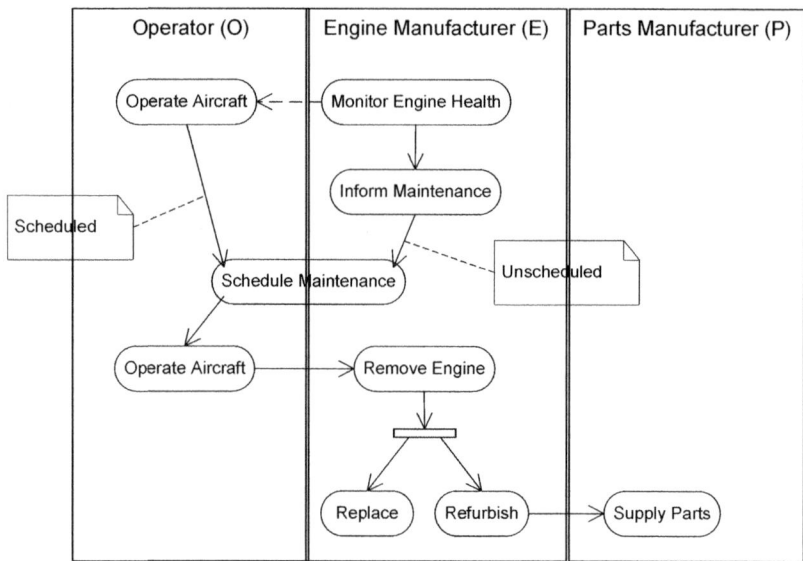

Fig. 3. A high-level model of the aerospace aftermarket process (verbatim from the Amoeba [5] paper, originally from CONTRACT project [15])

manufacturer. The engine manufacturer provides engines to the airline operator, and additionally services the engines to keep them operational; in return, the operator pays the manufacturer. If a plane waits on the ground for an engine to be serviced, the manufacturer pays a penalty to the operator. As part of the agreement, the operator regularly provides engine health data to the manufacturer, and may proactively request the manufacturer to perform schedule engine maintenance. The manufacturer analyzes the health data and informs the operator of any required unscheduled engine maintenance. As part of servicing the engine, the manufacturer can either refurbish or replace it. The manufacturer maintains a supply of engines by procuring parts from a parts manufacturer.

Table 1 describes the goals and commitments that model this scenario. For reasons of space, we exclude the airline manufacturer purchasing parts from the parts manufacturer. In the table, service_promised proposition represents creation of C_3 and C_4, and health_reporting_promised represents creation of C_5.

Table 2 describes a possible progression of the aerospace scenario. Each step shows the structural or practical reasoning rule that the airline manufacturer (MFG) or the operator (OPER) employ, and how their configurations progress. For readability, we place new or modified state elements in bold, and omit satisfied commitments and goals in steps subsequent to their being satisfied.

In Steps 1 and 2, the airline manufacturer and the operator consider and activate goals G_1 and G_2. In Step 3, the manufacturer entices (ENTICE rule) the operator to create C_1, which would enable the manufacturer to satisfy G_1. Notice how ENTICE causes manufacturer's configuration to reach the coherent state $\langle \{G_1^A\}, \{C_1^A\} \rangle$. Similarly in Step 4, operator creates C_2.

Table 1. Goals and commitments from the aerospace scenario

ID	Goal, Commitment, or Event	Description
G_1	G(MFG, T, T, payment_made ∧ health_reporting_promised, payment_made ∧ health_reporting_promised, insufficient_money)	Airline manufacturer's (MFG's) goal to receive the payment and the promise to provide the health report
G_2	G(OPER, T, T, engine_provided ∧ service_promised, engine_provided ∧ service_promised, engine_not_provided)	Operator's (OPER's) goal to receive the engine and the promise to provide the service
G_3	G(OPER, T, T, payment_made ∧ health_reporting_promised, payment_made ∧ health_reporting_promised, insufficient_money)	Operator's goal to make the payment and the promise to provide the health report
G_4	G(MFG, T, T, engine_provided ∧ service_promised, engine_provided ∧ service_promised, engine_not_provided)	Airline Manufacturer's goal to provide the engine and the promise to provide the service
$G_5[i]$	G(OPER, service_needed[i], T, service_requested[i], service_requested[i], service_not_requested[i])	Operator's goal to request the service; there is an instance of this goal for each occurrence of service needed
$G_6[i]$	G(MFG, service_requested[i], T, service_provided[i], service_provided[i], service_not_provided[i])	Manufacturer's goal to provide the service; there is an instance of this goal for each service request
$G_7[i]$	G(MFG, engine_down[i], T, penalty_paid[i], penalty_paid[i], penalty_not_paid[i])	Manufacturer's goal to pay the penalty if the engine is down; there is an instance of this goal for each engine down occurrence
C_1	C(MFG, OPER, payment_made ∧ health_reporting_promised, engine_provided ∧ service_promised)	Mfr's commitment to operator to provide the engine and service if operator pays and promises to provide the health report
C_2	C(OPER, MFG, engine_provided ∧ service_promised, payment_made ∧ health_reporting_promised)	Operator's commitment to the mfr to pay and to provide the health report if the mfr provides the engine and service
$C_3[i]$	C(MFG, OPER, service_requested[i] ∧ ¬expired, service_provided[i])	Mfr's commitment to the operator to provide the service if the operator requests service prior to the contract expiration
$C_4[i]$	C(MFG, OPER, engine_down[i] ∧ ¬expired, penalty_paid[i])	Manufacturer's commitment to the operator to pay penalty if the engine is down prior to the contract expiration; there is an instance of this commitment for each occurrence of the engine downtime
$C_5[i]$	C(OPER, MFG, health_report_requested[i] ∧ ¬expired, health_report_provided[i])	Operator's commitment to the manufacturer to provide the health report if the manufacturer requests the report; there is an instance of this commitment for each health report request

In Step 5, the manufacturer considers and activates G_4 to detach (DETACH rule) C_2. Observe how DETACH activates manufacturer's (debtor's) means goal G_4, which corresponds to the operator's (creditor's) end goal G_2. In Step 6, the operator considers and activates G_3 to detach C_1.

In Step 7, due to other priorities, the operator decides to suspend G_2. The operator suspends C_2 (SUSPEND OFFER rule) in Step 8, which transitions its configuration to the coherent state $\langle\{G_2^U\}, \{C_2^P\}\rangle$. In Step 9, the manufacturer suspends G_4 (BACK BURNER rule), which transitions its configuration to the coherent state $\langle\{G_4^U\}, \{C_2^P\}\rangle$. Observe how the practical reasoning rules cause the manufacturer (debtor) to suspend its means goal G_4 in response to the operator (creditor) suspending its end goal G_2. In Step 10–11, the operator reactivates G_2, and reactivates (REVIVE rule) C_2. In Step 12, the manufacturer reactivates (REVIVE rule) G_4.

In Steps 13–15, the manufacturer provides engine (engine_provided) to the operator and creates C_3 and C_4. Recall that service_promised means creation of C_3 and C_4, and satisfaction condition of G_2 and G_4 is engine_provided $\land$ service_promised. Therefore, in Step 15, G_2 and G_4 are satisfied. Further since engine_provided $\land$ service_promised is consequent of C_1 and antecedent of C_2, in Step 15, C_1 is satisfied and C_2 is detached. In Steps 16–17, operator pays the manufacturer (payment_made), and creates C_5 (health_reporting_promised). This satisfies G_1, G_3, and C_2. Observe how, in Step 17, the practical reasoning rules cause the manufacturer's and the operator's configuration to reach the coherent states $\langle\{G_1^S\}, \{C_1^S\}\rangle$ and $\langle\{G_2^S\}, \{C_2^S\}\rangle$.

A *service_needed* event occurs at Step 18; it instantiates the parameter i with the value 1. In response, the operator activates $G_5[1]$, an instance of G_5, to request the service in Step 19. By its requesting the service, in Step 20 the operator satisfies $G_5[1]$ and detaches $C_3[1]$, an instance of C_3. To deliver upon its commitment, the manufacturer activates $G_6[1]$ in Step 21, and provides the service in Step 22. This satisfies $G_6[1]$, and $C_3[1]$. Finally, in Step 23, only the recurring commitments C_3, C_4, and C_5 remain in the agent configurations.

6   Related Work

Chopra et al. [3] formalize semantic relationship between agents and protocols encoded as goals and commitments, respectively to verify at design time if a protocol specification (commitments) supports achieving goals in an agent specification, and vice versa. In contrast, our semantics applies at runtime, and we propose practical reasoning rules that agents may follow to achieve coherence between related goals and commitments. Dalpiaz et al. [4] propose a model of agent reasoning based on pursuit of *variants*—abstract agent strategies for pursuing a goal. We conjecture that their approach can be expressed as sets of practical reasoning rules, such as those we described above.

Winikoff [16] develops a mapping from commitments to BDI-style plans. He modifies SAAPL, an agent programming language, to include commitments in an agent's belief-base and operational semantics update the commitments. Our operational semantics addresses goals (more abstract than plans) and

Table 2. Progression of configurations in the aerospace scenario

#	Event Rule	or MFG's Action	MFG's State	OPER's Action	OPER's State
1	(structural)	consider(G_1) ∧ activate(G_1)	$\langle\{G_1^A\}\rangle$		$\langle\rangle$
2	(structural)		$\langle\{G_1^A\}\rangle$	consider(G_2) ∧ activate(G_2)	$\langle\{G_2^A\}\rangle$
3	ENTICE	create(C_1)	$\langle\{G_1^A\}, \{C_1^C\}\rangle$		$\langle\{G_2^A\}, \{C_1^C\}\rangle$
4	ENTICE		$\langle\{G_1^A\}, \{C_1^C, C_2^C\}\rangle$	create(C_2)	$\langle\{G_2^A\}, \{C_1^C, C_2^C\}\rangle$
5	DETACH	consider(G_4) ∧ activate(G_4)	$\langle\{G_1^A, G_4^A\}, \{C_1^C, C_2^C\}\rangle$		$\langle\{G_2^A\}, \{C_1^C, C_2^C\}\rangle$
6	DETACH		$\langle\{G_1^A, G_4^A\}, \{C_1^C, C_2^C\}\rangle$	consider(G_3) ∧ activate(G_3)	$\langle\{G_2^A, G_3^A\}, \{C_1^C, C_2^C\}\rangle$
7	(structural)		$\langle\{G_1^A, G_4^A\}, \{C_1^C, C_2^C\}\rangle$	suspend(G_2)	$\langle\{G_2^U, G_3^A\}, \{C_1^C, C_2^C\}\rangle$
8	SUSPEND OFFER		$\langle\{G_1^A, G_4^A\}, \{C_1^C, C_2^P\}\rangle$	suspend(C_2)	$\langle\{G_2^U, G_3^A\}, \{C_1^C, C_2^P\}\rangle$
9	BACK BURNER	suspend(G_4)	$\langle\{G_1^A, G_4^U\}, \{C_1^C, C_2^P\}\rangle$		$\langle\{G_2^U, G_3^A\}, \{C_1^C, C_2^P\}\rangle$
10	(structural)		$\langle\{G_1^A, G_4^U\}, \{C_1^C, C_2^P\}\rangle$	reactivate(G_2)	$\langle\{G_2^A, G_3^A\}, \{C_1^C, C_2^P\}\rangle$
11	REVIVE		$\langle\{G_1^A, G_4^U\}, \{C_1^C, C_2^C\}\rangle$	reactivate(C_2)	$\langle\{G_2^A, G_3^A\}, \{C_1^C, C_2^C\}\rangle$
12	REVIVE	reactivate(G_4)	$\langle\{G_1^A, G_4^A\}, \{C_1^C, C_2^C\}\rangle$		$\langle\{G_2^A, G_3^A\}, \{C_1^C, C_2^C\}\rangle$
13	(structural)	engine_provided	$\langle\{G_1^A, G_4^A\}, \{C_1^C, C_2^C\}\rangle$		$\langle\{G_2^A, G_3^A\}, \{C_1^C, C_2^C\}\rangle$
14	(structural)	create(C_3)	$\langle\{G_1^A, G_4^A\}, \{C_1^C, C_2^C, C_3^C\}\rangle$		$\langle\{G_2^A, G_3^A\}, \{C_1^C, C_2^C, C_3^C\}\rangle$
15	(structural)	create(C_4)	$\langle\{G_1^A, G_5^S\}, \{C_1^S, C_2^D, C_3^C, C_4^C\}\rangle$		$\langle\{G_2^S, G_3^A\}, \{C_1^S, C_2^D, C_3^C, C_4^C\}\rangle$
16	(structural)		$\langle\{G_1^A\}, \{C_2^D, C_3^C, C_4^C\}\rangle$	payment_made	$\langle\{G_3^A\}, \{C_2^D, C_3^C, C_4^C\}\rangle$
17	(structural)		$\langle\{G_1^S\}, \{C_2^S, C_3^C, C_4^C, C_5^C\}\rangle$	create(C_5)	$\langle\{G_3^S\}, \{C_2^S, C_3^C, C_4^C, C_5^C\}\rangle$
18	service_needed[1]		$\langle\{C_3^C, C_4^C, C_5^C\}\rangle$		$\langle\{C_3^C, C_4^C, C_5^C\}\rangle$
19	DETACH		$\langle\{C_3^C, C_4^C, C_5^C\}\rangle$	consider($G_5[1]$) ∧ activate($G_5[1]$)	$\langle\{G_5^A[1]\}, \{C_3^C, C_4^C, C_5^C\}\rangle$
20	(structural)		$\langle\{C_3^D[1], C_3^C, C_4^C, C_5^C\}\rangle$	service_requested[1]	$\langle\{G_5^S[1]\}, \{C_3^D[1], C_3^C, C_4^C, C_5^C\}\rangle$
21	DELIVER	consider($G_6[1]$) ∧ activate($G_6[1]$)	$\langle\{G_6^A[1]\}, \{C_3^D[1], C_3^C, C_4^C, C_5^C\}\rangle$		$\langle\{C_3^D[1], C_3^C, C_4^C, C_5^C\}\rangle$
22	(structural)	service_provided	$\langle\{G_6^S[1]\}, \{C_3^S[1], C_3^C, C_4^C, C_5^C\}\rangle$		$\langle\{C_3^S[1], C_3^C, C_4^C, C_5^C\}\rangle$
23			$\langle\{C_3^C, C_4^C, C_5^C\}\rangle$		$\langle\{C_3^C, C_4^C, C_5^C\}\rangle$

commitments. It will be interesting to combine Winikoff's work with ours to develop a joint semantics for commitments, goals, and plans.

Avali and Huhns [1] relate an agent's commitments to its beliefs, desires, and intentions using BDI_{CTL*}. In contrast, we relate an agent's commitments to its goals. We consider goal lifecycle in our semantics, and propose practical reasoning rules for coherence with commitments.

Telang and Singh [11] enhance Tropos, an agent-oriented software engineering methodology, with commitments. They describe a methodology that starts from a goal model and derives commitments. Our operational semantics complements by providing a formal underpinning.

Telang and Singh [12] propose a commitment-based business metamodel, a set of modeling patterns, and an approach for formalizing the business models and verifying message sequence diagrams with respect to the models. Our combined operational semantics of commitments and goals can provide a basis for how a business model can be enacted and potentially support the derivation of suitable message sequence diagrams.

van Riemsdijk et al. [9] and Thangarajah et al. [14] propose abstract architectures for goals, on which is based the simplified goal lifecycle that we consider. These and other authors formalize the goal operationalization. In contrast, our work formalizes the combined operational semantics of goals and commitments. A future extension of our work is to address the different goal types that have been suggested [9,18]. Our work is complementary also to exploration of goals that have temporal extent (e.g., [2,7]). Moreover, we have considered each goal to be private to an agent. Works that study coordination of agents via shared proattitudes, such as shared goals, include for example Grosz and Kraus [6] and Lesser et al. [8].

7 Conclusion and Future Work

This paper studied the complementary aspects of commitments and goals by establishing an operational semantics of the related lifecycles of the two concepts. We have distinguished the purely semantic aspects of their lifecycles from the pragmatic aspects of how a cooperative agent may reason, and stated desirable properties such as convergence of mental states. These proporties need to be formally proved. From the viewpoint of agent programming, we have sought to provide a foundational set of rules that is complete in a technical sense; their sufficiency in practice will be found through use.

Our work carries importance because of its formalization of the intuitive complementarity between goals and commitments. Directions for building on this foundation include considering a hierarchy of prioritized goals or commitments, and extending our semantics to include maintenance goals, shared goals, or plans. We are also interested in examining convergence properties when there are more than two agents working collaboratively.

Acknowledgments. We gratefully acknowledge the suggestions of the anonymous reviewers of the ProMAS'11 workshop and the post-proceedings volume, and the discussions with the participants at the workshop.

References

1. Avali, V.R., Huhns, M.N.: Commitment-Based Multiagent Decision Making. In: Klusch, M., Pěchouček, M., Polleres, A. (eds.) CIA 2008. LNCS (LNAI), vol. 5180, pp. 249–263. Springer, Heidelberg (2008)
2. Braubach, L., Pokahr, A.: Representing Long-Term and Interest BDI Goals. In: Braubach, L., Briot, J.-P., Thangarajah, J. (eds.) ProMAS 2009. LNCS, vol. 5919, pp. 201–218. Springer, Heidelberg (2010)
3. Chopra, A.K., Dalpiaz, F., Giorgini, P., Mylopoulos, J.: Reasoning about agents and protocols via goals and commitments. In: Proc. AAMAS, pp. 457–464 (2010)
4. Dalpiaz, F., Chopra, A.K., Giorgini, P., Mylopoulos, J.: Adaptation in Open Systems: Giving Interaction Its Rightful Place. In: Parsons, J., Saeki, M., Shoval, P., Woo, C., Wand, Y. (eds.) ER 2010. LNCS, vol. 6412, pp. 31–45. Springer, Heidelberg (2010)
5. Desai, N., Chopra, A.K., Singh, M.P.: Amoeba: A methodology for modeling and evolution of cross-organizational business processes. ACM Trans. Software Engineering and Methodology 19(2), 6:1–6:45 (2009)
6. Grosz, B., Kraus, S.: Collaborative plans for complex group action. Artificial Intelliegence 86(2), 269–357 (1996)
7. Hindriks, K.V., van der Hoek, W., van Riemsdijk, M.B.: Agent programming with temporally extended goals. In: Proc. AAMAS, pp. 137–144 (2009)
8. Lesser, V., Decker, K., Wagner, T., Carver, N., Garvey, A., Horling, B., Neiman, D., Podorozhny, R., NagendraPrasad, M., Raja, A., Vincent, R., Xuan, P., Zhang, X.: Evolution of the GPGP/TAEMS Domain-Independent Coordination Framework. J. Autonomous Agents and Multi-Agent Systems 9(1), 87–143 (2004)
9. van Riemsdijk, M.B., Dastani, M., Winikoff, M.: Goals in agent systems. In: Proc. AAMAS, pp. 713–720 (2008)
10. Singh, M.P.: An ontology for commitments in multiagent systems. AI and Law 7, 97–113 (1999)
11. Telang, P.R., Singh, M.P.: Enhancing Tropos with Commitments. In: Borgida, A.T., Chaudhri, V.K., Giorgini, P., Yu, E.S. (eds.) Conceptual Modeling: Foundations and Applications. LNCS, vol. 5600, pp. 417–435. Springer, Heidelberg (2009)
12. Telang, P.R., Singh, M.P.: Specifying and verifying cross-organizational business models. IEEE Trans. Services Comput. 4 (2011)
13. Telang, P.R., Singh, M.P., Yorke-Smith, N.: A coupled operational semantics for goals and commitments (2012), working paper
14. Thangarajah, J., Harland, J., Morley, D., Yorke-Smith, N.: Operational Behaviour for Executing, Suspending, and Aborting Goals in BDI Agent Systems. In: Omicini, A., Sardina, S., Vasconcelos, W. (eds.) DALT 2010. LNCS, vol. 6619, pp. 1–21. Springer, Heidelberg (2011)
15. van Aart, C.J., Chábera, J., Dehn, M., Jakob, M., Nast-Kolb, K., Smulders, J.L.C.F., Storms, P.P.A., Holt, C., Smith, M.: Use case outline and requirements. Deliverable D6.1, IST CONTRACT Project (2007), http://tinyurl.com/6adejz
16. Winikoff, M.: Implementing commitment-based interactions. In: Proc. AAMAS, pp. 873–880 (2007)
17. Winikoff, M., Padgham, L., Harland, J., Thangarajah, J.: Declarative and procedural goals in intelligent agent systems. In: Proc. KR, pp. 470–481 (2002)
18. Winikoff, M., Dastani, M., van Riemsdijk, M.B.: A unified interaction-aware goal framework. In: Proc. ECAI, pp. 1033–1034 (2010)

Part II

Multi-Agent Oriented Programming

Developing a Knowledge Management Multi-Agent System Using *JaCaMo*

Carlos M. Toledo[1], Rafael H. Bordini[2], Omar Chiotti[1], and María R. Galli[1]

[1] INGAR-CONICET, Avellaneda 3657, Santa Fe, Argentina
{cmtoledo,chiotti,mrgalli}@santafe-conicet.gov.ar
[2] FACIN–PUCRS, Porto Alegre RS, Brazil
rafael.bordini@pucrs.br

Abstract. Recent research on social and organisational aspects of multi-agent systems has led to practical organisational models and the idea of organisation-oriented programming. These organisational models help agents to achieve shared (global) goals of the multi-agent system. Having an organisational model is an important advance, but this model needs to be integrated to an environment infrastructure and agent-oriented programming platforms. *JaCaMo* is the first fully operational programming platform that integrates three levels of multi-agent abstractions: an agent programming language, an organisational model, and an environment infrastructure. For better showcasing the advantages of a fully-fledged multi-agent platform, this paper presents a concrete agent-based architecture to proactively supply knowledge to knowledge-intensive workflows which has been designed using *JaCaMo*.

Keywords: Multi-agent systems, organisations, workflow, knowledge management.

1 Introduction

For Multi-Agent Systems (MAS) to achieve shared global goals, the autonomous behaviour of individual agents sometimes needs to be constrained [12]. Thus, organisational models arise as a way to manage agents' behaviour, so that they can work as a coordinated team in order to achieve common goals.

Organisation-oriented programming has emerged as a result of recent research on social and organisational aspects of MAS; one practical example of such type of programming is made available by the *Moise* platform [13]. To address the issue of collective behaviour, *Moise* allows the definition of structural, functional, and normative aspects of agent organisations. Each agent in the system, if it chooses to participate in the organisation, must comply with organisational rules that constrain its autonomy. *Moise* proposes an organisational modelling language and principles for defining these rules, organising the system, and ensuring organisational constraints by means of notions such as roles, groups, schemes, missions, permissions, and obligations.

To characterise multi-agent oriented programming, an organisational model should be integrated with both an environment infrastructure and an agent

L.A. Dennis, O. Boissier, and R.H. Bordini (Eds.): ProMAS 2011, LNCS 7217, pp. 41–57, 2012.

programming platform. Agents can then reason about the organisation in which they are playing specific roles and interact with their shared environment. Recent research has focused on the integration of organisational models with agent-oriented programming platforms so as to provide practical solutions for MAS development [3,13,8,11,12]. With that purpose, the multi-agent programming platform called *JaCaMo* was developed. It allows users to take advantage of first-class abstractions and declarative language constructs that encompass the three main abstraction levels of a multi-agent system. It was developed through the integration of three independent existing MAS technologies addressing the agent, environment, and organisation levels respectively.

In this work, we present a MAS architecture developed using *JaCaMo*. This architecture allows the proactive supply of knowledge to knowledge-intensive workflows by integrating Business Process Management (BPM) and Knowledge Management (KM) infrastructures. The remainder of this paper is structured as follows. Section 2 describes the various features of *JaCaMo*. Section 3 presents an agent-based architecture for BPM and KM integration. In Section 4, the architecture based on *JaCaMo*'s features is described. Section 5 presents related work. Finally, Section 6 presents conclusions and future work.

2   *JaCaMo* Platform

JaCaMo[1] is a platform for multi-agent programming that combines three independent existing MAS technologies: *Jason*[2] [5], *CArtAgO*[3] [23], and *Moise*[4] [13]. *JaCaMo* allows developers to program organisation-aware BDI (Belief-Desire-Intention) agents supporting the Agent & Artifact (A&A) meta-model [18] for the implementation of environment-based coordination mechanisms and non-autonomous services and tools [28]. It should be highlighted that *JaCaMo* is more than a set of MAS technologies, it is a unified and fully operational platform that supports the three main levels of MAS abstractions of a MAS: agent, environment, and organisation. The following subsections detail each of the main components of the *JaCaMo* platform.

2.1   Organisational Model

JaCaMo uses the *Moise* model for the specification of MAS organisations. *Moise* provides an organisational modelling language, an organisation management infrastructure, and supports organisation-based reasoning mechanisms at the agent level. *Moise* defines three dimensions that deal with various aspects of an organisational specification: *structural*, *functional*, and *normative*.

The *structural dimension* deals with the more static aspects of the organisational model, and it is built on three levels: the *individual level*, which deals with

---

[1] Available at http://jacamo.sourceforge.net/
[2] Available at http://jason.sourceforge.net/
[3] Available at http://cartago.sourceforge.net/
[4] Available at http://moise.sourceforge.net/

the responsibilities an agent assumes when it adopts a role; the *social level*, which describes acquaintance, communication, and authority links between roles; and the *collective level* responsible for the aggregation of roles into groups.

At the *individual level*, agents adopt roles in organisational groups, accepting some behavioural constraints related to such roles. This adoption is constrained by compatibility relations between roles, so that an agent can play two or more roles only if they are compatible. At the *collective level*, agents are divided into groups and sub-groups. Groups and sub-groups are considered well-formed if they comply with the constraints referred to maximum and minimum numbers of members playing each role. At the *social level*, roles are linked through authority, communication, and acquaintance relationships. These relationships indicate the influence or the rights an agent has over agents playing roles related through such links. Relationships can be intra-group or inter-group depending on whether their linked roles belong to the same or different groups.

The *functional dimension* deals with the dynamic aspects of the organisational specification. It aims at making agents work together to achieve global goals. This dimension is composed of a set of *schemes* in which a goal is decomposed into social plans and distributed to agents through *missions* [13]. These schemes are modelled by trees in which the root is a global goal and the leaves are goals that agents can achieve individually.

Schemes specify execution plans that define partial orders for goal achievements. The execution of goals of a plan can be sequential, parallel, or alternative. In a sequence, a goal can be achieved only if the preceding goal has been previously achieved. In a parallel decomposition, two goals can be achieved at the same time. In an alternative decomposition, a goal is deemed achieved if any of its sub-goals has been achieved.

Each scheme may include a number of missions. A mission is a set of goals that an agent playing a particular roles can/must achieve [13] within a given amount of time. Agents commit to missions, so they are responsible for their fulfilment (i.e., the achievement of a set of goals included in that mission).

The *normative dimension* links the *structural dimension* (i.e., roles and groups) with the *functional dimension* (i.e., the schemes). It limits the autonomy of the agents by defining which missions an agent who plays a role in the organisation is permitted to take on and to what missions it is obliged to commit. A relationship $permission(r, m)$ specifies that the agents that play role r *can* commit to mission m, while a relationship $obligation(r, m)$ specifies that the agents that play role r *must* commit to mission m.

2.2   Agent Platform

To develop the agents, *JaCaMo* uses the *Jason* MAS platform [5], which is based on an interpreter for an extended version of the AgentSpeak programming language [22], one of the best-known languages for BDI agents. *Jason* allows the creation of user-defined internal actions and the customisation of agent features such as perception, action, AgentSpeak selection functions, trust, belief bases, and communication. Furthermore, *Jason* supports the notion of a multi-agent environment and the ability to deploy a MAS distributed over a network, for example using JADE [4] as middleware. Communication mechanisms allow agents to communicate with one another through high-level protocols based on speech-act and performatives similar to the well-known Knowledge Query and Manipulation Language (KQML). For more details, see [5]. At this abstraction level, belief, goals, and plans are some of the main concepts.

2.3 Environment as a First-Class Abstraction

Ideally, MAS environments should not be just the source of agent perceptions and the target of agent actions. It should be also considered as an active abstraction, i.e. a first-class entity that encapsulates functionalities and services, supporting coordination, agent mobility, communication, security, and non-autonomous special functions [28].

JaCaMo provides an infrastructure to program MAS environments adopting the A&A meta-model as implemented by the *CArtAgO* technology [23]. *JaCaMo* uses the environment to access external hardware/software resources hiding away low-level aspects. The environment also provides mechanisms to access shared resources and mediate the interaction between agents.

With *JaCaMo*, users can program the environment by means of a set of first-class entities called artifacts. Each artifact represents a resource or tool that agents can instantiate, share, use, and perceive at runtime [18]. Artifacts are non-autonomous and function-oriented entities, whereas agents are autonomous and goal-oriented entities. Artifacts are at the appropriate level of abstraction for agent interaction in declarative approaches to programming MAS.

Agents and artifacts interact through *actions* and *perceptions*. Agents execute *actions* (or operations) of the artifact's *usage interface* in order to modify the artifact state or to request a service. Changes in the state of an artifact are perceived by agents through observable events, which potentially become agent beliefs.

Artifacts can be linked to work together, accomplishing their purposes by executing operations of the *link interfaces* of other artifacts. When an agent or another artifact executes an operation over an artifact, the operation request is suspended while the invoked operation is executed and a result (success or failure) is returned. Artifacts handle all aspects of concurrency control for the operations they provide.

Agents and artifacts are grouped in workspaces that act as logical containers. Workspaces, which define the environment topology, can be distributed while agents and artifacts work together by means of direct communication and sharing artifacts. An artifact belongs to a single workspace whereas an agent can inhabit one or more workspaces and share artifacts. Agents working in the same workspace can use the same artifacts.

2.4 Three-Level Abstraction Integration

The three main MAS levels of abstractions (agent, organisation, and environment) are available in *JaCaMo*. Agents join a particular workspace and can then use the artifact operations and sense the observable properties of artifacts. It allows heterogeneous agents to work in the same artifact-based environment, sharing actions and observable events.

The organisation-environment integration is based on the ORA4MAS infrastructure [11]. This infrastructure for organisational management was developed as a set of *organisational artifacts* and *organisational agents*. They are responsible for encapsulating functionalities concerning the management and enactment of the organisation specification, implementing and controlling regimentation and enforcement mechanisms. Regimentation aims to prevent agents from performing actions that are forbidden by an organisational norm, whereas enforcement aims to provide tools for detecting possible norm violations, for checking whether they were violations or not, and imposing the appropriate sanctions if they were [11].

In ORA4MAS, there are two main types of *organisational artifacts*: *scheme* and *group*. They are responsible for implementing the structural, functional, and normative dimensions of *Moise* through a set of operations that allows agents to adopt a role, join or leave a group, commit to a mission, etc.

Organisational agents are responsible for the creation and management of organisational artifacts and for performing *enforcement* activities. If a norm is violated, artifacts should detect and show this violation, and the organisational agents should deal with it. Both organisational agents and organisational artifacts are described in detail in [15].

The agent-organisation integration is carried out by a mapping of agents' actions into operations of the organisational artifacts. That is, an agent performs an operation (such as to adopt a role, leave a mission, etc.) of an organisational artifact by means of its repertoire of environment actions. This mapping provides a unified mechanism for normal actions (e.g., to move a robotic arm) as well as organisational actions (e.g., to adopt a role).

3 An Agent-Based Architecture for BPM and KM Integration

These days, many companies coordinate their activities through business processes. To accomplish the tasks involved in a business process, workers may need information that is scattered throughout the company. This need for information should be attended to in a contextualised way and be suitably delivered through the company's Knowledge Management (KM) infrastructure [21]. Business Process Management (BPM) and KM are closely interrelated and are both important elements of any corporation.

Enterprise activities orchestrated through a business process and automated by a Workflow Management System (WfMS) should be considered as an opportunity to provide a KM infrastructure in order to bring the right knowledge to the right people in the right form and at the right time [10]. A WfMS defines, manages, and executes structured business processes by arranging task executions through a computational representation of the workflow logic. It should be a trigger of KM support activities and a distributor of enterprise knowledge that provides the participants (e.g., an employee responsible for a particular task within the company) with the necessary information for them to make better decisions.

Some tasks of a business process require intensive information flow. For such tasks, participants of the business process would benefit from the WfMS automatically and proactively offering the relevant knowledge required for the task to be accomplished [17]. When someone selects a task to be executed, the system should make available all the relevant information, avoiding any time waste in searching for such information.

The integration between KM and BPM has been addressed in many research efforts. However, most existing approaches are conceptual proposals without specific solutions [21]. Other existing frameworks define static systems in which the knowledge domains are tied with the architecture, failing to support the current diversity of knowledge domains [1,14].

Toledo et al. [27] proposed an agent-based architecture for the integration of business processes orchestrated by a WfMS with the enterprise knowledge repository managed by ontology-driven KM systems (Figure 1). The architecture is based on a distributed enterprise memory [24] and the KM conceptual model proposed in [2]. This architecture consists of three main types of components: an *enterprise knowledge repository*, *knowledge intensive workflows*, and a *knowledge exchange infrastructure*.

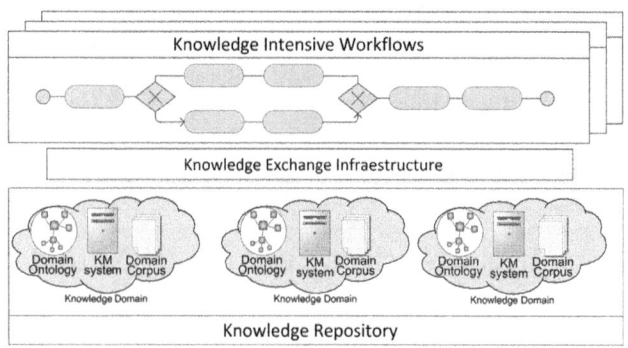

Fig. 1. Enterprise Knowledge Management Architecture

In the *knowledge repository*, the corporation is seen as a set of interrelated functional units defined through its structure, informal groups, or communities of practice. Each of these units is considered an enterprise knowledge domain executing activities that produce and consume information.

KM systems are responsible for storing knowledge produced in their respective domains and for providing information to requests related to their own knowledge domain coming from other knowledge domains, and, in the case of this proposal, to WfMSs as well. The set of all knowledge domains of the enterprise constitutes the *enterprise knowledge repository*, i.e., the enterprise memory [16].

Each knowledge domain implements its own KM system. This KM system is part of a distributed enterprise memory [24]. KM systems typically use an ontology to annotate and retrieve information to/from the domain corpus.

The *knowledge intensive workflows* automate a set of business processes composed of one or more tasks that require and/or produce valuable enterprise knowledge. These tasks are called Knowledge Intensive Tasks (KITs). Relevant information should be proactively provided to each KIT for its execution, considering the participants' behaviour in previously performed tasks and the KIT context including the participant's profile and role, as well as the task specification. Also, relevant information produced as a result of a KIT execution should be stored in a suitable knowledge domain. The tasks of knowledge intensive workflows are orchestrated by a WfMS.

The *knowledge exchange infrastructure*, implemented as a MAS, supports the knowledge exchange between the knowledge repository and the workflows. Through interaction protocols, agents can exchange and control the information that the participants require in order to perform the tasks involved in the business processes. Conventional workflows are extended by including automatic tasks for KM support, which execute instances of software agents. These agents are responsible for retrieving knowledge from the repository and storing results within it.

MAS technology was used in this system for three main reasons. First, it is an open system: new workflows and knowledge domains can be added on-the-fly. Each domain can manage the local knowledge and choose the representation mechanisms and management policies. Second, agents can use machine learning techniques to improve the knowledge provision and storing processes. Third, the involved entities should have autonomous behaviour in deciding the most convenient way to store the generated information, and the most suitable knowledge sources to consult.

4   The Architecture Specification

The proposed architecture was specified using the *JaCaMo* platform. Details of its specification are described following.

4.1   Environment Specification

The proposed MAS architecture is composed of a set of distributed artifact-based workspaces [20], which can be classified into three types: *KIT workspaces*, *knowledge domain workspaces*, and the *knowledge integration workspace*. Each workspace contains agents and artifact instances that supply agents with information and help them to coordinate their activities. Artifacts also encapsulate other non-autonomous services, such as the *KM system artifact* which is responsible for managing the local domain knowledge (see Figure 2).

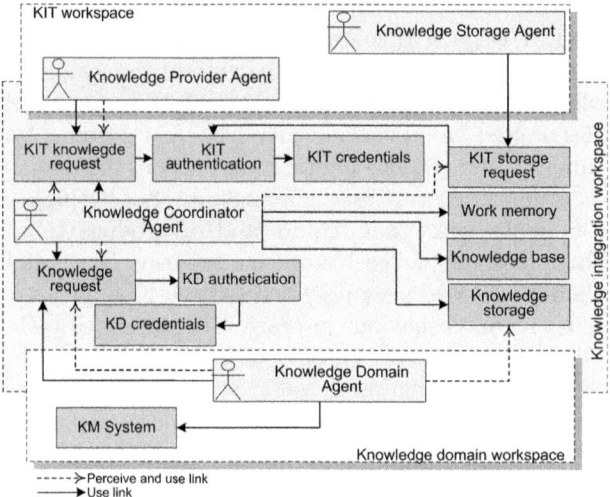

Fig. 2. MAS Topology

Each *KIT workspace* models the enactment of a KIT, and contains instances of artifacts and agents responsible for providing and storing information relevant to the KIT. The KIT workspace contains the *knowledge provider agent* and the *knowledge storage agent*. The former is responsible for retrieving information relevant to the KIT, taking into account the parameters of the participant profile specification artifact, the participant role specification artifact, and the KIT specification artifact. For details about those agents, see [27]. The latter agent is responsible for collecting results obtained from the KIT execution. Once the information has been collected, the agent establishes the necessary communication for storing results in the appropriate knowledge domain. To determine the knowledge domain in which results will be stored, configuration parameters of the KIT specification artifact are taken into account.

The knowledge provider agent and the knowledge storage agent join the KIT workspace as well as the knowledge integration workspace. This allows agents to use artifacts of both workspaces and exchange data, enabling integration within this architecture.

Each knowledge domain workspace represents an enterprise knowledge domain. Therefore, in the architecture, there are as many knowledge domain workspaces as there are knowledge domains in the corporation or company where the system is to be deployed. Each knowledge domain workspace includes its own KM system that is responsible for providing and storing the domain knowledge. An approach for its implementation was detailed in [26]. The *knowledge domain agent* uses operations of the KM system artifact to consult information and then provides this information to a KIT through the *knowledge coordinator agent*. The knowledge domain agent joins the knowledge domain workspace and the knowledge integration workspace as well.

Finally, the MAS architecture has a single instance of the *knowledge integration workspace* which makes the integration between enterprise knowledge repositories and knowledge intensive workflows possible by means of artifact-based coordination and agent communication. The knowledge coordinator agent is responsible for the exchange of knowledge between workflows and knowledge domains, and can pro-actively offer knowledge to KIT participants. This agent also manages the MAS organisation by applying sanctions and rewards, and controlling the access of KITs and knowledge domains to the system.

The knowledge integration workspace is populated by a set of artifacts that enable the system to authenticate KITs and knowledge domains (the KIT authentication and KD authentication artifacts), store access credentials (the KIT credentials and KD credentials artifacts), coordinate agents and exchange knowledge (the KIT storage request, KIT knowledge request, Knowledge request, and Knowledge storage artifacts), and help the knowledge coordinator agent to fulfil its responsibilities (the Work memory and Knowledge-base artifacts). The code in Figure 3 shows how the knowledge coordinator agent creates and focuses on the artifacts in its environment.

```
+!create_artifacts: true
 <- makeArtifact("KnowledgeProvider","kiWorkspace.KnowledgeProvider",[],KnowledgeProviderID);
    makeArtifact("KITAutentication","kiWorkspace.KITAutentication",[],KITAutenticationID);
    makeArtifact("KDAutentication","kiWorkspace.KDAutentication",[],KDAutenticationID);
    makeArtifact("KDCredentials","kiWorkspace.KDCredentials",[],KDCredentialsID);
    makeArtifact("KITCredentials","kiWorkspace.KITCredentials",[],KITCredentialsID);
    makeArtifact("KITStorageRequest","kiWorkspace.KITStorageRequest",[],KITStorageRequestID);
    makeArtifact("KnowledgeBase","kiWorkspace.KnowledgeBase",[],KnowledgeBaseID);
    makeArtifact("WorkMemory","kiWorkspace.WorkMemory",[],WorkMemoryID);
    makeArtifact("KnowledgeRequest","kiWorkspace.KnowledgeRequest",[],KnowledgeRequestID);
    makeArtifact("KnowledgeResponse","kiWorkspace.KnowledgeResponse",[],KnowledgeResponseID);
    makeArtifact("KnowledgeStorage","kiWorkspace.KnowledgeStorage",[],KnowledgeStorageID);
    focus(KnowledgeProviderID);
    focus(KITStorageRequestID);
    focus(KnowledgeRequestID);
    focus(KnowledgeResponseID).
```

Fig. 3. Artifact Creation

The knowledge coordinator agent also creates two organisational artifacts to manage the organisational model: the *group* and *scheme* artifacts (for the sake of clarity, these are not shown in Figure 2). The scheme artifact (see Section 2.4) keeps track of which goals are feasible and creates the respective obligations for agents, whereas the group artifact manages the organisation groups. The organisational specification (groups, goals, roles, etc.) is defined in the *organisation.xml* file, as referenced in the code in Figure 4.

Workspaces with their artifacts define the MAS environment. Agents can only access artifacts of workspaces to which they have joined. As agents can join more than one workspace, this enables the coordination and communication between agents belonging to different workspaces through artifacts. The code in Figure 5 shows how the knowledge domain agent discovers the relevant artifacts when it enters the system.

```
+!create_organisational_artifacts: true
  <- makeArtifact("Scheme", "ora4mas.nopl.SchemeBoard",
       ["organisation.xml", scheme, false, true], SchemeID);
     makeArtifact("Group", "ora4mas.nopl.GroupBoard",
       ["organisation.xml", group, false, true], GroupID);
     focus(SchemeID);
     focus(GroupID).
```

Fig. 4. Organisational Artifacts

```
+!enter_kmArchitecture: true
  <- joinWorkspace("KnowledgeIntegration",kiID);
     !discover_artifact("Scheme");
     !discover_artifact("Group");
     !discover_artifact("KnowledgeRequest");
     !discover_artifact("KnowledgeStorage").
+!discover_artifact(ArtifactName): true
  <- lookupArtifact(ArtifactName,ArtifactId);
     focus(ArtifactId).
```

Fig. 5. Entering the System

4.2   Structural Specification

In order to achieve global goals, agents' autonomy should be controlled by means
of behavioural constraints [12]. These constraints are defined in the organisational specification that is part of the system design. As described in Section 2,
the *JaCaMo* platform, based on the *Moise* model, allows an organisational structure to be assigned to the system through the specification of groups, roles, and
shared goals.

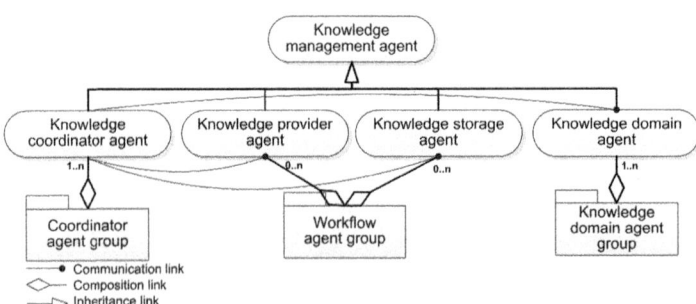

Fig. 6. *Moise* Structural Specification Diagram

At the *collective level* of the *Moise*'s structural dimension, three agent groups
are defined: *coordinator agents, workflow agents,* and *knowledge domain agents*
(see Figure 6). The coordinator agent group is composed of at least one agent
playing the role of knowledge coordinator. The workflow agent group can be

composed of agents playing two types of roles: knowledge provider and knowledge storage. The architecture allows zero, one, or more KITs; each of them has a knowledge provider agent and a knowledge storage agent. The knowledge domain agent group is composed of one or more agents playing the role of knowledge domain manager. All those agents inherit the properties of the knowledge management agent role.

At the *social level* of *Moise*'s structural dimension, inter-group communication relationships specify that two agents of different groups may exchange information. The structural specification diagram in Figure 6 shows that the knowledge coordinator agent can communicate with other agents, allowing the exchange of information between various KITs and knowledge domains.

4.3   Functional and Normative Specifications

The MAS behaviour is specified as social plans that agents should execute together so as to achieve global goals. The *Moise* functional dimension decomposes global goals into simpler goals and distributes them by assigning *missions* (i.e., a set of goals) to agents [13]. The architecture proposed for the case study presented in this paper has two global goals: *Store relevant information* and *Provide relevant information*.

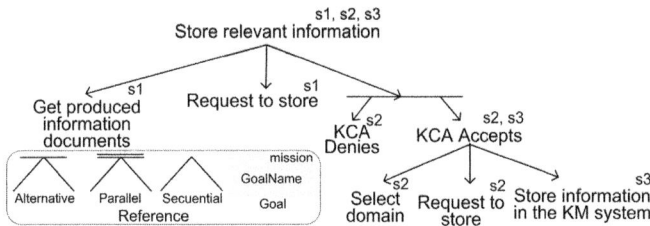

Fig. 7. *Moise* Functional Specification Diagram for the "Store relevant information" Goal

The functional decomposition of the "Store relevant information" goal is shown in Figure 7. This goal is decomposed into tree missions to be assigned to the agents. Mission s1 includes goals *Get produced information* and *Request to store*. Mission s2 includes goals to decide whether the request to store is *Denied* or *Accepted*, to *Select domain*, and to send a *Request to store*. Mission s3 has only the goal to *Store information in the KM system*.

When a participant performs a task within a workflow that creates or modifies a document, the knowledge storage agent can trigger the "Store relevant information" goal by committing to carry out mission s1. In that case, other agents must commit to the another missions. Table 1 presents the corresponding rules of the normative specification.

The agents interact in the following way (see Figure 2): the *knowledge storage agent* (mission s1 in Figure 7) creates a request to store information in the

KIT storage request artifact (Figure 2). This request includes storing criteria, information about the workflow instance, and the information document to be stored.

The KIT storage request artifact validates the request. If the request comes from an authorised agent, the artifact generates an environment property that is then perceived by the *knowledge coordinator agent*.

The *knowledge coordinator agent* (mission s2 in Figure 7) receives the request and decides whether to deny or accept it. If it is accepted, based on information about the KIT and its own knowledge (currently active knowledge domains, preferred domains, frequently consulted domains, etc.), the agent decides the knowledge domains to which the information will be sent to be stored. Then, it creates a storage request in the corresponding Knowledge storage artifact (Figure 2).

When the *knowledge domain agents* (mission s3 in Figure 7) receive environment perception they check whether any of the percepts is directed to them. The agent to which the storage request is directed stores the information in its KM System (Figure 2).

The functional decomposition of the "Provide relevant information" goal is divided into six missions: pp1, pp2, pp3, pr1, pr2, and pr3, as shown in Figure 8.

When a participant selects a KIT to perform, agents interact for providing knowledge in a proactive way, as follows. The *knowledge provider agent* (mission pp1 in Figure 8) makes a request through the respective operation in the KIT knowledge request artifact (Figure 2), providing the KIT specification, information about the workflow instance, the participant's profile, and the participant's role. The KIT knowledge request artifact validates the request. If the request comes from an authorised agent, it generates an environment property that is perceived by the knowledge coordinator agent.

The *knowledge coordinator agent* (mission pp2 in Figure 8) receives the request. Based on the KIT specification, participant's profile, participant's role, and its own knowledge, this agent decides the knowledge domains from which the information will be obtained.

Once the target domains were selected, the agent creates a knowledge request in the knowledge request artifact. The knowledge domain agent (mission pp3 in Figure 8) retrieves the required information from its KM system and sends it to the knowledge coordinator agent. The knowledge coordinator agent than supplies the information to the knowledge provider agent that made the request.

Participants can also request knowledge through Natural Language Queries (NLQs). In that case, the query is sent to knowledge domains to be processed and the information that answers the query can be retrieved (missions pr1, pr2, and pr3 in Figure 8). The process through which agents interact to provide the knowledge is similar to the previous case.

The features of both MAS technology and particularly the *JaCaMo* platform enable the knowledge coordinator agent, through machine learning strategies and recommendation mechanisms [29], to improve the quality of knowledge supply. Also, the knowledge storage mechanism can be improved by making available

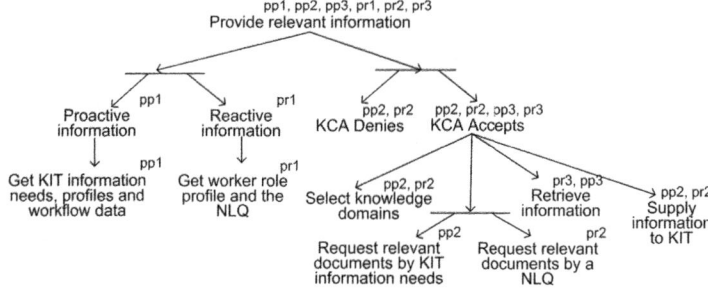

Fig. 8. *Moise* Functional Specification of the "Provide relevant information" Goal

Table 1. *Moise* Normative Specification

role	deontic relation	mission
Knowledge Coordinator Agent (KCA)	obligation	s2
Knowledge Coordinator Agent (KCA)	obligation	pp2
Knowledge Coordinator Agent (KCA)	obligation	pr2
Knowledge Domain Agent (KDA)	obligation	s3
Knowledge Domain Agent (KDA)	obligation	pp3
Knowledge Domain Agent (KDA)	obligation	pr3
Knowledge Storage Agent (KSA)	permission	s1
Knowledge Provider Agent (KPA)	permission	pp1
Knowledge Provider Agent (KPA)	permission	pr1

information about reliability, security, confidence, and so forth; the Knowledge coordinator agent could use that information for deciding in which domains the information should be stored or consulted.

The use of MAS and the encapsulation of the KM systems into artifacts allow knowledge domains to implement different information retrieval strategies. Some such strategies can be found in [2] and [26].

5   Related Work

Related work was analysed from the MAS and KM-BPM integration viewpoints. The MAS approaches related to this work are as follows.

Baldoni et al. [3] propose a formal model that represents agents and the environment in terms of rules of interaction, conventions, resources, tools, and services for supporting direct and indirect forms of communication. They propose the use of the A&A meta-model to define artifacts that implement commitment protocols and verify the interaction of the agents. It remains future work the implementation of an infrastructure supporting that model.

The MASQ meta-model [25] is based on a 4-quadrant approach: the interior-individual quadrant deals with emotions, beliefs, desires, and intentions of an individual agent; the exterior-individual quadrant models the physical bodies, objects, and their behaviour; the exterior-collective quadrant deals with concepts of the organisation such as group and systems; and, the interior-collective quadrant describes collective representations, ontologies, and social norms. MASQ provides a unified model for physical and social environment focusing on the modelling of MAS. A software infrastructure to support the model is not yet available either.

Dastani et al. [7] present a programming language to implement MAS based on *norms* as a programming construct and a logic approach to verify properties of multi-agent system programs. The language provides constructs to specify the effects of agents' actions, and also monitoring and sanctioning mechanisms to determine the effects of actions performed in shared environments. This approach lacks a full integration platform to develop complete systems.

The KM and BPM integration approaches related to this work are as follows. Papavassiliou et al. [19] propose a framework for weakly-structured and knowledge-intensive business processes. This approach extends the workflow meta-model including KM tasks and knowledge objects. Two types of tasks are defined: normal tasks, related to the work structure; and KM tasks, such as knowledge storage, knowledge distribution, knowledge generation, and knowledge application. Through this extension, KM tasks are integrated into the workflow model, but the approach does not provide any features for proactive knowledge supply and there is no integration with the enterprise KM system.

Abecker et al. [1] present the VisualOffice and KnowMore projects for the integration of KM and BPM. VisualOffice employs workflow context data to integrate paper-based information in workflows. Context information, scanned document analysis, and a system able to understand information are used to provide knowledge to people participating in the processes. Relevant information about the workflow is collected so as to use such information for document retrieval. KnowMore is focused on delivering relevant and context-sensitive information to people who work on KITs. It recommends information to them, and records results of their task executions together with context data. These approaches do not consider open environments, i.e., knowledge domains and workflows are unknown in advance.

Jung et al. [14] define an architecture for integrating BPM and KM based on their lifecycle requirements. The objective is to consolidate KM and BPM lifecycle by extending it to include process knowledge. Three types of knowledge to support KITs are defined: process template knowledge that contains the information collected during process creation, modelling, and evolution; knowledge of process instances composed of information collected during and after the process enactment phase; and process-related knowledge. The approach also assumes a closed environment in which knowledge domains and workflows are known in advance.

Han et al. [9] propose a framework for process-centred knowledge model, develop an enterprise ontology that links enterprise concepts for future knowledge retrieval, and implement a KM system that support the framework. The proposal intends to provide knowledge enriched by the context for improving task execution. The model defines process knowledge objects that provide guidelines and tools for task execution as well as task support knowledge such as documents, business rules, expert consulting, and on-line forum. The approach was developed for closed environments and does not provide services for proactive knowledge supply.

6   Conclusions and Future Work

The KM and BPM integration problem addressed in this work requires a MAS architecture with complex autonomous agents, each playing different roles into dynamic organisations situated in environments with special features. The autonomous behaviour of the agents should be constrained in appropriate ways as agents must work as a coordinated team to achieve common goals. To satisfy these requirements, approaches that integrate organisational models with both environment infrastructures and an agent programming platform were found to be useful.

The *JaCaMo* platform was the only complete MAS platform available that was able to satisfy all those requirements, through first-class abstractions and declarative language constructs that encompass the three main abstraction levels of a multi-agent system. Using this platform, a MAS architecture was developed. This architecture allows the proactive supply of knowledge to knowledge-intensive workflows by integrating BPM and KM infrastructures. This also served as one of the first case study for the platform.

The use of *JaCaMo* allowed us to develop an open system able to evolve at runtime, enabling human designers or agents themselves changing the high-level specifications of particular agents, the organisation, or the environment. Through this case study, *JaCaMo* has proved to be a fully-fledged MAS development platform that facilitates the development of complex multi-agent applications.

Performance analysis of the MAS developed will be reported in future work. This requires results of at least six months of operation in real-world situations. Currently, the system implementation is being improved to operate in a real-world environment under controlled conditions for evaluation purposes. Furthermore, due to the current lack of a suitable modelling tools, it would be interesting to develop a modelling approach, for example based on MAS-ML [6], which will allow the description of all static and dynamic aspects of *JaCaMo*. Such modelling language is likely to use the OMG's Meta Object Facility (MOF).

References

1. Abecker, A., Bernardi, A., Maus, H., Sintek, M., Wenzel, C.: Information supply for business processes: coupling workflow with document analysis and information retrieval. Knowledge-Based Systems 13(5), 271–284 (2000)
2. Ale, M.A.: An Organizational Knowledge Management Conceptual Model. PhD in information systems, National Technological University (2009)

3. Baldoni, M., Baroglio, C., Bergenti, F., Boccalatte, A., Marengo, E., Martelli, M., Mascardi, V., Padovani, L., Patti, V., Ricci, A., et al.: MERCURIO: An Interaction-oriented Framework for Designing, Verifying and Programming Multi-Agent Systems. In: 11th Inter. Workshop on Coordination, Organization, Institutions and Norms in MAS, France (2010)
4. Bellifemine, F.L., Caire, G., Greenwood, D.: Developing Multi-Agent Systems with JADE. Wiley (2007)
5. Bordini, R., Hübner, J., Wooldridge, M.: Programming multi-agent systems in AgentSpeak using Jason. Wiley (2007)
6. da Silva, V.T., Choren, R., de Lucena, C.J.P.: Using the MAS-ML to Model a Multi-agent System. In: Lucena, C., Garcia, A., Romanovsky, A., Castro, J., Alencar, P.S.C. (eds.) SELMAS 2003. LNCS, vol. 2940, pp. 129–148. Springer, Heidelberg (2004)
7. Dastani, M., Grossi, D., Meyer, J.-J.C., Tinnemeier, N.: Normative Multi-agent Programs and Their Logics. In: Meyer, J.-J.C., Broersen, J. (eds.) KRAMAS 2008. LNCS, vol. 5605, pp. 16–31. Springer, Heidelberg (2009)
8. Esteva, M., Rosell, B., Rodríguez-Aguilar, J.A., Arcos, J.L.: AMELI: An agent-based middleware for electronic institutions. In: International Joint Conference on Autonomous Agents and MAS, vol. 1, pp. 236–243 (2004)
9. Han, K.H., Park, J.W.: Process-centered knowledge model and enterprise ontology for the development of knowledge management system. Expert Systems with Applications 36(4), 7441–7447 (2009)
10. Hollingsworth, D.: The workflow reference model. Tech. Rep. TC00-1003, Workflow Management Coalition (1995)
11. Hübner, J., Boissier, O., Kitio, R., Ricci, A.: Instrumenting multi-agent organisations with organisational artifacts and agents. AAMAS 20, 369–400 (2010)
12. Hübner, J.F., Sichman, J.S., Boissier, O.: S-Moise$^+$: A Middleware for Developing Organised Multi-agent Systems. In: Boissier, O., Padget, J., Dignum, V., Lindemann, G., Matson, E., Ossowski, S., Sichman, J.S., Vázquez-Salceda, J. (eds.) ANIREM 2005 and OOOP 2005. LNCS (LNAI), vol. 3913, pp. 64–78. Springer, Heidelberg (2006)
13. Hübner, J.F., Sichman, J.S., Boissier, O.: Developing organised multiagent systems using the Moise+ model: programming issues at the system and agent levels. Inter. Journal of Agent-Oriented Software Engineering 1(3/4), 370–395 (2007)
14. Jung, J., Choi, I., Song, M.: An integration architecture for knowledge management systems and business process management systems. Computers in Industry 58(1), 21–34 (2007)
15. Kitio, R., Boissier, O., Hübner, J.F., Ricci, A.: Organisational Artifacts and Agents for Open Multi-Agent Organisations: "Giving the Power Back to the Agents". In: Sichman, J.S., Padget, J., Ossowski, S., Noriega, P. (eds.) COIN 2007 Workshops. LNCS (LNAI), vol. 4870, pp. 171–186. Springer, Heidelberg (2008)
16. Kühn, O., Abecker, A.: Corporate memories for knowledge management in industrial practice: Prospects and challenges. Journal of Universal Computer Science 3(8), 929–954 (1997)
17. Lai, J., Fan, Y.: Workflow and Knowledge Management: Approaching an Integration. In: Han, Y., Tai, S., Wikarski, D. (eds.) EDCIS 2002. LNCS, vol. 2480, pp. 16–29. Springer, Heidelberg (2002)
18. Omicini, A., Ricci, A., Viroli, M.: Artifacts in the A&A meta-model for multi-agent systems. Autonomous Agents and Multi-Agent Systems 17(3), 432–456 (2008)

19. Papavassiliou, G., Mentzas, G., Abecker, A.: Integrating knowledge modelling in business process management. In: ECIS 2002 Conference: The Xth European Conference on Information Systems (2002)
20. Piunti, M., Ricci, A.: Cognitive Use of Artifacts: Exploiting Relevant Information Residing in MAS Environments. In: Meyer, J.-J.C., Broersen, J. (eds.) KRAMAS 2008. LNCS, vol. 5605, pp. 114–129. Springer, Heidelberg (2009)
21. Raghu, T., Vinze, A.: A business process context for knowledge management. Decision Support Systems 43(3), 1062–1079 (2007)
22. Rao, A.: AgentSpeak (L): BDI Agents Speak Out in a Logical Computable Language. In: Van de Velde, W., Perram, J.W. (eds.) MAAMAW 1996. LNCS, vol. 1038, pp. 42–55. Springer, Heidelberg (1996)
23. Ricci, A., Piunti, M., Viroli, M.: Environment programming in multi-agent systems: An artifact-based perspective. Autonomous Agents and MAS, 1–35 (2010)
24. Souza, R.G.S.: Agent-oriented constructivist knowledge management. Ph.D. thesis, University of Twente, Enschede (2006)
25. Stratulat, T., Ferber, J., Tranier, J.: MASQ: towards an integral approach to interaction. In: Proceedings of the 8th International Conference on Autonomous Agents and Multiagent Systems. International Foundation for Autonomous Agents and Multiagent Systems, vol. 2, pp. 813–820 (2009)
26. Toledo, C.M., Ale, M., Chiotti, O., Galli, M.R.: An agent-based architecture for ontology-driven knowledge management. In: The V International Conference on Knowledge, Information and Creativity Support Systems, Thailand (2010)
27. Toledo, C.M., Chiotti, O., Galli, M.R.: Towards business process management and knowledge management integration through an agent-based architecture. In: XXIX International Conference of the Chilean Computer Society JCC 2010, Chile (2010)
28. Weyns, D., Omicini, A., Odell, J.: Environment as a first class abstraction in multiagent systems. Autonomous Agents and Multi-Agent Systems 14, 5–30 (2007)
29. Zhen, L., Huang, G.Q., Jiang, Z.: Recommender system based on workflow. Decision Support Systems 48(1), 237–245 (2009)

Notes on Pragmatic Agent-Programming with *Jason*

Radek Píbil[1,2], Peter Novák[1], Cyril Brom[2], and Jakub Gemrot[2]

[1] Agent Technology Center, Department of Computer Science and Engineering
Faculty of Electrical Engineering, Czech Technical University in Prague
Czech Republic
[2] Department of Software and Computer Science Education
Faculty of Mathematics and Physics, Charles University in Prague
Czech Republic

Abstract . *AgentSpeak(L)*, together with its implementation *Jason*, is one of the most influential agent-oriented programming languages. Besides having a strong conceptual influence on the niche of BDI-inspired agent programming systems, *Jason* also serves as one of the primary tools for education of and experimentation with agent-oriented programming. Despite its popularity in the community, relatively little is reported on its practical applications and pragmatic experiences with adoption of the language for non-trivial applications.

In this paper, we present our experiences gathered during an experiment aimed at development of a non-trivial case-study agent application by a novice *Jason* programmer. In our experiment, we tried to use the programming language *as is*, with as few customisations of the *Jason* interpreter as possible. Besides providing a structured feedback on the most problematic issues faced while learning to program in *Jason*, we informally propose a set of ideas for solving the encountered design problems and programming language issues.

1   Introduction

Jason [8] is an agent-oriented programming system implementing the agent programming language *AgentSpeak(L)* [19]. *AgentSpeak(L)* was proposed as a theoretical language, an articulation and operationalization of the Bratman's Belief-Desire-Intention architecture [9]. *Jason* is nowadays one of the popular approaches in the group of theoretically-rooted agent-oriented programming languages (APLs). Some other members of this group include also *2APL, 3APL, GOAL, Golog, Jazzyk*, etc. (for an overview consult e.g., [5,6,7,16]). Building on the foundations of formal logics, these languages serve as vehicles for study of both theoretical issues in agent systems (language features, generic programming constructs, reasoning, coordination, etc.), as well as practical aspects of their design and implementation (e.g., modularity, design, debugging, or code maintenance). To enable program verification, or model checking for more rigorous reasoning about agent programs, *Jason*, together with the majority of APLs in this class, puts a strong emphasis on their rooting in computational logic and rigorous formal semantics. Unlike the more pragmatic approaches, such as *Jadex*, or *JACK* (cf. [18,20]), these APLs were designed from scratch. While providing the advantages we have discussed, this has also created serious shortcomings with respect to the practicality of their use, such as those discussed in this paper.

L.A. Dennis, O. Boissier, and R.H. Bordini (Eds.): ProMAS 2011, LNCS 7217, pp. 58–73, 2012.

On one hand, pragmatic problems of agent design and implementation, such as code modularity, are gaining a more prominent role in the research community. On the other hand, a feedback on practical use of such APLs in more elaborated settings is rather scarce. *AgentSpeak(L)* often serves as a basic APL for various extensions and integration with 3rd party tools. However, little is reported on its practical applications and experiences with its use, be it in more involved applied research projects, or in more significant close-to-real-world applications (cf. also the *Jason* related projects website [14]). To date, the only report on pragmatic issues of *Jason* in a more involved context is the study by Madden and Logan [15] in which the authors deal with problems of modularity in their application and in turn propose corresponding improvements of the language itself. At the same time, to our knowledge, the most elaborated applications of the *Jason* programming system include the entries to the *Multi-Agent Programming Contest*, which already witnessed eight submissions in years 2006-2010 altogether by three independent research groups [1,2]. The reports on development of these applications do not include a discussion of practical issues of an agent program implementation, but rather focus on the analysis and design aspects with an emphasis on the multi-agent coordination.

In this paper we discuss our experiences gathered during an experiment aimed at developing a non-trivial case-study multi-agent application by a novice *Jason* programmer. The main goal of the undertaking was an exploration of basic problems in multi-agent coordination in a simple simulated environment using the *Jason* programming system. In particular, we have implemented an application involving a team of eight agents collaboratively exploring a grid maze and subsequently traversing the environment while cooperatively maintaining a formation. Our experiment aimed at a naïve, and relatively conservative use of the *Jason* programming system. We tried to use the programming language *as is*, with as few customisations of the *Jason* interpreter as possible. In contrast, most involved example applications published at the *Jason* project website [14] and submissions to the *AgentContest* employ extensive customisations of the *Jason* interpreter as an inherent part of the system implementation.

The contribution of the presented paper is twofold. Firstly, we provide a structured feedback on the most problematic issues faced while learning to program in *Jason*. Secondly, without an ambition to provide conclusive technical solutions, we rather informally propose a set of ideas aimed at solving the discussed design problems and programming language issues.

After a brief introduction of *AgentSpeak(L)* and *Jason* in Section 2 the subsequent Section 3 provides a description of the implemented case-study. In Section 4, the core of this paper, we discuss a selection of problems we have faced during the experiment. For each discussed issue, we firstly motivate and explain the problem on the background of the introduced case-study application, or its extension, and then we discuss possible solutions. The topics covered in the discussion include implementation of a simple loop design pattern, handling interactions between several plans and interruptibility thereof, and usage of mental notes as local variables in plans. We also discuss two technical issues arising from implementation of agents embodied in dynamic environments and the unclear boundary between *Jason* programming language itself and its underlying customisation API in *Java*. We conclude the paper by final remarks in Section 5.

2   AgentSpeak(L) and Jason

AgentSpeak(L) is a theoretical agent-oriented programming language introduced by Rao in [19]. It can be seen as a flavour of logic programming implementing the core concepts of the BDI agent architecture, a currently dominant approach to design of intelligent agents. Structurally, an *AgentSpeak(L)* agent is composed of a *belief base* and a *plan library*. The belief base, essentially a set of belief literals, provides the initial beliefs of the agent. The plan library serves as a basis for action selection, as well as for steering the evolution of the agent's mental state over time. The plans of the agent are rules of the form:

$$\texttt{event : context} \leftarrow \texttt{plan}$$

The rule denotes a plan, a sequence of basic actions and/or subgoals, which is applicable in reaction to the triggering event if the context condition, a conjunction of belief literals, is satisfied.

AgentSpeak(L) agents are reactive planning systems which react to events occurring in their environment, or are generated as subgoals internally by the agent as a result of a deliberative change in its own goals. The dynamics of the agent system is facilitated by i) instantiation of abstract plans as intentions relevant in particular contexts, and subsequently ii) gradual execution of the intentions leading to their subsequent decomposition into more and more concrete subgoal invocations and finally atomic action executions. In each deliberation cycle, such an agent performs the following sequence of steps:

1. *perceive* the environment and update the belief base accordingly,
2. *select an event* to handle,
3. retrieve all *relevant plans*,
4. *select an applicable plan* and *update the intentions* accordingly,
5. *select an intention* for further execution,
6. *execute one step* of an intention and modify the intention base and the set of events accordingly.

Jason is a *Java*-based programming system implementing *AgentSpeak(L)* with various extensions. It also includes an integration with several multi-agent middleware platforms such as *JADE*, or *Moise+*. In its original incarnation, *AgentSpeak(L)* is underspecified in several points of the deliberation cycle. In particular, in how exactly its three selection functions $\mathcal{S}_{\mathcal{E}}$, $\mathcal{S}_{\mathcal{P}}$ and $\mathcal{S}_{\mathcal{I}}$, denoting the selection of events, applicable plans and intentions respectively, are implemented. In *Jason*, these are customizable functions that can be implemented as *Java* methods. Furthermore, *AgentSpeak(L)* disregards the implementation details of agent's interaction with its environment. That is, the interpreter assumes that the belief base is updated according to agent's percepts at the beginning of each deliberation cycle. *Jason* extends the framework for reasoning about agent's beliefs in that it incorporates a *Prolog* interpreter in the belief base and also provides a toolbox for implementation of custom belief bases, such as the topology of environments, or interface to relational databases. Finally, *Jason* provides a framework for an implementation of perception handlers and external events as *Java* methods, together with an API for implementation of customised exogenous actions embodying the behaviours of the agent.

The customisation interfaces of the *Jason* interpreter provide means to tailor the deliberation cycle to the domain specific requirements, as well as to improve the efficiency of the agent program execution. Our motivation in the presented experiment was to explore the issues faced in the course of agent program implementation using the vanilla *Jason* interpreter. The main requirement underlying the experiment was to make only minimal customisations of the interpreter required to make the implemented agents interact with their environment.

3   The Case-Study

The *Cows & Cowboys* problem of the *Multi-Agent Programming Contest* editions 2009 and 2010 (cf. [4], scenarios for the 2009-10 editions) is a challenging scenario for cooperative multi-agent teams benchmarking. In the *Cows & Cowboys* scenario, two teams of agents, herders, compete for a shared resource, cows. The environment is a grid, usually a square with a side approximately 100 cells. Each cell can be either empty, or can contain an object which can be either a tree, a fence, an agent, or a cow. Trees serve as obstacles in the environment and are arranged so that the freely traversable space forms a kind of a maze. The agents can move between empty cells and can open fences, by standing at the edge of a fence. Similarly to the agents, cows also roam around through empty cells, however their movement is controlled by the environment. It takes into account their mutual distances, as well as distances from the agents and trees the cow can see. The agents and cows have a limited view, and in each simulation step receive a perception containing cells in their vicinity. The task of each agent team is to herd as many cows as possible into a corral belonging to the team. Because cows are afraid of the agents, they can be pushed by a coordinated movement of a team of agents.

For purposes of this case-study, we have considered a fragment of the *Cows & Cowboys* scenario. The concrete problem was to implement a team of agents, which cooperatively explore the maze, find some pre-determined landmarks and then traverse the maze from one landmark to another while maintaining a formation of a particular shape.

The simulated environment was provided by the MASSim server [3]. The architecture of the implemented system is depicted in Figure 1.

During every simulation step the belief base is updated with new perceptions and an action from the previous timestep is marked as executed, if there was any. *Jason* thread is then allowed to continue its deliberation based on the new percepts. Subsequently, the agent's control thread goes to sleep for 2000 milliseconds (the server sends new percepts every 2500 milliseconds) unless it is woken up by the *Jason* thread upon an invocation of an exogenous action from within an intention of the agent. Finally, the indicated action to perform is validated by checking whether it is intended for the current timestep and if found valid, it is sent back to the server. The only exogenous actions the agent can execute are moves in the eight directions: *north, east, south, west* and the diagonal moves *north-east, north-west, south-east* and *south-west*.

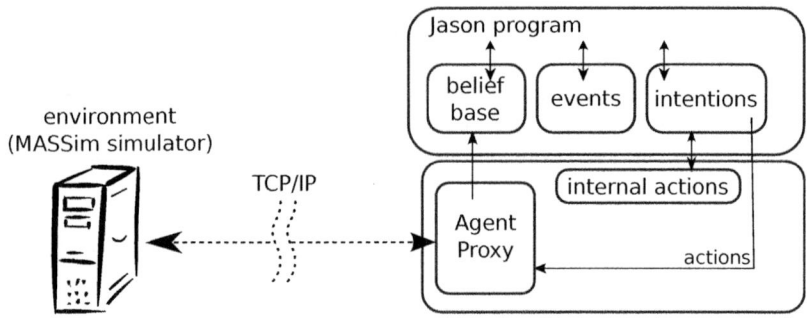

Fig. 1. The architecture of a single *Jason* agent interacting with the simulated environment

The toolbox of internal actions includes, most importantly, the implementation of the path planning algorithm A*, together with a few auxiliary functions such as a lottery-like mechanism for choosing the formation leader, queries for contents of map cells, etc.

One of the most important decisions for the implementation of the case-study was that we did not customise the *Jason* interpreter itself, nor the event, plan, and intention selection functions $S_\mathcal{E}$, $S_\mathcal{P}$, $S_\mathcal{I}$.

4   Issues Faced

In the following, we discuss a set of problems we encountered in the course of implementing the case-study described above in Section 3. The programmer involved in the experiment was new to BDI-style agent-oriented programming and was learning the *Jason* language along the way. We used the book *Programming Multi-Agent Systems in AgentSpeak Using Jason* [8] as the authoritative source and documentation for *Jason*. For clarity, the discussion of each issue includes a brief motivation and explanation of the particular design problem, subsequently followed by a discussion of the available solutions, their consequences and wherever appropriate an informal proposal for an improved solution to the issue.

4.1   Loop Implementation

Quite often a programmer needs to implement some kind of a loop design pattern. In a maze-like environment, the agent calculates a path from point A to point B using a path planning algorithm and then it follows the path. This pattern could be implemented by the following algorithm in an imperative language:

```
before-loop-code
while not loop-condition do
    loop-body
end
after-loop-code
```

As of conducting the here reported experiment, *Jason* did not feature a loop programming construct per se, but it could be implemented by the following *Jason* code:

```
event: context ←
        !before−loop−plan;
        !loop;
        !after−loop−plan.
+!loop: not loop−condition ←
        !loop−body;
        !loop.
```

This pattern implements the idea of tail recursion. The interpreter does not feature a special treatment of tail recursion though. According to the language semantics, this pattern unfolds into a growing intention stack. At the bottom of the stack there is the after−loop−plan goal. Above it in the stack, there is a series of invocations of !loop of a length equal to the number of iterations of the loop. In order to facilitate correct plan failure handling, *Jason* interpreter does not remove the top-level invocation from the intention stack. In the path-following scenario, if the path is of length 1000, the intention stack would grow to the size 1000 plus the length of after−loop−plan. Notice that several tenths of thousands path steps are not that unrealistic for large grid environments. In cases with an extremely high number of loop iterations, the intention stack growth can lead to a high memory consumption. Perhaps even more importantly, the following clean-up of the intention stack, may take an undesirably long time. The execution of after−loop−plan may therefore be heavily delayed. Possibly even missing some important timing window. This issue is the same as with the depth-first search algorithm (DFS). There are two main approaches to the DFS implementation: an exclusive stack and a recursive function call. The exclusive stack solution requires only the to-be-explored nodes, while the recursive function call solution requires the activation records of the recursive function to be present on the program stack as well.

A naïve attempt by a novice programmer could be a loop implementation using the asynchronous goal invocation !!loop. A straightforward application is inappropriate in this context though as besides invoking the loop, it would lead to an immediate continuation with the after−loop−plan.

We propose the following implementation of the loop design pattern, which uses higher order variables feature of *Jason* (cf. [8], Chapter 3) to implement a kind of a callback scheme:

```
event: context ←
        before−loop−plan;
        !!loop(after−loop−event).
+!after−loop−event: true ← after−loop−plan.
+!loop(Callback): not loop−condition ←
        loop−body;
        !!loop(Callback).
+!loop(Callback): loop−condition ← !!Callback.
```

The above loop implementation is well-formed and a valid program according to the *Jason* syntax and semantics. Instead of a synchronous event invocation, we invoke the loop in a asynchronous manner using !!loop and provide it with an argument, which is a string denoting the event, which should be invoked after the loop finishes – in this case after−loop−event. When the loop termination condition becomes true, the pattern simply invokes the event stored as the callback. The advantage of this loop implementation is that it does not lead to the intention stack growth, while at the same time it still allows for plan failure handling as in the standard loop implementation.

In the pattern above, the loop has a callback argument. This callback is added as a goal upon the loop's successful termination. An extension of this callback design solution allows a programmer to introduce a powerful plan failure handling mechanism as follows:

```
event: context ←
        before−loop−plan;
        !!loop(after−loop−event, fail−loop−event).
+!after−loop−event: true ←
        after−loop−plan.
+!fail−loop−event: true ←
        loop−failure−plan.
+!loop(SuccessCallback, FailCallback): not loop−condition & loop−continuation−condition ←
        loop−body;
        !!loop(SuccessCallback, FailCallback).
+!loop(_, FailCallback): not loop−condition & not loop−continuation−condition ←
        !!FailCallback.
+!loop(SuccessCallback, _): loop−condition ←
        !!SuccessCallback.
```

A loop is a handy and a frequently used design pattern in imperative programming. However, for a novice programmer, a loop implementation in *Jason* is rather unintuitive and it often leads to a confusion. One of the straightforward solutions, well in the spirit of BDI architecture, would be to use persistent goals, such as in 3APL. Another way to deal with this would be to implement a built-in loop programming construct, or a macro pre-processor construction similar to the various types of goals and commitment strategies discussed in [8], Chapter 8, or in [17].

To conclude, in the course of writing up and submission process of this paper, a new version of *Jason* interpreter was released. In the most recent version of the interpreter (from ver. 1.3.4 on), *Jason* includes a loop construct in the form of two internal actions for (foreach) and while. As a result, this point is no longer a pressing issue for *Jason*, yet the more general solution of the problem presented above might come handy as a standalone pattern.

4.2   Interruptions and Intention Interactions

Among other desirable properties, intelligent agents are supposed to be able to follow long term goals, but at the same time should be reactive to events in the environment and proactively seek opportunities for action whenever they arise in an appropriate context. Consider the following slight extension of the case-study scenario. The team of agents is moving through the environment in a formation, however, agents are also capable of picking up objects, let's say garbage, from the cells they stand on. Let's also assume, an agent perceives the object to pick, only when it is located in the same cell as the object and it can pick up an object only after it has closely inspected it. In *Jason*, a straightforward and naïve implementation of the two behaviours would look like as follows:

```
+!formation_loop : not aligned ←
        /∗ calculate the move action towards formation position ∗/
        move;
        !formation_loop.
```

```
+see(Object) : true ←
       inspect(Object);
       pick(Object).
```

The above naïve implementation does not work properly using the vanilla *Jason* interpreter. The reason is that after the new intention leading to picking up the object from the cell is formed, it is not ensured that in the same deliberation cycle, the intention selection function S_I selects the same intention for execution. In the case S_I selects for execution first the intention for keeping the formation aligned, it can happen that at the moment the agent wants to inspect, or pick up the object, the plan fails since the agent is no more located in the same cell as the object – the plan for keeping the formation aligned moved it away.

The implementation problem described above is that of interacting intentions (run-time plans) that can mutually interrupt each other. In *Jason*, similarly to most state-of-the-art BDI-based agent programming languages, intentions are implicitly considered interruptible. However, having several intentions involved in the same context, i.e., modifying the same aspect of agent's state, the problem is *how to determine the priority of execution of the corresponding intentions?* Below, we discuss several different solutions to this problem.

A straightforward approach would be to use some kind of plan synchronisation mechanism. *Jason* provides atomic, a pre-defined plan annotation construct ensuring that the intention instantiated from an atomic plan is executed without interruption until it finishes. The following code presents a usage of this construct:

```
@object_picking[atomic]
+see(Object) : true ←
       inspect(Object);
       pick(Object).
```

While simple and straightforward, this solution of the plan interaction does not scale with the number of involved interacting intentions. Consider that our agent should be able to quickly renegotiate the details of formation location and its heading with the team. While interdependent with the formation alignment behaviour, it is independent to the object picking behaviour. As a result, we would like to impose the following ordering on the three behaviours: the formation alignment behaviour is preceded by the opportunistic object picking, which is in turn preceded by the negotiation. However, the atomic construct applied to the object picking behaviour would cause it to be non-interruptible, hence the negotiation could not take place.

Another possibility to deal with interacting intentions would be to let the program handle the situations, in which they can be interrupted, not the intentions themselves. By that we mean that all plans would be considered implicitly non-interruptible and at every point in which an intention can be interrupted by a higher-priority event, there would be an explicit check for all possibilities of such interruptions, followed by a synchronous invocation of the interrupting event and an explicit check for preconditions of the remaining plan. The following code snippet demonstrates a use of such a technique:

```
+!formation_alignment : context ←
       align−plan−start;
       !pick_object; !negotiation;
       align−plan−rest.
+!pick_object : see(Object) ←
       pick−plan−start;
```

```
        !negotiation;
        pick−plan−rest.
    +!negotiation: request(Sender, Msg) ←
        negotiation−plan.
```

Obviously, this technique leads to implementation of agent behaviours in terms of finite state machines and consequently to a brittle, non-elaboration-tolerant, code. In order to add a new behaviour, interactions with all the other existing behaviours have to be considered and these have to be modified accordingly.

An alternative solution supported by the *Jason* interpreter is to employ .suspend and .resume internal functions which facilitate suspension and resuming of intentions respectively. The previous example could then be reformulated as follows:

```
    +!formation_alignment : context ←
        align−plan.
    +!pick_object : see(Object) ←
        .suspend(formation_alignment);
        pick−plan;
        .resume(formation_alignment).
    +!negotiation: request(Sender, Msg) ←
        .suspend(pick_object); suspend(formation_alignment);
        negotiation−plan;
        .resume(pick_object); .resume(formation_alignment).
```

The presented code should be considered in comparison with the previous example which involved explicit invocation of the possible higher-priority interruptions. In this case, the approach is to rather let the lower-priority plans to proceed freely, while the higher-priority behaviours should care for suspending and resuming the possibly running lower-priority plans. Clearly, both solutions suffer from the same problems and lead to a brittle code in which plans for various independent behaviours have to be informed and have to depend on each other for the program to execute correctly.

The only scalable and flexible mechanism for the problem of interacting plans is a customization of the intention selection function S_I. The modified function would prioritise the intentions appropriately according to the particular application domain. The downside of this, rather heavyweight, solution is that it renders the resulting *Jason* program ambiguous and not understandable in isolation. An important part of the program semantics is this way shifted to the *Java* side and the *Jason* program cannot be fully comprehended without understanding the *Java* code functionality.

Finally, in [8] authors discuss the plan annotation priority reserved for future use. The annotation is intended to instruct the plan selection and intention selection functions S_P and S_I about the plan and intention selection priority respectively. They also note that the mechanism is not implemented in *Jason* programming system yet and do not provide enough technical detail on its functionality.

Above, we have tried to show that the problem of steering plan interactions and interruptions is an important one, yet not solved appropriately in the current incarnation of *Jason*. On one hand, an intuitive and clean mechanism for intention interaction is vital in BDI-style agent programming, where several intentions might be running in parallel and interleave their executions. On the other, intentions can interact in many different ways. To strike balance between the two requirements, as an informal attempt, we suggest a conservative extension of *Jason* allowing to impose partial ordering of plans and intentions in a program. While certainly not a mechanism general enough (consider e.g., a specification of the priorities of the program modules, similar to the one proposed in [15]), such a mechanism, would help to avoid customisation of the intention selection function $\mathcal{S}_\mathcal{I}$, which we consider a bad design practice for the reasons discussed above.

4.3 Mental Notes and Plan Destructors

Mental notes are beliefs added to an agent's belief base from inside its intention. This way the agent can remind itself about status of its own execution and partially solve the problem of intention interactions discussed in the previous section. The main reason to employ mental notes is to provide a way to transfer complex information between two behaviours, usually between a behaviour and its invoked subgoals. As a result, the mental notes can be used as a kind of local variables of plans. The belief base may have to be cleaned up upon an intention completion by retracting these "local variables" corresponding to the intention. If implemented carefully, *Jason* provides a means to implement such a mechanism. Consider the following code:

```
+!event: context ←
      +event(note1);
      ...;
      +event(note2);
      ...;
      .abolish(event(_)).
```

Each mental note local to the intention triggered by the event event is of a particular form, allowing a bulk retract of all the beliefs of one argument and name event using the internal action .abolish.

While relatively straightforward, this technique can lead to difficulties in the case of an intention failure. The involved problems are quite similar to those involved in handling run-time exceptions in imperative programming languages. Upon an intention failure, the local mental notes have to be cleaned up as well. A variation of the following can be used to achieve that:

```
−!event: context ←
      ...;
      .abolish(event(_)).
```

Besides code duplication, a naïve *Jason* programmer can simply forget to implement the appropriate failure plan. Another issue of this technique is that it might be necessary to use different mental note forms for alternative plans handling the event event. However, upon an intention failure it is no longer possible to infer, which particular intention has failed.

We informally propose a language extension similar to the exception handling programming construct try−catch−finally present in many imperative languages, as well as in some niche agent programming languages, such as *StorySpeak* [12]. Consider the following code snippet:

```
+!event: context ←
      try {
          plan−body;
      } finally {
          .abolish(event(_));
      }.
```

The code in the finally block should include a plan destructor, a subplan which should be invoked upon the plan termination, regardless of its success, or a failure. The advantage of this construct is that the plan destructor is associated with the particular plan variant handling event +!event, unlike the standard *Jason* plan failure event −!event. Obviously the syntax of the proposed extension is not in line with the declarative spirit of *AgentSpeak(L)* and *Jason*, but it illustrates the point well.

4.4   Jason Agents vs. External Environment

In the implemented case-study, agents had a time limit imposed on their deliberation. They had 2500ms to choose their next action. If the action is not chosen within this timeframe, the simulated environment continues as if the agent executed the action skip and discards any action reply delivered after the timeout. However, in such environments, it is vital for an agent programmer, to optimise the speed of the agent's deliberation as much as possible. Speeding up the deliberation itself is often not enough. The agent may then have to restart the whole intention (or just a single instantiated plan) to take the new state of the environment into account.

In the implemented case-study, it was necessary for agents to reason about complex aspects of the environment, such as relative positions of teammates in the formation. In order to speed up the deliberation of the agent, we have implemented a relatively complex caching mechanism in the belief base. Upon each belief update, the agent triggers an event for a plan pre-calculating answers to often-queried plan context predicates and stores them as mental notes in his belief base. While speeding up the execution, this mechanism led to relatively large set of belief base updating plans within the agent. However, even with this optimisation, the agent was not able to reply to the server within the set time limit in some situations.

To solve the problem of a prolonged deliberation, we propose two extensions of the *Jason* programming system. Prolonged reasoning over the agent's beliefs is often caused by rule context conditions (deliberation over complex aspects of the environment, such as the form of obstacles ahead, path calculation, etc.). In order to speed up such *Prolog* query evaluations, we propose to implement a RETE-style mechanism [11] for context conditions and their caching. As a result, they would be treated as constant queries for the rest of the deliberation cycle.

To deal with the intention restart problem, *Jason* provides constructs for explicit management of the intention base. Current implementation of the *Jason* programming system provides the internal action .drop_intention facilitating forceful intention drop from within a plan of the agent. A straightforward use of this mechanism is, however, not well suited for the case-study application. It would require an implementation of a recurring goal, a loop like pattern, regularly checking whether the timeout already passed, or not. Another option would be to add the timestep mechanism handling to the environment implementation, annotate the relevant plans with a particular name pattern and finally enhance the agent program with a plan similar to the following one:

```
+timestep: true ←
    .drop_intention(...);
    /* possibly restart some of the intentions */.
```

However, such design solutions, as the two introduced in the previous paragraph, would interact with other plans as discussed in Subsection 4.2 and would therefore be difficult to implement without an appropriate customisation of the intention selection function. More importantly, in the case of the first solution, regularly checking the timeout could lead to further slow-down of the deliberation cycle.

We propose an extension of the *Jason* annotation mechanism allowing for annotations of agent's intentions with timestamps. At the point when the system timestamp value is incremented, either by the agent program itself, or from within the underlying *Java* code, all the intentions annotated with a lower timestamp should automatically fail as they become irrelevant.

To conclude this part, let's consider interaction between the *Jason* interpreter and an external environment in general. In its current incarnation, *Jason* is rather *introverted*, as are many other agent-oriented programming languages. In particular, the programming system implicitly assumes that the agent acts in a synchronous manner with respect to the environment. This assumption holds when the speed of the agent's deliberation is higher, or at least matching the rate of change, the update frequency, of the environment. However, in cases where the agent deliberation struggles to match the frequency imposed by the environment, the current implementation of the *Jason* programming system does not provide enough optimisation mechanisms to deal with the issue (in [13], we discuss some possibilities dealing with this problem in the context of videogame bots).

4.5   Jason vs. Java

Jason programming system is tightly integrated with the underlying *Java* infrastructure. This setup allows for interfacing the implemented agents with their environments in a very flexible way. It also facilitates extensive customisation of the language interpreter for the particular application domain. As we already noted above, *Jason* allows for custom belief bases, as well as adaptation of the event, plan and intention selection functions $S_{\mathcal{E}}$, $S_{\mathcal{P}}$ and $S_{\mathcal{I}}$, respectively.

We argue that the flexibility of this setup might also be a drawback. The reason is that such extensive customisations may lead to a fuzzy boundary between *Java* and *Jason* parts of the implemented agent program. Significant and important parts of the agent program functionality are often implemented in *Java* code, but this approach tends to render the *Jason* (*AgentSpeak(L)*) program difficult to understand in isolation.

In this context, a point especially relevant for novice *Jason* programmers, is the question *what are the guidelines regarding which aspects of the agent program should be implemented in Java and which in Jason?* In an extreme case, one could consider a trivial *Jason* program of the following form:

```
!main.
+!main: true ← .main.
```

There is a single event invoked at the start of the program, which leads to an invocation of an internal action main implementing the whole functionality of the agent as a *Java* code. In contrast to this approach, we may have the A* search algorithm implemented exclusively in *Jason*. While both these *Jason* programs are extreme and absurd to consider, they illustrate the point.

The ability to shift pieces of functionality between *Java* and *Jason*, and at the same time not having clear guidelines regarding what belongs where, leads to confusion of inexperienced *Jason* programmers. Bordini, Hübner and Wooldridge briefly mention this issue in [8], Chapter 11. They seem to take a puristic stance, since they argue that programmers should resist the temptation to enhance environments with "fake" actions and other user customisations leading to "cheating" in *Jason* programming. While this point is fair, the pragmatic use of the *Jason* language by a relatively inexperienced programmer facing design issues such as those discussed above in this section might lead to a growing frustration and finally a solution through the path of "minimal effort". The programmer might simply revert to a more familiar tool, in this case the *Java* programming language.

A similar issue has been addressed by J. J. Bryson in the context of the *POSH* reactive planner [10]. She proposes a methodology for a behavioural design, which, besides other things, states explicitly, which parts of behavioural code belong to the underlying *Java* (or *Python*) components and which to the *POSH* program itself.

4.6   Minor Technical and Methodological Issues

Finally, let us conclude the core discourse by listing some minor technical issues a programmer learning *Jason* encounters. While of relatively low importance, improvement on these fronts could have a considerable impact on overall usability of the *Jason* programming system.

Debugging. Debugging BDI agent systems is a topic often discussed within the community. Apart from deeper discussion on particular debugging methods, one of the issues are the appropriate tools available for the particular programming platform. *Jason* provides a tool for stepping through the agent's reasoning cycle, display its current belief base, the pursued intentions and events awaiting evaluation. Apart from problems with stability of the tool, one of the main difficulties with this style of program debugging is that in situations with relatively short time limit on an agent's deliberation, this approach is inapplicable. A more appropriate technique in such situations is to use a logging facility.

In *Jason* ver. 1.3.3, which has been used for this study, the provided logger does not expose enough information to the programmer. It is not comprehensible enough, because it only reports selected events and plans, percepts, execution control messages and user defined outputs. It would be useful to dump/export the whole current state of the agent when needed. Additionally, the user should be allowed to specify different levels of detail for logging (even dynamically during the execution), as output of whole states could be space intensive.

Integrated Development Environment. Even though the provided *Eclipse* plug-in is reasonably comfortable, it does not follow some of the established patterns for plug-ins of the same category for *Eclipse* IDE. Instead of adding program run options directly to the project options menu, it has them attached to the context menu of a *mas2j* file. An ordinary *Eclipse* plug-in would try and replicate the selection of main class of *Java* program, which has essentially the same objectives.

Another minor issue is the lack of code completion function in the standard *Jason* IDE, which rather slows down the agent program implementation.

Educational Material. One of the most difficult aspects of programming in *Jason* was actually learning it. There is only a limited material freely available. Thus, along with generated documentation for the source code (*javadoc*), examples and demos, the most useful resource is the book *"Programming Multi-Agent Systems in AgentSpeak Using Jason"* [8]. While the book provides a complete description of the programming system itself, it is still relatively difficult to use as a pedagogical tool. It imposes a strong emphasis on the theoretical part of *Jason*, without introducing the student into pragmatics of building more complex agent systems first. To improve the situation, we would appreciate several authoritative tutorials on incremental building of complex agent systems teaching the correct techniques of programming in *Jason*. As of now, the initial barrier between first working plans and first complex interacting plans is tremendous and requires a lot of trial and error approach on the side of the novice *Jason* programmer. In our opinion, the hurdle is much greater than those of other, especially imperative, languages such as *Java*, *C++* or *Python*.

5   Final Remarks

We have discussed some of the most problematic issues we have faced during the experiment. In particular, the experiment aimed at an implementation of a relatively complex case-study application by a programmer without a prior knowledge of *Jason* language. To keep the experience as relevant to *Jason*-style agent programming as possible, one of the goals was to try to use *Jason* programming system as is, with as few customisations as possible. In particular, we decided not to customise the deliberation cycle of the *Jason* interpreter and to limit the code written in *Java*. The features implemented in a form of a *Java* code were those facilitating the interaction with the simulated environment, such as a set of internal actions providing an access to the path planning algorithm.

Since we have used the *Cows & Cowboys* simulated environment for the *Multi-Agent Programming Contest* (*AgentContest*), the complexity of the implemented case-study is directly comparable to the implementations of *AgentContest* entries in its last few editions. For comparison, our implementation resulted in a codebase involving 1127 lines of code, while the *AgentContest* entries to editions 2009 and 2010, presented by teams involving the Jason platform developers, included 1416 and 1648 lines of code respectively. The *AgentContest* entries, however, aimed at the full-featured cows herding scenario, while our case-study implemented only a fragment of the scenario, environment exploration and movement in a formation through the environment. The independent entry to the 2010 edition of the *AgentContest* by the team of the *Technical University of Denmark* featured only 173 lines of *Jason* code and most of the team functionality was thus implemented on *Java* side. If our assumption that the *AgentContest* entries are the largest publicly available applications written to date is correct, then our case-study resulted in one of the most extensive *Jason* codebases to date.

In parallel to creating the *Jason* implementation reported in this paper, several students implemented the same case-study application in *Java* in the context of Multi-Agent Systems course at CTU in Prague. Interestingly, while most of them considered the task quite work-intensive and reported a workload in range of 40-60 hours of programming and testing to complete the undertaking, the *Jason* implementation took more than 100 hours to complete for an experienced *Java* programmer. The average *Java* codebase resulting from the exercise involved more than 4000 lines of code. While no hard conclusion can be drawn from this remark, it may serve as an indicator that learning *Jason* on a non-trivial example application is definitely a difficult task and that the community should invest more effort into educational material such as more extensive tutorials on teaching of agent-oriented programming.

The discussion in this paper does not aim at providing a significant scientific contribution. However, we believe that reports such as this contribute to the on-going discussion in the community on usefulness, relevance and pragmatics of agent-oriented programming systems, tools and languages, as well as to the future developments of the field. We would like to emphasize that the issues discussed in this paper are those we found to be important while developing a concrete experimental case-study. The conclusions drawn here, even if generic as they are, should be considered with caution in the context of the particular application domain. To study the subject in a more depth and more rigorously, further studies on larger groups of test subjects should take place and should also consider some established methodologies like Agent-Oriented Software Engineering.

Acknowledgements. We are grateful to Jomi F. Hübner (*Federal University of Santa Catarina*, Brasil) and Jørgen Villadsen (*Technical University of Denmark*) for the permission to study and use the code of their entries to the AgentContest.

Authors of the presented work were supported by the *Czech Ministry of Education* grants MSM6840770038 and MSM0021620838; the *Grant Agency of the Czech Technical University in Prague* grant SGS10/189/OHK3/2T/13; the *Grant Agency of Czech Republic* grant P103/10/1287 and the *Grant Agency of Charles University in Prague* grant 0449/2010/A-INF/MFF.

References

1. Multi-agent programming contest 2010 (2010),
   http://www.multiagentcontest.org/2010
2. Behrens, T.M., Dastani, M., Dix, J., Köster, M., Novák, P.: The multi-agent programming contest from 2005-2010 - from gold collecting to herding cows. Ann. Math. Artif. Intell. 59(3-4), 277–311 (2010)
3. Behrens, T.M., Dix, J., Dastani, M., Köster, M., Novák, P.: MASSim: Technical Infrastructure for AgentContest Competition Series (2009),
   http://www.multiagentcontest.org/
4. Behrens, T.M., Dix, J., Dastani, M., Köster, M., Novák, P.: Multi-Agent Programming Contest (2009), http://www.multiagentcontest.org/
5. Bordini, R.H., Braubach, L., Dastani, M., El Fallah Seghrouchni, A., Gomez-Sanz, J.J., Leite, J., O'Hare, G., Pokahr, A., Ricci, A.: A survey of programming languages and platforms for multi-agent systems. Informatica 30, 33–44 (2006)

6. Bordini, R.H., Dastani, M., Dix, J., El Fallah-Seghrouchni, A. (eds.): Multi-Agent Programming: Languages, Tools and Applications. Springer, Berlin (2009)
7. Bordini, R.H., Dastani, M., Dix, J., El Fallah-Seghrouchni, A.: Multi-Agent Programming Languages, Platforms and Applications. Multiagent Systems, Artificial Societies, and Simulated Organizations, vol. 15. Kluwer Academic Publishers (2005)
8. Bordini, R.H., Hübner, J.F., Wooldridge, M.: Programming Multi-agent Systems in Agent-Speak Using Jason. Wiley Series in Agent Technology. Wiley-Blackwell (2007)
9. Bratman, M.E.: Intention, Plans, and Practical Reason. Cambridge University Press (March 1999)
10. Bryson, J.J.: Intelligence by design: Principles of Modularity and Coordination for Engineering Complex Adaptive Agent. PhD thesis (2001)
11. Forgy, C.: Rete: A fast algorithm for the many patterns/many objects match problem. Artif. Intell. 19(1), 17–37 (1982)
12. Gemrot, J.: Joint behaviour for virtual humans. Master's thesis, Faculty of Mathematics and Physics. Charles University, Prague (2009)
13. Gemrot, J., Brom, C., Plch, T.: A Periphery of Pogamut: From Bots to Agents and Back Again. In: Dignum, F. (ed.) Agents for Games and Simulations II. LNCS, vol. 6525, pp. 19–37. Springer, Heidelberg (2011)
14. Jason Developers. Jason, a Java-based interpreter for an extended version of AgentSpeak (2011), http://jason.sourceforge.net/
15. Madden, N., Logan, B.: Modularity and Compositionality in Jason. In: Braubach, L., Briot, J.-P., Thangarajah, J. (eds.) ProMAS 2009. LNCS, vol. 5919, pp. 237–253. Springer, Heidelberg (2010)
16. Novák, P.: Jazzyk: A Programming Language for Hybrid Agents with Heterogeneous Knowledge Representations. In: Hindriks, K.V., Pokahr, A., Sardina, S. (eds.) ProMAS 2008. LNCS, vol. 5442, pp. 72–87. Springer, Heidelberg (2009)
17. Novák, P., Jamroga, W.: Code patterns for agent-oriented programming. In: Proceedings of the Eighth International Conference on Autonomous Agents and Multi-Agent Systems, AAMAS, IFAAMAS (2009)
18. Pokahr, A., Braubach, L., Lamersdorf, W.: Jadex: A BDI Reasoning Engine. In: [7]. Multiagent Systems, Artificial Societies, and Simulated Organizations, ch. 6, vol. 15, pp. 149–174 (2005)
19. Rao, A.S.: AgentSpeak(L): BDI Agents Speak Out in a Logical Computable Language. In: Van de Velde, W., Perram, J.W. (eds.) MAAMAW 1996. LNCS, vol. 1038, pp. 42–55. Springer, Heidelberg (1996)
20. Winikoff, M.: JACK^{TM} Intelligent Agents: An Industrial Strength Platform. In: [7]. Multiagent Systems, Artificial Societies, and Simulated Organizations, ch. 15, vol. 15, pp. 175–193 (2005)

Integrating Expectation Monitoring into BDI Agents

Surangika Ranathunga, Stephen Cranefield, and Martin Purvis

Department of Information Science, University of Otago,
PO Box 56, Dunedin 9054, New Zealand
{surangika,scranefield,mpurvis}@infoscience.otago.ac.nz

Abstract. Although expectations play an important role in designing cognitive agents, monitoring for agent expectations is not explicitly being handled in most common agent programming environments. There are techniques for monitoring fulfilment and violation of agent expectations, however they are not linked with common agent programming environments so that agents can be easily programmed to respond to these circumstances. This paper investigates how to delegate this aspect of agent practical reasoning to an expectation monitoring tool integrated with a BDI agent platform. We exemplify this using the Jason BDI agent interpreter by extending it with built-in actions to initiate and terminate monitoring of expectations. This delegation enables agents to monitor for the fulfilment and violation of their expectations without relying on a centralised monitoring mechanism. This way, it is possible for agents to have plans that respond to the identified fulfilments and violations of their expectations.

1 Introduction

Expectations represent the anticipatory mental component of an agent, thus they resemble an important part of cognitive agents. When an agent bases its practical reasoning on the assumption that one or more of its expectations will hold, it somehow has to ensure that it is aware of when these expectations are fulfilled and/or violated. Agent expectations are often discussed in a social context. Expectations have been identified as an important concept for social reasoning, with the argument that expectations can support agents for maintaining beliefs regarding components of a multi-agent system that are not directly observable [15]. Expectations have also been identified as useful in modeling social interactions, by striking a balance between the autonomy of black-box agents and the normative social-level exertion of control [11].

Much research can be found on techniques for monitoring fulfilment and violation of various types of social-level future expectation such as those based on norms, commitments, and contracts (see reference 8 for a brief survey of the existing monitoring techniques). Despite this, we do not see much research on providing support for these monitoring techniques in common agent programming environments. However, to successfully implement normative multiagent

L.A. Dennis, O. Boissier, and R.H. Bordini (Eds.): ProMAS 2011, LNCS 7217, pp. 74–91, 2012.

systems using these agent programming environments, it is important that they support techniques to monitor for fulfilments and violations of these expectations to help in the development of socially aware multiagent systems, and to provide better testbeds for experimenting with new monitoring techniques.

In this work, we present an approach for tightly integrating expectation monitoring with the Belief-Desire-Intension (BDI) agent paradigm, by providing an interface to initiate and terminate monitoring of expected constraints on the future and by defining specific belief types to represent detected fulfilments and violations of expectations. This enables agents to initiate application-specific monitoring of expectations and to respond to future events representing the fulfilment and violation of these expectations. We demonstrate this using the Jason BDI agent development platform [4] integrated with an expectation monitor developed in previous work [7]. The interface between Jason and the expectation monitor is implemented using Jason's support for defining new built-in agent actions, and this interface is designed to be generic so that any third party expectation monitoring tool can be integrated with Jason. We also present extended operational semantics for BDI agents incorporating expectation monitoring, with an emphasis on Jason-related semantics.

Our mechanism allows agents to choose to delegate to an expectation monitor service the monitoring of rules that specify conditional constraints on the future. These rules may be based on published norms, agreed contracts, commitments created through interaction with other agents, or personally inferred regularities of behaviour. Multiple instances of the monitoring service may be active on behalf of different agents at any time. At some future time, fulfilments and violations of an agent's expectations may occur and will be detected by the monitor. These result in new expectation fulfilment and violation beliefs for the agent and these can be handled in a flexible way by creating plans that are triggered by those belief additions.

The benefit of using a monitoring service available within the BDI platform rather than using an external monitoring agent is that it is easier to apply this monitoring mechanism to different applications. The only requirements for agent system developers to understand and use our approach are (i) understanding of the abstract idea of monitoring for fulfilments and violations of future-oriented expectations, (ii) the signatures of the interface constructs that connect the agent platform with the monitoring system (e.g. the method signatures of the two new internal actions in Jason), and (iii) to be provided with the customised logic needed to connect a given monitoring technique with the agent platform. This is in contrary to monitoring mechanisms based on specialised monitoring agents, such as the work of Meneguzzi et al. [10]. In that work, a norm monitoring tool for a specific domain was implemented as an agent and agent-level communication was used between the monitor agent and its client (a Jason agent). This can be seen as an application pattern that can be reused for different domains, but this reuse requires understanding of the function of the monitor agent, the protocols used for communication, and the Jason plans used to handle communication with the monitor agent. Furthermore, while that approach is suitable for providing an official monitor for norms and contracts defined at the institutional level, it would introduce undesirable communication overhead if used as an architecture for agents wanting their own individual expectations monitored, for use in their own personal reasoning processes.

However, it should be noted that our approach does not rule out the use of a single designated monitoring agent to monitor expectations (e.g. norms) applying to a whole society. Such a monitor agent can also make use of the techniques discussed in this paper.

The rest of the paper is organised as follows. Section 2 gives an overview of agent expectations and related work. Section 3 gives an overview of the Jason platform, and Section 4 contains an overview of the expectation monitor used in this work. Section 5 lays out the introduced extensions to BDI, and in Section 6 we demonstrate these by means of an example implemented in Jason. Finally, Section 7 concludes the paper.

2   Expectations of Cognitive Agents

Expectations represent the anticipatory mental component of an agent. Castelfranchi et al. described expectations as "hybrid mental configurations whose components entail not only beliefs but also converging goals that those beliefs will be realised" [6] and provided a formal account of that intuition. According to Castelfranchi [5], the belief component of an expectation is a mental anticipation of a future state or event. In addition, the expectation includes a goal (which can be any motivational mental state, such as a wish, desire or an intention[1]) to know whether the anticipated state or event occurs. This means that the agent has to monitor what is happening, and it should compare this received information with its mental representation of the belief in order to satisfy the goal to know whether the world actually is as anticipated.

Along with perceptions, expectations play a very important role in generating emotions of agents such as hope, fear, frustration, disappointment, and relief [5]. For example, if the agent had been expecting something bad, and the received punishment is less than what was expected, it generates the emotion *relief.* If the agent achieved a lesser result than what was expected, it leads to the emotional state *disappointment.*

Expectations also have an important role to play in the social context of multi-agent systems. They can be seen as a precursor to the development of social norms, conventions, and commitments [6] as well as social trust [9]. Alberti et al. have proposed an approach to modelling agent interaction protocols using an explicit representation of expectations [1]. Protocols are expressed using logical rules that define how future expectations on agents' communicative acts

---

[1] In our approach, we provide a mechanism for the agent programmer to directly create an intention to monitor an expectation that is delegated to an external expectation monitoring tool. The belief component of the expectation is a declarative representation of the expectation in the language used by the monitor, e.g. a conditional rule encoded in temporal logic.

arise from observations of current and past communicative acts. An abductive proof procedure can be used to verify agents' compliance with protocols. It has also been shown how the deontic logic concepts of obligation, prohibition and permission can be mapped to expectations in this approach [2].

Nickles et al. [11] introduce the notion of *expectation-oriented modelling*, in which explicit representations of agent expectations are used both as part of the agent design process and agents' run-time execution. Agents' interactions with other agents are defined using a graph-based formalism called *expectation networks* in which nodes represent event occurrences and annotated edges encode information about how the occurrence of events result in expectations of other subsequent events.

Wallace and Rovatsos [15] have developed a framework for practical social reasoning in multi-agent systems, focusing on social expectations of agents. They define an expectation as "a conditional belief regarding a statement whose truth status will be eventually verified by a test and reacted upon by the agent who holds it" [15]. Each expectation is represented by a condition under which a certain proposition should be believed, along with a test condition to be monitored and separate sets of expectation activation and deactivation actions to be performed when the test condition is believed to be true or believed to be false. A set of expectation rules is used to define how an agent's beliefs should be revised based on its local beliefs and social beliefs. Another set of "behaviour" rules specify when agent actions should be generated based on conditions on the agent's current beliefs and an "expectation graph" that encodes the possible transitions between belief sets that are implicit in the expectation rules. The resulting formalism can be executed to control an agent's social reasoning, in conjunction with a BDI agent program that provides the agent's practical reasoning [16].

In our work we consider expectations as conditional constraints on the observed history of the agent that should be continuously monitored for fulfilment or violation as new states are generated during the agent's execution [7,8]. We do not currently address the definition of domain-specific rules dictating when expectations should arise as a result of following agent interaction protocols or other forms of social reasoning. Our focus is on modelling and monitoring expectations with a complex temporal structure and we therefore use a formalism for expectations (outlined in Section 4) based on linear temporal logic. To this we add operators allowing the explicit representation of an expectation being active, fulfilled or violated in a given state, and we adopt two key principles for representing and tracking the state of expectations over time: i) that there should always be an explicit representation of an active expectation from the viewpoint of the current state (thus *formula progression* is used to carry forward to the next state any expectations that have not been fulfilled or violated), and ii) determining the fulfilment or violation of an expectation in a given state should not take any future information into account (this is important when performing offline monitoring such as the examination of audit trails). These principles are directly reflected in the semantics of our new operators, but a discussion of this is out of the scope of this paper. Here, the focus is the integration of an expectation monitor (in general) with a BDI agent platform, in order to allow plans to be defined to respond to the fulfilment and violation of specific expectations. Although we illustrate this integration using our specific logic and its associated monitor tool, the interface is defined to encompass any expectation representation that has a notion of conditional expectations that may be determined to be fulfilled or violated at some time in the future.

3   Jason

Jason [4] is a Java-based interpreter for an extended version of the AgentSpeak agent programming language [14], which is based on the BDI model. Jason is open source, can be easily customisable, and is commonly used in multi-agent systems research and teaching. It is a well documented and well supported platform with an active user community.

A Jason agent program consists of plans that are executed in response to the events received. These events are generated by the addition or deletion of the beliefs and goals of an agent. A belief is the result of a percept the agent retrieves from its environment or it could be based on a message received from another agent. A goal could be internally generated by the agent, or it could be the result of a request from another agent. While executing a plan, an agent might generate new goals, act on its environment, create mental notes to itself or execute internal actions.

3.1   Jason Agent Reasoning Cycle

An agent operates in a continuous cycle called the reasoning cycle, consuming a stream of belief update events that are produced as the agent perceives its environment. The Jason semantics define the following steps for interpreting AgentSpeak programs, as shown in Figure 1 [4]. First, the reasoning cycle checks for messages received by the agent and selects one of the messages to process further (ProcMsg). Then one event from the many pending events is selected to be processed further in that reasoning cycle (SelEv). This is followed by the selection of the relevant plans for the given event (RelPl). Next, the applicable plans are generated (ApplPl)—these are the plans with context conditions that evaluate to true given the agent's current beliefs. Then, one plan from the set of applicable plans (the intended means) is selected for execution (SelAppl), and the new intended means is added to the set of intentions (AddIM). The reasoning cycle then chooses one of the pending intentions (SelInt), executes one step of that intention (ExecInt), and clears the intended means that may have finished in the previous step (ClrInt).

Most of the aforementioned steps are directly customisable and since the Jason source is freely available, other functionalities of the Jason interpreter can also be changed as needed.

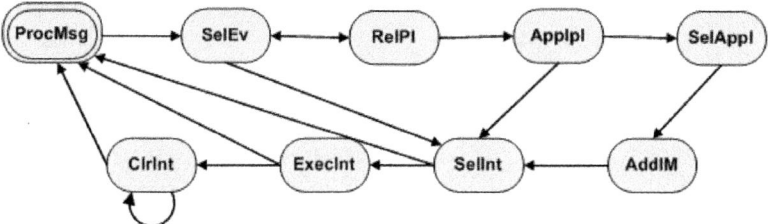

Fig. 1. Possible Jason state transitions within one reasoning cycle [4]

4   The Monitoring Tool

In this paper we selected an expectation monitor developed in previous research [7] to handle expectation monitoring for agents. This expectation monitor is designed for monitoring expectations that encode complex temporal constraints as opposed to many other monitoring techniques that handle only propositions that must come true by a deadline[2].

The language that the expectation monitor accepts is based on a hybrid temporal logic and includes the following operators relating to conditional rules of expectation[3]:

- Exp(*Condition, Expectation*)
- Fulf(*Condition, Expectation*)
- Viol(*Condition, Expectation*)

where *Condition* and *Expectation* are formulae in a form of linear propositional temporal logic. *Condition* expresses a condition on the past and present, and *Expectation* is a constraint that may express an expectation on the future or a check on the past (or both). Expectations become active when their condition evaluates to true in the current state. These expectations are then considered to be fulfilled or violated if they evaluate to true in a state.

However, this evaluation must be done without using any information from future states in the model. For example, when examining a model representing an audit trail, the expectation that a certain party will never access a certain file ($\mathsf{Exp}(true, \Box \neg bob\_accessed\_file)$) should *not* be deemed to be violated before any state (s_9, say) in which that prohibited access occurs, even though $\Box \neg bob\_accessed\_file$ would evaluate to *false* in any state up to and including s_9. Thus the semantics for Fulf and Viol include a notion of truncating the model at the current state and using "strong" finite model semantics to evaluate the expectation [7]. In this way, the language provides declarative semantics for

---

[2] A comparison with other approaches used for monitoring expectations and related concepts such as norms and commitments is out of the scope of this paper, but is presented elsewhere [8].

[3] In previous work these operators were named ExistsExp, ExistsFulf and ExistsViol, but we use simplified names here.

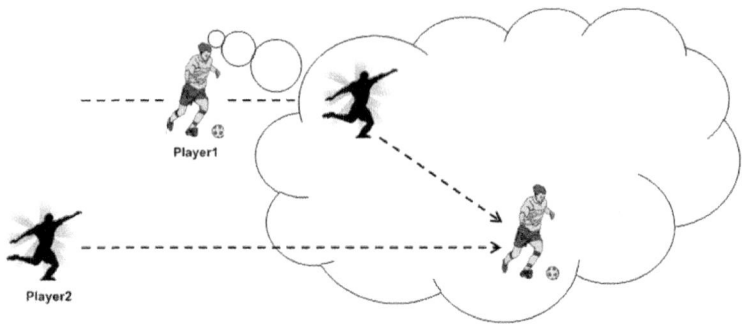

Fig. 2. The "give and go" team play scenario in football

expectations and their fulfilment and violation can be applied to both offline monitoring such as examining audit trails, and online monitoring where states are added incrementally to the model.

An expectation remains active in the following state in a "progressed" form if it is not fulfilled or violated in the current state. Formula progression involves partially evaluating the formula with respect to the current state and re-expressing it from the viewpoint of the next state [3]. In other words, if p is true in the current state, an expectation that "p is true and q is true in the next state" progresses to "q is true in the current state".

Although this expectation monitor supports monitoring for states in which a given expectation exists (i.e. is active), as well as for fulfilments and violations, we currently handle only the fulfilment and violation of an expectation in our extension of Jason. We intend to modify our extension to support monitoring for the existence of an expectation in a future version.

As an example, consider the football team play scenario "give and go" illustrated in Figure 2. This team play scenario involves two players where one player (player 2 in the figure) passes the ball to her team mate (player 1). Player 1 then adopts an expectation that player 2 will run down to an advantageous field position (which was agreed upon according to the team tactic). The intention of player 1 is to pass the ball back to player 2 when she fulfills this expectation. If player 2 was not able to fulfill this expectation, player 1 has to initiate a new tactic.

As player 1 has to focus on advancing down the field while avoiding opposition players, the expectation monitor can be delegated to monitor player 2, to check whether she fulfils (or violates) the defined expectation of player 1. The fulfilment and violation of this expectation can be expressed using the following two formulae, where we assume that player 2 is supposed to advance towards goal A in the field *until* she reaches the penalty area in front of goal A.

$$\text{Fulf}(s10, advanceToGoalA(player2) \cup penaltyA(player2))$$
$$\text{Viol}(s10, advanceToGoalA(player2) \cup penaltyA(player2))$$

The first argument in the formulae refers to the condition that triggers the expectation, as explained earlier. As Player 1 wants to begin monitoring the expectation as soon as the ball is received, this condition is given as a *nominal* (a proposition that is true in only one state) that 'names' the current state (state 10, in this example). This ensures that the rule is fired precisely once, immediately[4].

The first formula above evaluates to true in any state in which the rule is fulfilled (i.e. player 2 reaches the penalty A area), and the second formula will be true in any state in which the rule is violated (e.g. player 2 moves in the opposite direction from goal A or stops moving before reaching the penalty area). In these cases, the monitor sends a notification back to player 1 to inform it that this rule was fulfilled or violated. Player 1 can generate a belief addition event with respect to this notification.

5   Expectation Monitoring in BDI Agents

5.1   New Interface to Start and Stop Expectation Monitoring

An important feature of our monitoring mechanism is the ability to use any third-party monitoring tool in conjunction with agent plans. Therefore the interface between the BDI agent and an expectation monitor was designed to be more abstract than the logic described in the previous section. This helps to switch to different expectation monitor techniques without changing the agent logic that initialises or terminates expectation monitoring. Our intention is to provide a generic interface that would suit a range of monitoring tools.

Initiating Expectation Monitoring: The interface construct corresponding to the initialisation of expectation monitoring is the *start_monitoring* action. Currently each call to *start_monitoring* creates a new instance of the monitor. This is due to a current limitation of the monitor implementation that it only handles one rule at a time. This introduces a limitation to the flexibility of *start_monitoring*, as a monitor started later in an agent's reasoning process may not be aware of the past states that occurred before its initialisation. However, pragmatically, we believe that in most situations in which an agent wishes to begin monitoring an expectation, the past states will not be of relevance to the agent's intentions; otherwise it would have chosen to monitor the expectation earlier. Also, in future work, we plan to have a single monitor handling multiple rules at a time, eliminating this limitation.

The *start_monitoring* action has the following parameters:

monitoring_mode: This is either "fulf" or "viol" to indicate whether the rule of expectation is to be monitored for fulfilment or violation. For example, for the expectation monitor we are currently employing, a Fulf formula is created in

---

[4] In practice, we do not require the agent to know the nominal for the current state— we allow a special keyword "#once" to be used as the condition of a rule, and this is replaced by a nominal for the current state when the rule is sent to the monitor (see Section 6).

the monitor if the value of this parameter is "fulf" and a Viol formula is created if the value is "viol".

expectation_name: This specifies a name for the expectation, for ease of future reference.

monitor_tool: This identifies the monitoring tool that should be used to monitor this expectation.

condition: This specifies the requirements on the past and present that activate monitoring for the expectation.

expectation: This specifies the actual expectation.

context_information_list: This argument can be used to assign any other contextual information that might be useful for monitoring an expectation. For example, we can specify a specific agent or a group of agents that are responsible for the fulfilment of the expectation. This information is added as a Jason annotation to any fulfilment belief or violation belief related to this expectation.

Terminating Expectation Monitoring: We have made it possible for an agent to stop monitoring for an expectation if the need arises to do so during its reasoning process. The *stop_monitoring* action stops the monitoring of the expectation. It takes the following parameters:

expectation_name: The name of the expectation

monitor_tool: The monitor that is checking for the specified expectation.

Implementation of these actions depends on the selected BDI platform. Many of the currently available BDI agent development platforms such as JACK and Jason provide capability to link external logic with the agent programs. For a given BDI agent development platform, this capability should be exploited to implement the interface constructs for start and termination of expectation monitoring.

For example, internal actions in the Jason platform help programmers to extend agent capabilities by defining them in the Java programming language. Internal actions are appropriate to use when the corresponding logic cannot be expressed in AgentSpeak language constructs (e.g. integrating Jason with an external program) or involve computations of a procedural nature that are more conveniently expressed in Java.

The new internal actions needed to extend the Jason platform were directly added to the standard internal actions library, enabling any agent program to refer to them. Thus an agent programmer does not have to know how to design these internal actions. However, if the custom logic related to an expectation monitor is included in these internal actions, the agent programmer has to change the standard Jason code each time when integrating a new expectation monitor type. Therefore we have made it possible to store this custom code in a Java class that is included inside the same Java package as the related agent program. The internal actions expect the existence of this customised class to handle the specific logic related to a given expectation monitor. The internal actions decode the parameter values sent by an AgentSpeak program, and send these values to this customised class, to be processed according to the selected expectation monitor.

5.2   Representing Expectation Fulfilments and Violations

An important design consideration is how to encode notifications related to fulfilments and violations identified by the external expectation monitor to be used by a BDI agent. Essentially, these notifications should be converted to beliefs to be processed by the agent.

Following the previous section, in order to generate a belief using a received notification, it suffices to have the monitoring mode, name of the expectation, and the identifier for the state in which the actual fulfilment or violation of the expectation occurred. The notion of a state is important because fulfilments and violations arise in a particular temporal context that is encapsulated by the state identifier. The explicit notion of a state is also useful because we do not assume synchronisation between the agent platform and the monitor. It is up to the monitor to provide an appropriate form of state identifier.

Apart from these mandatory components, other constructs that can be included in a belief are the rule related to the expectation, the state at which the condition part of the expectation came true, and any other related contextual information.

For example, in Jason we define the structure of beliefs based on the detected fulfilments and violations as follows:

$$\text{fulf}(Name, StateId)[rule(Cond, Exp), rule\_triggered\_in\_state(OldStateId),$$
$$context(Context)]$$

$$\text{viol}(Name, StateId)[rule(Cond, Exp), rule\_triggered\_in\_state(OldStateId),$$
$$context(Context)]$$

Here, fulf encodes the fulfilment of an expectation, while viol represents a violation.

The variable *Name* represents the name assigned to a particular fulfilment or violation detected, and the *StateId* represents the identifier for the state in which the actual fulfilment or violation of the expectation occurred.

In Jason, a percept with the same content as an already existing belief will not lead to the generation of a new belief. However, we want a fulfilment or a violation detected in one iteration of the Jason reasoning cycle to be distinct from the same fulfilment or violation detected in the previous cycle (e.g. two different robberies in consecutive states are two different crimes). This requirement can be accomplished with the state identifier associated with the fulfilment (and violation) beliefs.

When creating beliefs in Jason, an agent programmer can add optional additional information using 'annotations'. These annotations can be omitted when specifying the triggering event for a plan if the context and the body of the corresponding plan do not need this information. In the above predicates, we have used three annotations to incorporate the aforementioned non-mandatory belief constructs into a Jason agent belief. The first annotation records the rule that was fulfilled or violated. It has two parameters: the condition that triggers the expectation and the actual expectation. These can be defined in any format according to the expectation monitor in use. The second annotation is 'rule_triggered_in_state', which identifies the state in which the condition of the expectation became true. The third annotation is the list of contextual information that is related to this identified fulfilment or violation. The context information list that was generated for the related expectation when it was initiated by *start_monitoring* internal action is used to provide this information.

The Environment class in Jason acts as the interface to integrate the Jason platform with outside simulation environments. Therefore the Environment class was selected as the best option to communicate the detected fulfilments and violations to Jason agents. Just like percepts, these result in new beliefs that lead to the execution of plans that handle the detected fulfilment or violation.

5.3   Extended Semantics for Expectation Monitoring

In this section, we present an extension of Jason semantics that includes the operation of the expectation monitor. In our semantics, an expectation monitor has its own state, which is different from an agent's state. For simplicity, we only model a single expectation monitor in the semantics. Incorporating multiple monitors is a straightforward extension.

An expectation monitor can have many 'monitor tasks', distinguished by their unique name. Each monitor task is comprised of a rule (a rule resembles an expectation, and its triggering condition), and a property that states whether the rule should be monitored for its fulfilment or violation. Associated with a monitor, there is also a history component, which resembles the set of input states received by the monitor. We also define a *set of notifications*, which becomes the output of the expectation monitor. The set of notifications resembles the set of states where the expectation monitor recorded a fulfilment or violation for any of the monitor tasks that are currently being monitored. These notifications are eventually consumed by the agent.

An expectation monitor is represented by the triple $\langle H, MTs, Ns \rangle$, where:

- H is the history of the monitor. As mentioned earlier, H resembles the set of input states received by the monitor. The input states have a state identifier, and some associated information about the agent's environment in a representation specific to the expectation monitor being used.
- MTs is the set of monitor tasks associated with the expectation monitor. A monitor task MT is a 4-tuple of the form $\langle Na, Cn, Ex, Pr \rangle$. Here Na is the unique name assigned to the monitor task. The Cn and Ex parameters represent a rule, where Cn represents the condition specifying when an expectation becomes active and Ex refers to the actual expectation. Pr is the property with two possible values, $FULF$ or $VIOL$, meaning that the property refers to the fulfilment or violation of a rule, respectively.
- Ns is the map of notifications generated by the expectation monitor as the output. This map associates state identifiers with sets of pairs $\langle Na, Pr \rangle$

where each pair expresses the information that in the given state, the monitor task named Na resulted in a detected event of type Pr ($FULF$ or $VIOL$).

This abstract model of a monitor can be related to the semantics of a specific monitor tool as shown by the following example rule. This shows how the model theoretic semantics (top left) of our chosen monitor [7] is related to the emission of a fulfilment notification (a similar rule can be defined to explain the emission of violation notifications).

$$\frac{H, \varnothing, |H| \models \mathsf{Fulf}(Cn, Ex) \quad \langle Na, Cn, Ex, FULF \rangle \in MTs}{\langle H, MTs, Ns \rangle \rightarrow \langle H, MTs, Ns' \rangle}$$

where

$Ns' = Ns \cup (|H| \mapsto \langle Na, FULF \rangle)$ if $|H|$ is not a key in Notifications,

or

$Ns' = map\_update(Ns, |H|, Ns[|H|] \cup \langle Na, FULF \rangle)$ otherwise.

In this rule, we assume that history states are identified by their (1-based) indices, so $|H|$ (the length of the history H) is the identifier for the final state in the history.

The rule states that when a fulfilment formula logically holds in the logic used by the monitor[5], and the corresponding rule is being monitored, a fulfilment notification is emitted for the current state (the last in the history). The notification map is updated either by adding a new mapping $|H| \mapsto \langle Na, FULF \rangle$ to the monitor notifications, or by adding $\langle Na, FULF \rangle$ to the notifications for state $|H|$ if any exist.

To define the semantics of our extension we must address three issues: i) the effect of the new interface constructs *start_monitoring* and *stop_monitoring*, ii) how notifications emitted from the monitor are communicated to an agent as beliefs, and iii) defining the process that adds states to the monitor's history. How these issues can be addressed heavily depends on the selected BDI agent platform. Therefore the designed solutions can be well explained with respect to a selected BDI agent platform, and we use Jason for this purpose. However, the underlying concepts are quite general to BDI paradigm, and therefore they can be easily tailored for other BDI agent platforms.

In Jason, the state of an agent is determined by the *belief base*, the *set of events*, the *plan library* and the *set of intentions*. In Jason semantics, the transition relation of an agent's configuration is given by a set of conditional rules that change the agent's configuration in each of the steps of the reasoning cycle. The configuration for an agent is represented by the tuple $\langle ag, C, M, T, s \rangle$ [4], where:

- ag refers to the agent program, which consists of a set of beliefs and a set of plans
- C is an agent's circumstance, denoted by the tuple $\langle I, E, A \rangle$, with I being the set of intentions, E the set of events and A being the set of actions to be performed in the environment.

---

[5] The details of this particular monitor's semantics [7] are outside the scope of this paper.

- *M* is a tuple $\langle In, Out, SI \rangle$ that registers different aspects of communicating agents. Here, *In* is the message inbox of an agent, *Out* is the out-going message box, and *SI* keeps track of the suspended intentions related to the communication messages that are currently being processed.
- *T* is a structure that stores temporary data required in various steps of the reasoning cycle. This is a tuple $\langle R, Ap, i, \epsilon, \rho \rangle$, where *R* represents the relevant plans, *Ap* represents the set of applicable plans, and i, ϵ, ρ respectively represent an intention, event and an applicable plan that are being considered along the execution of one reasoning cycle.
- *s* is the current step (or state) in the agent reasoning cycle shown in Figure 1, where:
  $s \in \{$ProcMsg, SelEv, RelPl, ApplPl, SelAppl, AddIM, SelInt, ExecInt, ClrInt$\}$.

Subscripts are used to identify individual components of tuples, e.g. C_E denotes the events set within a configuration C, and the notation $i[p]$ is used to denote an intention consisting of plan p on top of intention i.

Now the extended system configuration comprising the Jason agent and the monitor can be defined by the pair $\langle AG, EM \rangle$, where $AG = \langle ag, C, M, T, s \rangle$ and *EM* represents the expectation monitor as defined above.

From the aforementioned list of issues related to our extension, here we address the implementation details of the first two issues. We consider the third issue as being out of the scope of these semantics. This is because the Jason agent is not responsible for sending percepts to the monitor. The monitor may have its own separate mechanism for obtaining information from the system in which the Jason agent is situated, or it may receive state information from the Jason environment object[6].

Start_monitoring: Through the *start_monitoring* internal action, an expectation monitor is started and is added to the set of active expectation monitors of the agent. This takes place during the ExecInt step in the reasoning cycle in Figure 1, when the body of an agent plan is being executed and this internal action becomes the current intended means to be executed. The action executes completely (i.e. without suspension, which is the normal procedure for executing internal actions) and returns.

The Jason semantics for this action is shown below.

$$\frac{T_i = i[head \leftarrow start\_monitoring(Mm, En, Cn, Ex); h]}{\langle \langle ag, C, M, T, \mathsf{ExecInt} \rangle, EM \rangle \rightarrow \langle \langle ag, C, M, T', \mathsf{ClrInt} \rangle, EM' \rangle}$$

where:

- Parameters Mm, En, Cn, and Ex respectively refer to the monitoring_mode, expectation_name, condition, and expectation as defined in Section 5.1[7].

---

[6] This first situation is used in our work on integrating this extended version of Jason with the Second Life virtual world [12], and the second situation is demonstrated in an extended version of this framework [13]

[7] Note that here we have omitted some parameters of *start_monitoring* internal action defined in Section 5.1, because they do not contribute to the semantics of the internal action.

- Here $EM'_{MTs} = EM_{MTs} \cup \{\langle En, Cn, Ex, Mm \rangle\}$
- $T'_i = i[head \leftarrow h]$

As in the standard Jason semantics, where a transition is defined as transforming a structure S into a new version S', all components of S' are assumed to be the same as those in S except where otherwise specified.

Stop_monitoring: The *stop_monitoring* internal action also takes place when the body of an agent plan is being executed, and this internal action becomes the current intended means to be executed. This refers to the ExecInt step in the reasoning cycle, and it moves the transition to the state ClrInt.

$$\frac{T_i = i[head \leftarrow stop\_monitoring(En); h]}{\langle\langle ag, C, M, T, \text{ExecInt}\rangle, EM\rangle \rightarrow \langle\langle ag, C, M, T', \text{ClrInt}\rangle, EM'\rangle}$$

where:

- Parameter En refers to the expectation_name as defined in Section 5.1[8]
- $EM'_{MTs} = EM_{MTs} \setminus \{MT\}$. In other words, the *stop_monitoring* internal action removes the monitor task MT referenced by En (here, the expectation_name refers to the unique name of the monitor task) from the expectation monitor.
- $T'_i = i[head \leftarrow h]$

Though not included in the paper, we also modify the condition of the existing Jason semantic rule for handling internal actions to exclude it from applying the standard operational semantics in the case that the selected action a is *start_monitoring* or *stop_monitoring*.

Handling Fulfilment and Violation Notifications
Whenever the monitor identifies the fulfilment or violation of a rule defined in it, it sends a notification to the BDI agent platform. At the agent platform, these notifications have to be converted to beliefs. We define the function *NotBels* to denote the process that converts monitor notifications into agent beliefs using the syntax defined in Section 5.2. These notifications are treated as Jason percepts and subsequently result in new belief events, as defined by the following rule:

$$\frac{EM_{Ns} \neq \varnothing}{\langle\langle ag, C, M, T, s\rangle, EM\rangle \rightarrow \langle\langle ag, C', M, T, s\rangle, EM'\rangle}$$

In this rule, $EM'_{Ns} = \varnothing$ and $C'_E = C_E \cup NotBels(EM_{Ns})$.

Here, EM'_{Ns} refers to the set of notifications belonging to all the monitor tasks active for that expectation monitor.

This rule is not executed as part of the Jason agent's reasoning cycle. Rather, it represents a separate process that consumes notifications from the monitor and adds them as new events for the agent to process. This process runs concurrently with the Jason interpreter, and we do not assume any sychronisation between

---

[8] Here also we omit the monitor_tool parameter, as it is not referenced in the semantics.

the two processes (except to avoid concurrent modification of the agent's input event set C_E). Therefore this rule can be applied in any state of the agent[9].

6   Example Scenario - A Jason Agent Engaged in the Football Team Play Scenario "Give and Go"

We have integrated this Jason extension with the popular virtual world Second Life[10] using a framework we have developed [12] for integrating agents with Second Life.

In this example, we demonstrate how the ability of a Jason agent to monitor and detect fulfilments and violations of its expectations is useful in its decision making process. We implement this example in the SecondFootball[11] virtual simulation in Second Life, which enables playing virtual football. This system provides scripted stadium and ball objects that can be deployed inside Second Life, as well as a "head-up display" object that an avatar can wear to allow the user to initiate kick and tackle actions.

In this example, we implement the "give and go" team play scenario described in Section 4. Here, the Jason agent Ras_Ruby deployed in Second Life is engaged in the give and go team play scenario with the human-controlled player Su_Monday. When Ras_Ruby receives the ball, it gets the expectation that Su_Monday should run until she reaches the PenaltyA area, so that it can pass the ball back to Su_Monday for her to attempt a goal score.

When the system starts, the Jason agent corresponding to Ras_Ruby is initialised. When the Jason agent starts executing, it first tries to log itself into Second Life. After sending its login request, the agent has to wait till it gets the confirmation of the successful login. When it receives the successful login notification, the agent adopts the new goal to run to the area MidfieldA2. The corresponding plan for this goal addition is shown below (+! denotes a goal addition event, a context condition appears after the colon, and the arrow operator separates the head and body of the plan).

```
+!check_connected: connected  <-
    action("run", "MidfieldA2").
```

Once in the area MidfieldA2, the agent Ras_Ruby waits for Su_Monday to kick and pass the ball to it. Once it successfully receives the ball, the agent gets the "successful_kick(su_monday, ras_ruby)" percept (which is generated by our Second Life integration framework and states that Su_Monday successfully passed the ball to Ras_Ruby through a kick), and this triggers the corresponding plan related to this belief addition, as given below.

---

[9] In practice, the monitor's notifications are recorded as percepts in the Jason Environment object, and the agent perceives them via Jason's belief update phase. However, Jason's operational semantics do not include a step for perceiving the environment, so here we model the connection between the monitor and the agent as a separate process that pushes fulfilment and violation beliefs to the agent.

[10] http://secondlife.com

[11] http://www.secondfootball.com

```
+successful_kick(su_monday,ras_ruby)
  <- //internal actions
   .start_monitoring("fulf",
    "move_to_target","expectation_monitor","#once",
    "('U','advanceToGoalA(su_monday)','penaltyA(su_monday)')",[]);
   .start_monitoring("viol",
    "move_to_target","expectation_monitor","#once",
    "('U','advanceToGoalA(su_monday)','penaltyA(su_monday)')",[]).
```

This plan uses the new internal actions introduced in Section 5.1 for monitoring for the fulfilment and violation of the agent's expectation. Here, in the first parameter we define the type of expectation; in the first call to the internal action, it is of the type 'fulfilment' (fulf), and in the second, it is of the type 'violation' (viol). In the second parameter, the name of the expectation is given as 'move_to_target'. The third parameter is the name of the expectation monitor used. The fourth parameter is the triggering condition for the expectation, and here it is a keyword with a special meaning (#once). The BDI execution cycle only executes a single step of a plan at each iteration, and any knowledge of the current state of the world retrieved by the plan may be out of date by the time the monitor is invoked. Therefore the #once keyword instructs the monitor to insert a nominal for the current state of the world just before the rule begins to be monitored. The expectation formula referred by the fifth parameter resembles the formulae presented in Section 4, and it states that Su_Monday should advance towards GoalA (`advanceToGoalA(su_monday)`), until (`'U'`) she reaches PenaltyA, denoted by `'penaltyA(su_monday)'`. We do not use the optional sixth parameter in this example.

The fulfilment of this expectation occurs when Su_Monday advances towards GoalA until she reaches PenaltyA. Similarly, the violation of this expectation occurs if Su_Monday stopped somewhere before reaching PenaltyA, or she moves in the opposite direction before reaching PenaltyA area[12].

If Su_Monday fulfilled Ras_Ruby's expectation, the expectation monitor detects this and reports back to the Jason agent, which results in a fulfilment belief. The following plan handles this detected fulfilment and instructs the avatar to carry out the kick action.

```
+fulf("move_to_target", X)
   <- //Calculate kick direction and force, turn, then ...
      action("animation", "kick").
```

If Su_Monday violated the expectation, the expectation monitor reports the violation to the Jason agent, generating a violation belief for the agent. The agent uses the first plan below to decide the agent's reaction to the detected violation, which creates a goal to choose a new tactic for execution. The second

---

[12] The conditions and expectations are defined in temporal logic and we do not wish to elaborate on them in the scope of this paper. These are written as nested Python tuples, as this is the input format for the expectation monitor written in Python.

plan (responding to this new choose_and_enact_new_tactic) is then triggered, and the agent adopts the tactic of attempting to score a goal on its own by running towards the PenaltyA area with the ball.

```
+viol("move_to_target",X)
    <- !choose_and_enact_new_tactic.

+!choose_and_enact_new_tactic
    <- action("run", "penaltyB").
```

7 Conclusion

This paper addressed the importance of agents having the capability to directly monitor their expectations and detect the fulfilments and violations of these expectations, and respond accordingly. As expectation monitoring in complex environments is far from being trivial, we present an approach to delegate the practical reasoning related to expectation monitoring to an outside monitoring mechanism, which is the main contribution of the paper. With this approach, while BDI agents can respond to received events, we provide functionality to initiate program specific monitoring for future events, and send notification of fulfilments and violations of expectations back to the agents.

We demonstrated a tight integration of expectation monitoring in the BDI agent model and presented an implemented mechanism to monitor expectations of individual agents in the Jason agent model. Also, we identified this as an approach to focus on monitoring at the individual agent level, as opposed to the organisational level monitoring that has received the main focus in the past research. With our approach, individual BDI agents can monitor for the fulfilment and violation of their own expectations, and can react to the identified fulfilments and violations by having plans that are triggered by those events.

As future work, it is interesting to investigate how monitoring of expectations with a complex temporal structure can be integrated with other BDI agent development platforms and BDI-related expectation-based social reasoning frameworks such as the ESB framework [16]. We also plan to investigate the use of other expectation monitors.

References

1. Alberti, M., Gavanelli, M., Lamma, E., Chesani, F., Mello, P., Torroni, P.: Compliance verification of agent interaction: a logic-based software tool. Applied Artificial Intelligence 20(2), 133–157 (2006)
2. Alberti, M., Gavanelli, M., Lamma, E., Mello, P., Torroni, P., Sartor, G.: Mapping deontic operators to abductive expectations. Computational & Mathematical Organization Theory 12, 205–225 (2006)
3. Bacchus, F., Kabanza, F.: Using temporal logics to express search control knowledge for planning. Artificial Intelligence 116(1-2), 123–191 (2000)

4. Bordini, R.H., Hubner, J.F., Wooldridge, M.: Programming multi-agent systems in AgentSpeak using Jason. John Wiley & Sons Ltd. (2007)
5. Castelfranchi, C.: Mind as an anticipatory device: For a theory of expectations. In: De Gregorio, M., Di Maio, V., Frucci, M., Musio, C. (eds.) BVAI 2005. LNCS, vol. 3704, pp. 258–276. Springer, Heidelberg (2005)
6. Castelfranchi, C., Giardini, F., Lorini, E., Tummolini, L.: The prescriptive destiny of predictive attitudes: From expectations to norms via conventions. In: Proceedings of the 25th Annual Meeting of the Cognitive Science Society, pp. 222–227 (2003)
7. Cranefield, S., Winikoff, M.: Verifying social expectations by model checking truncated paths. Journal of Logic and Computation 21(6), 1217–1256 (2011)
8. Cranefield, S., Winikoff, M., Vasconcelos, W.: Modelling and monitoring interdependent expectations. In: Proceeedings of the 12th International Workshop on Coordination, Organizations, Institutions and Norms in Agent Systems (COIN), pp. 31–45 (2011), http://coin-aamas2011.iiia.csic.es/COIN_PreProceedings.pdf
9. Lorini, E., Falcone, R.: Modeling expectations in cognitive agents. In: Castelfranchi, C., Balkenius, C., Butz, M., Ortony, A. (eds.) AAAI 2005 Fall Symposium: From Reactive to Anticipatory Cognitive Embodied Systems, pp. 114–121. AAAI Press (2005)
10. Meneguzzi, F., Miles, S., Luck, M., Holt, C., Smith, M.: Electronic contracting in aircraft aftercare: a case study. In: Proceedings of the 7th International Conference on Autonomous Agents and Multiagent Systems, pp. 63–70. IFAAMAS (2008)
11. Nickles, M., Rovatsos, M., Weiss, G.: Expectation-oriented modeling. Engineering Applications of Artificial Intelligence 18, 891–918 (2005)
12. Ranathunga, S., Cranefield, S., Purvis, M.: Interfacing a cognitive agent platform with a virtual world: a case study using Second Life. In: International Workshop on the Uses of Agents for Education, Games and Simulations (AEGS 2011), pp. 1–16 (2011)
13. Ranathunga, S., Cranefield, S., Purvis, M.: Identifying events taking place in Second Life virtual environments. Applied Artificial Intelligence 26, 137–181 (2012), doi:10.1080/08839514.2012.629559
14. Rao, A.: AgentSpeak(L): BDI agents speak out in a logical computable language. In: Perram, J., Van de Velde, W. (eds.) MAAMAW 1996. LNCS, vol. 1038, pp. 42–55. Springer, Heidelberg (1996)
15. Wallace, I., Rovatsos, M.: Bounded practical social reasoning in the ESB framework. In: Proceedings of the 8th International Conference on Autonomous Agents and Multiagent Systems, pp. 1097–1104. IFAAMAS (2009)
16. Wallace, I., Rovatsos, M.: Executing specifications of social reasoning agents. In: Omicini, A., Sardina, S., Vasconcelos, W. (eds.) DALT 2010. LNCS, vol. 6619, pp. 112–129. Springer, Heidelberg (2011)

Part III

Model Checking

Abstraction for Model Checking Modular Interpreted Systems over ATL

Michael Köster[1] and Peter Lohmann[2]

[1] Computational Intelligence Group, Clausthal University of Technology
Julius-Albert-Str. 4, 38678 Clausthal-Zellerfeld, Germany
`mko@tu-clausthal.de`
[2] Theoretical Computer Science, Leibniz University Hannover
Appelstr. 4, 30167 Hannover, Germany
`lohmann@thi.uni-hannover.de`

Abstract. We present an abstraction technique for model checking multi-agent systems given as modular interpreted systems (MIS) (introduced by Jamroga and Ågotnes). MIS allow for succinct representations of compositional systems, they permit agents to be removed, added or replaced and they are modular by facilitating control over the amount of interaction. Specifications are given as arbitrary ATL formulae: We can therefore reason about strategic abilities of groups of agents.

Our technique is based on collapsing each agent's local state space with handcrafted equivalence relations, one per strategic modality. We present a model checking algorithm and prove its soundness: This makes it possible to perform model checking on abstractions (which are much smaller in size) rather than on the concrete system which is usually too complex, thereby saving space and time. We illustrate our technique with an example in a scenario of autonomous agents exchanging information.

Keywords: Model Checking, Abstraction, Temporal and Strategic Logics, Multiagent Systems, Verification.

1   Introduction

Multi-agent systems (MAS) and their logical frameworks have attracted some attention in the last decade. Agent logics have been used to reason about knowledge, time, strategic abilities, coordination and cooperation [13,10,1]. An important technique for verifying properties of a system is model checking [5], which has been refined and improved over the last years.

While an important feature of a MAS is its modularity, e.g., removing, replacing, or adding an agent, only a few of the existing compact representations are both modular, computationally grounded [22] and allow the system designer to represent knowledge and strategic ability. Among these few approaches are Modular Interpreted Systems (MIS) [17], which we modify a bit, and use it to apply our abstraction techniques. MIS are inspired by interpreted systems [12,13]

L.A. Dennis, O. Boissier, and R.H. Bordini (Eds.): ProMAS 2011, LNCS 7217, pp. 95–113, 2012.
© Springer-Verlag Berlin Heidelberg 2012

but achieve a modularity and compactness property much like concurrent programs [18], i.e., they are modular, compact and computationally grounded while allowing at the same time to represent strategic abilities.

Although explicit models (and symbolic representations [21,20]) achieve the second part very well (because the semantics are defined over them) some problems arise with the first part: Usually temporal models have an exponential number of states and, in addition, they do not support modularity since there is no easy way to remove or replace an agent. Interpreted systems [12,13], however, have a modular state space. But they use a joint transition function for modelling temporal aspects of the system and are thus not modular wrt actions. In contrast, concurrent programs [18] are both modular and compact not only wrt the states but also wrt the actions. However, in the context of a MAS it is important that actions can have side effects on the states of other agents as well and this behaviour is difficult to model with concurrent programs ([17] contains a detailed comparison). Finally, our choice of using MIS to model MAS is, although motivated by the above reasons, still arbitrary to some extent and our techniques could certainly be used with other formalisms as well.

A major obstacle to model checking real systems is the state explosion problem. As model checking algorithms require a search through the state space of the system, the efficiency of any algorithm highly depends on the size of this state space. While for small problems this is still feasible, for larger state spaces it soon becomes intractable. We therefore need to eliminate irrelevant states by using appropriate abstraction techniques [4] which guarantee that the property to be verified holds in the original system if it holds for the abstract system. We present such an abstraction technique for MIS. More precisely, we reduce the local state space of each agent in a MIS. We do this by using hand crafted equivalence relations because, clearly, there cannot be a generic automatizable abstraction technique: Model checking ATL for MIS is *EXPTIME*-complete, therefore in the worst case there are instances where no abstraction technique at all is applicable.

While abstraction of reactive systems for temporal properties is a lively research area [2,3,7,19], there are only a few approaches when it comes to MAS and even fewer concerning an abstraction technique for dealing with strategic abilities. One interesting approach by Cohen et al. [6] achieves an abstraction that preserves temporal-epistemic properties. However, the abstraction is based on an interpreted system to model the MAS and therefore limits the modularity of the MAS. Several other abstraction approaches for epistemic properties (cf. [8,11]) are either not computationally grounded or use an explicit representation of the model.

Another approach by Henzinger et al. [15] shows how to use abstraction for symbolic model checking of alternating-time μ-calculus formulae over MAS given as alternating transition systems. Their technique is quite similar to ours but still more restricted in an important way. They assume that there are only two agents present and then use a single abstraction to model check the whole formula. Our approach allows for multiple agents and for many abstractions (one per strategic operator). Hence, we allow for a much finer control over what information is abstracted away but still preserve soundness of our model checking algorithm.

Note that we will assume the existence of handcrafted equivalence relations, e.g. generated from manual annotations of program code, since any automatic abstraction generation or refinement (as in [14] for two-player games) can only work in typical cases but not in the worst case. That is also the reason why we do not work out how our algorithms can be implemented fully symbolically: in the worst case it will be as bad as a non-symbolic algorithm. We are not trying to neglect the usefulness of either of those techniques but our focus lies on something else: a provable upper bound for the runtime which is exponential in the sum of the sizes of the abstract systems but linear in the size of a succinct representation of the concrete system (see Theorem 1). The exponential part of this is not as bad as it sounds because, as argued above, our technique allows for more than one abstraction and therefore each abstraction can be quite small and still much of the relevant information of the whole concrete system can be preserved for the overall model checking process.

Finally, the abstraction for MIS which we present in this paper is motivated by the idea of an IT ecosystem [9], i.e., a system composed of a large number of distributed, decentralized, autonomous, interacting, cooperating, organically grown, heterogeneous, and continually evolving subsystems. In such an ecosystem, which can be seen as a MAS, it is important to verify safety, fairness and liveness properties in order to control the stability of it. A non-trivial demonstrator (mentioned in [9]) describes one instance of such a system by introducing a fictional scenario, namely a smart airport. In that airport there exist many agents doing different things, e.g., carrying your bags, buying flight tickets or exchanging pictures about the travel destination. Among many other things some agents at the airport want to share some information with other agents. Assuming that no direct agent-to-agent connection is possible, the agents have to send the information to some middleman that forwards the message. Obviously this communication protocol raises some questions about safety, fairness and liveness properties. While examining these properties, i.e., model checking the whole system (consisting of many agents and therefore many states), is intractable, model checking a MIS allows us to concentrate on just the agents that have to communicate. Using our abstraction method it is sufficient to model-check a fairly small subset of the original system. We will use this scenario as a running example throughout the paper.

The structure of the paper is as follows: First we present the background of our work. Section 2 recalls the MIS framework and describes our modifications. We extend this section by formulating the communicating agents example as a MIS. In Section 3 we introduce the logic ATL. The main contributions of this paper are in Section 4, Section 5 and Section 6: We design an abstraction technique for MIS, then construct a model checking algorithm based on this technique and conclude with a soundness proof as well as a complexity analysis of the algorithm. Section 7 illustrates the abstraction technique by an example. Finally, Section 8 summarizes the results and discusses future work.

2   Modular Interpreted Systems

We model multi-agent systems in the framework of Modular Interpreted Systems (MIS) [17]. Each agent is described by a set of possible local states, i.e., states it can be in, and a function that calculates the available actions in a certain state. A local transition function specifies how an agent evolves from one local state to another. States are labeled with a set of propositional symbols by an associated labeling function. Finally, an agent is equipped with a function that defines the possible influences of an agent's action on its environment, i.e. the other agents, and a function for the influence of the environment on this particular agent.

Definition 1. *A Modular Interpreted System (MIS) is a tuple $S = (\text{Agt}, \text{Act}, \mathcal{I}n)$ where Act is the set of actions all agents can perform. $\mathcal{I}n$ is called inter-action alphabet. It describes the interaction between the agent and its environment. Finally, $\text{Agt} = \{a_1, \ldots, a_k\}$ is a set of agents where an agent is a tuple $a_i = (St_i, d_i, out_i, in_i, o_i, \Pi_i, \pi_i)$ with*

- *St_i is the local state space. It is a non-empty set of possible local states for agent a_i.*
- *$d_i : St_i \to \mathcal{P}(Act)$ defines for each state in St_i the available actions for agent a_i. With $\mathcal{P}$ we denote the power set.*
- *$out_i : St_i \times Act \to \mathcal{P}(\mathcal{I}n)$ defines the possible influences (one is then chosen non-deterministically) of agent a_i's action (executed in a certain local state) on its environment.[1] Intuitively, this describes the external effect of an action which agent a_i is executing.*
- *$in_i : St_i \times \mathcal{I}n^{k-1} \to \mathcal{P}(\mathcal{I}n)$ defines the possible influences (one is then chosen non-deterministically) of its environment on this agent.[1] It maps the external effects of the actions of all other agents to the influence these actions might have on the agent in a particular state.*
- *$o_i : St_i \times Act \times \mathcal{I}n \to \mathcal{P}(St_i)$ is a local (non-deterministic) transition function.[2].*
- *Π_i are the local propositions, where Π_i and Π_j are disjoint when $i \neq j$.*
- *$\pi_i : St_i \to \mathcal{P}(\Pi_i)$ is a valuation (local labeling function) of these propositions.*

The global state space is defined as $St := St_1 \times \cdots \times St_k$.

Example 1. We consider a system with several autonomous agents which can gather information about their environment and share that information between each other if they are in communication range. We consider groups of them working together as teams.

Our example consists of six agents $\{a_1, a_2, a_3, a_4, b_1, b_2\}$ partitioned in two teams $A = \{a_1, a_2, a_3, a_4\}$ and $B = \{b_1, b_2\}$ and where the agents' locations are

---

[1] This is different from the original MIS definition in so far as we have a set of possible influences and the authors had one deterministic influence symbol; it is changed to cope with possible ambiguities when doing abstraction later.

[2] Non-deterministic as opposed to in the original definition; it inherits the non-determinism from in_i and adds additional non-determinism to cope with abstraction of states later.

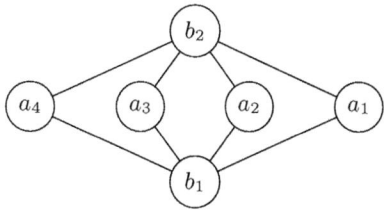

Fig. 1. Communication graph of the six agents

such that each agent a_i can reach each agent b_j but no two agents from the same team can reach each other (see Figure 1). Agents of team A can send a message (if they already know it) to b_1 or b_2 or choose to do nothing. Agents of team B, however, are not allowed to send a message back to its sender agent. Once an agent a_i sent a message to an agent b_j the agent b_j is not allowed to send it to a_i in any future round. Additionally, if an agent b_j has received a message from a_i then it has to send it to some agent a_k in the following round (unless this contradicts the former rule) and if possible k has to be greater than i.

Now agent a_1 has learned something and wants to communicate its newly gathered knowledge to its team member a_4. The difficulty is that the message has to pass through an agent of the other team. But we will see that it is still possible for team A to ensure that a_4 will know the message eventually. Formally we have the following MIS

$$S := (\mathbb{A}gt = \{a_1, a_2, a_3, a_4, b_1, b_2\}, Act = \{\text{send}_x \mid x \in \mathbb{A}gt\} \cup \{\text{noop}\},$$
$$\mathcal{I}n = \{\textbf{nothing}, \textbf{m}_{\textbf{a}_1}, \textbf{m}_{\textbf{a}_2}, \textbf{m}_{\textbf{a}_3}, \textbf{m}_{\textbf{a}_4}\}$$
$$\cup \mathcal{P}(\{\textbf{m}_{\textbf{a}_i\textbf{b}_j} \mid i \in \{1, \ldots, 4\}, j \in \{1, 2\}\}))$$

with $a_i := (St_{a_i}, d_{a_i}, out_{a_i}, in_{a_i}, o_{a_i}, \Pi_{a_i}, \pi_{a_i})$ where

- $St_{a_i} = \{k(nown), u(nknown)\}$
- $\Pi_{a_i} = \{\text{known}_{a_i}, \text{unknown}_{a_i}\}$
- $\pi_{a_i} : k \mapsto \{\text{known}_{a_i}\}, \quad u \mapsto \{\text{unknown}_{a_i}\}$
- $d_{a_i} : k \mapsto \{\text{send}_{b_1}, \text{send}_{b_2}, \text{noop}\}, \quad u \mapsto \{\text{noop}\}$
- $out_{a_i} : (k, \text{send}_{b_j}) \mapsto \{\textbf{m}_{\textbf{a}_i\textbf{b}_j}\}$
    $(k, \text{noop}) \mapsto \{\textbf{nothing}\}$
    $(u, \text{noop}) \mapsto \{\textbf{nothing}\}$
    for all $j \in \{1, 2\}$,
- $in_{a_i} : (s, \gamma_1, \ldots, \gamma_5) \mapsto \begin{cases} \{\textbf{m}_{\textbf{a}_i}\} & \text{if } \textbf{m}_{\textbf{a}_i} \in \{\gamma_1, \ldots, \gamma_5\} \\ \{\textbf{nothing}\} & \text{else} \end{cases}$
    for all $s \in St_{a_i}, \gamma_1, \ldots, \gamma_5 \in \mathcal{I}n$,
- $o_{a_i} : (k, \alpha, \gamma) \quad \mapsto \{k\}$
    $(u, \alpha, \textbf{nothing}) \mapsto \{u\}$
    $(u, \alpha, \textbf{m}_{\textbf{a}_i}) \quad \mapsto \{k\}$
    for all $\gamma \in \mathcal{I}n$ and $\alpha \in Act$.

For the agents b_j we have $b_j := (St_{b_j}, d_{b_j}, out_{b_j}, in_{b_j}, o_{b_j}, \Pi_{b_j}, \pi_{b_j})$ where

- $St_{b_j} = \mathcal{P}(\{r_1,\ldots,r_4\}) \times \mathcal{P}(\{n_1,\ldots,n_4\})$,
- $\Pi_{b_j} = \{\mathsf{known}_{b_j}, \mathsf{unknown}_{b_j}\}$,
- $\pi_{b_j} : (R,N) \mapsto \begin{cases} \{\mathsf{known}_{b_j}\} & \text{if } R \neq \emptyset \\ \{\mathsf{unknown}_{b_j}\} & \text{else} \end{cases}$,

- $d_{b_j} : (R,N) \mapsto \begin{cases} \{\mathsf{noop}\} & \text{if } R = \emptyset \\ \left\{\mathsf{send}_{a_i} \middle| \begin{array}{l} r_i \notin R \text{ and there is no } k \geq i: \\ n_k \in N \text{ and } \exists \ell > k: r_\ell \notin R \end{array}\right\} \\ \quad\cup \begin{cases} \{\mathsf{noop}\} & \text{if } N = \emptyset \text{ or } R = \{r_1,\ldots,r_4\} \\ \emptyset & \text{else} \end{cases} & \text{else} \end{cases}$,

- $out_{b_j} : ((R,N), \mathsf{send}_{a_i}) \mapsto \{\mathbf{m_{a_i}}\}$
  $\phantom{out_{b_j} :} ((R,N), \mathsf{noop}) \mapsto \{\mathbf{nothing}\}$
  for all $i \in \{1,\ldots,4\}$,

- $in_{b_j} : ((R,N), \gamma_1, \ldots, \gamma_5) \mapsto$
  $\begin{cases} \{\mathbf{m_{a_i b_j}} \mid \{\mathbf{m_{a_i b_j}}\} \in \{\gamma_1,\ldots,\gamma_5\}\} \\ \quad \text{if there is } i \in \{1,\ldots,4\} \text{ with } \{\mathbf{m_{a_i b_j}}\} \in \{\gamma_1,\ldots,\gamma_5\} \\ \{\mathbf{nothing}\} \quad \text{else} \end{cases}$
  for all $\gamma_1,\ldots,\gamma_5 \in \mathcal{I}n$,

- $o_{b_j} : ((R,N), \alpha, M) \qquad\quad \mapsto (R \cup \{r_i \mid \mathbf{m_{a_i b_j}} \in M\}, \{r_i \mid \mathbf{m_{a_i b_j}} \in M\})$
  $\phantom{o_{b_j} :} ((R,N), \alpha, \mathbf{nothing}) \mapsto (R, \emptyset)$
  for all $\alpha \in Act$, $\emptyset \neq M \subseteq \{\mathbf{m_{a_1 b_j}}, \ldots, \mathbf{m_{a_4 b_j}}\}$,

for all $(R,N) \in St_{b_j}$. R stands for "received (now or some time ago)" while N means "received **now**".

Figure 2 shows the agent a_1. Each arrow is denoted by an action, an incoming and an outgoing interaction symbol. The state u is labeled with $\mathsf{unknown}_{a_1}$ and k with known_{a_1}. The agents a_i are fairly simply structured, they consist of two states representing whether the agent knows the message (k) or it does not know it (u). In the former case the agent can send the message to one of the opponents or just do nothing. In the latter case it has to wait for some agent of team B sending the message to it.

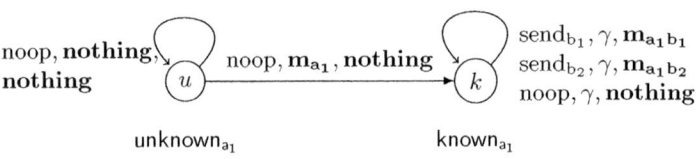

Fig. 2. Graph of agent a_1

The structure of the agent b_j however is more complex since it consists of 256 states. Every state is labeled with known_{b_j} if the state name contains at least one r_i, i.e., the agent received some time ago the message from agent a_i. Consequently, states that do not have any r_i are marked as $\mathsf{unknown}_{b_j}$. Intuitively, while the agent is waiting for a message it does nothing. When it receives a message, i.e., the state contains a n_i it has to send the message to one of the opponents with a higher number than i and with the condition that this agent did not send it to b_j before. If the state contains all r_1 to r_4 the agent does nothing.

We will come back to this concrete example when presenting the logic and the model checking algorithm.

3   Specification Logic ATL

After having outlined the framework with which we model our MAS, we now have to specify a logic to talk about strategic properties of such a system. We recall the syntax of ATL, define some abbreviations and sketch the semantics of ATL for MIS.

Definition 2. *Alternating-time temporal Logic (ATL) [1] is a logic that enables reasoning about temporal and strategic abilities of multi-agent systems. The syntax of plain* ATL *is defined by (with $A \subseteq \text{Agt}$)*

$$\varphi ::= \mathsf{p} \mid \neg\varphi \mid \varphi \vee \varphi \mid \langle\langle A \rangle\rangle \mathbf{X}\varphi \mid \langle\langle A \rangle\rangle \mathbf{G}\varphi \mid \langle\langle A \rangle\rangle \varphi \mathbf{U}\varphi.$$

Informally, $\langle\langle A \rangle\rangle \mathbf{X}\varphi$ means that agents A have a collective strategy to enforce that in the next step φ holds. The operator $\mathbf{X}$ is read "in the next state", the symbol $\mathbf{G}$ means "globally" and $\mathbf{U}$ "until". Other Boolean operators are defined by macros in the usual way.

For the model checking algorithm presented in Section 5 we need to split a formula into subformulae.

Definition 3. *For an ATL formula φ we write $\text{qsf}(\varphi)$ for the multiset of all subformulae of φ which start with a quantifier $\langle\langle A \rangle\rangle$.*

Note that identical formulae occurring in two different places inside φ occur twice in $\text{qsf}(\varphi)$ and if φ itself begins with a quantifier it is in the multiset as well.

Finally, we need the following notions.

Definition 4. *For a formula $\varphi = \langle\langle A \rangle\rangle \psi$ we write $[\![\varphi]\!]$ for the set A of agents. For an arbitrary formula φ and an arbitrary $\psi \in \text{qsf}(\varphi)$ let $\varphi(\psi, w)$ denote the formula resulting from φ by replacing all occurrences of ψ simultaneously with the new proposition w.*

Example 2. Considering the communicating agents example (cf. Example 1) we can ask the following question: Is it possible for team A to ensure that a_4 will know the message eventually? Written in ATL this corresponds to the question whether

$$S, \mathsf{q} \models \langle\langle A \rangle\rangle (\top \mathbf{U}\mathsf{known}_{\mathsf{a}_4})$$

with $A = \{a_1, a_2, a_3, a_4\}$ and q is the global state where a_1 is in state k, all other agents from team A are in state u and the agents from team B are in state $(\emptyset, \emptyset)$, i.e. where only a_1 knows the message.

3.1 Semantics of ATL for MIS

Modular Interpreted Systems can be easily transformed into *concurrent game structures* (CGS, cf. [1]) as shown for deterministic CGS in [17]. The notion of a CGS is a very universal formalism to model MAS but it comes at the cost of not being modular, i.e., CGS have an unstructured global state space. Also, just as MIS, they have for every agent i a function $d : \text{Agt} \times St \to \mathcal{P}(Act)$ expressing which actions are available to agent i in a certain global state. The global transition function of a CGS takes as input a global state and for every agent a permissible action and outputs a set of possible successor states (one is then chosen non-deterministically), i.e., the influences of an agent on its environment are implicitly given and there is no way to measure or limit that influence in the framework of CGS. In order to provide the formal semantics we firstly introduce CGS and the formal notion of a strategy and then describe the semantics. We conclude with the translation of a MIS to a CGS.[3]

Definition 5. *A CGS is a tuple* $M = (\text{Agt}, St, \Pi, \pi, Act, d, o)$, *consisting of a set of agents* Agt, *a set of states* St, *a set of propositions* Π *and a set of actions* Act. *Additionally, it has a valuation function* $\pi : St \to \mathcal{P}(\Pi)$ *and a function* $d : \text{Agt} \times St \to \mathcal{P}(Act)$ *defining for each agent in* Agt *and each state in* St *the available actions. Finally,* o *is a transition function that maps a state* $q \in St$ *and an action profile* $\langle \alpha_1, \ldots, \alpha_k \rangle \in Act^k$, $\alpha_i \in d(i, q)$ *to another state* $q' = o'(q, \alpha_1, \ldots, \alpha_k)$.

Definition 6. *A (memoryless) strategy of agent* i *is a function* $s_i : St \mapsto Act$ *such that* $s_i(q) \in d(i, q)$. *A collective strategy* S_A *for a team* $A \subseteq \text{Agt}$ *specifies an individual strategy for each agent* $i \in A$. *The outcome of strategy* S_A *of state* q *is defined as the set of all computations that may result from executing* S_A *from* q *on:*

$$out(q, S_A) = \{\lambda = q_0 q_1 q_2 \ldots \mid q_0 = q \text{ and for every } j = 1, 2, \ldots \text{ there exists}$$
$$\langle \alpha_1^{j-1}, \ldots, \alpha_k^{j-1} \rangle \text{ such that } \alpha_i^{j-1} = S_A(i)(q_{j-1}) \text{ for each } i \in A,$$
$$\alpha_i^{j-1} \in d(i, q_{j-1}) \text{ for each } i \notin A, \text{ and } o(q_{j-1}, \alpha_1^{j-1}, \ldots, \alpha_k^{j-1}) = q_j\}.$$

The semantics is as follows:

- $M, q \models \mathsf{p}$ iff $q \in \pi(\mathsf{p})$
- $M, q \models \neg\varphi$ iff $M, q \not\models \varphi$
- $M, q \models \varphi \vee \psi$ iff $M, q \models \varphi$ or $M, q \models \psi$
- $M, q \models \langle\langle A \rangle\rangle \mathbf{X}\varphi$ iff there is a collective strategy S_A such that, for every $\lambda \in out(q, S_A)$, we have $M, \lambda[1] \models \varphi$.
- $M, q \models \langle\langle A \rangle\rangle \mathbf{G}\varphi$ iff there exists S_A such that, for every $\lambda \in out(q, S_A)$, we have $M, \lambda[j] \models \varphi$ for every $j \geq 0$

---

[3] We do not provide the full semantics for MIS here but follow the same approach as in [17], i.e., translating the MIS to a CGS and using the semantics for CGS.

– $M, q \models \langle\langle A \rangle\rangle \varphi \mathbf{U} \psi$ iff there exists S_A such that, for every $\lambda \in out(q, S_A)$, there is a $j \geq 0$, for which $M, \lambda[j] \models \psi$, and $M, \lambda[l] \models \varphi$ for every $0 \leq l \leq j$.

Finally, we describe the translation from MIS to CGS.

Definition 7. *For a MIS $S = (\{a_1, \ldots, a_k\}, Act, \mathcal{In})$ with $a_i = (St_i, d_i, out_i, in_i, o_i, \Pi_i, \pi_i)$ ($1 \leq i \leq k$) the corresponding (non-deterministic) concurrent game structure $ncgs(S) = (\mathbb{A}gt', St', \Pi', \pi', Act', d', o')$ is defined as follows:*

– $\mathbb{A}gt' := \{1, \ldots, k\}$
– $St' := \prod\limits_{i=1}^{k} St_i$
– $\Pi' := \Pi_1 \cup \cdots \cup \Pi_k$
– $\pi'(p) := \{(q_1, \ldots, q_i, \ldots, q_k) \mid q_i \in \pi_i(p)\}$
– $Act' := Act$
– $d_i'((q_1, \ldots, q_k)) := d_i(q_i)$
– $o'((q_1, \ldots, q_k), \alpha_1, \ldots, \alpha_k) :=$
$\{(q_1', \ldots, q_k') \mid \forall 1 \leq i \leq k : q_i' \in o_i(q_i, \alpha_i, \gamma_i) \text{ for a } \gamma_i \in in_i(q_i, \gamma_1, \ldots, \gamma_{i-1}, \gamma_{i+1}, \ldots, \gamma_k) \text{ for some } \gamma_1, \ldots, \gamma_{i-1}, \gamma_{i+1}, \ldots, \gamma_k \text{ with } \gamma_j \in out_j(q_j, \alpha_j)\}$

Note that our concurrent game structures extend the definition from [1] in two ways. Firstly we use labeled actions instead of plain numbers. Secondly we allow the transition relation to be non-deterministic. The semantics of a formula $\langle\langle A \rangle\rangle \varphi$ over a non-deterministic CGS is defined with the non-determinism working against the agents in A. The rationale behind this is that $\langle\langle A \rangle\rangle \varphi$ means "the agents A have a combined strategy which enforces φ". Now, to enforce φ this strategy needs to ensure that in each of the possible runs of the system – determined by the other agents' choices and the non-deterministic branching – the formula φ holds.

Model checking ATL for deterministic MIS is *EXPTIME*-complete as stated in [16] and for deterministic CGS it is *PTIME*-complete as stated in [1]. These results still hold for the non-deterministic versions of the structures. This is because in the model checking algorithm from [1, Chapter 4.1] introducing non-determinism only changes the function $\text{Pre}(A, \rho)$ (which for a given set ρ of system states and a given set A of agents outputs the set of system states from which the agents A can enforce that the next state in any run will lie in $\rho)^4$. And computing Pre does not get more difficult with non-determinism because even in the case of deterministic systems it is already necessary to take into account all transitions in order to compute Pre.

Having defined MIS and ATL we can now present our new abstraction technique.

---

[4] The pre-image operator Pre is similar to the one of CTL [10]. However, it works on game structures instead of Kripke structures. For details see Section 4 in [1].

4   Abstraction for MIS

In general, multi-agent systems have large associated state spaces and even if
they are symbolically represented it is infeasible to verify properties by considering *all* reachable states. Nevertheless, interesting properties often only refer to
parts of a system. Under this assumption it makes sense to reduce the state space
by removing irrelevant states and/or by combining them. Due to the modularity
of MIS, we can in a first step easily remove the obviously non-relevant parts of
the global state space by removing particular agents while keeping the others.
Secondly, we reduce the state space of each agent by abstraction. As in [4] and
[6] we do this by partitioning the state space into equivalence classes: Each class
collects all concrete states that are equivalent and forms one new abstract state.
This new state is labeled by those propositions which are shared by all concrete
states. We define the local transition functions of the abstract system in such
a way that it behaves just as the concrete one. The set of available actions in
an abstract state is decreased so that it only contains actions available in every
one of the equivalent concrete states. Finally we show how to handle the interaction with an agents' environment. We start by introducing the definition of an
abstraction relation.

Definition 8. *An* abstraction relation *for a MIS is a product* $\equiv\; =\; \equiv_1 \times \cdots \times \equiv_k$
where each $\equiv_i\; \subseteq\; St_i \times St_i$ *is an equivalence relation for the states* St_i *of
agent* a_i.

For $q \in St_i$, *we write* $[q]_{\equiv_i}$ *for the equivalence class of the local state* q *with
respect to* $\equiv_i$. *And for* $q \in St = St_1 \times \cdots \times St_k$, *we write* $[q]_{\equiv}$ *for the equivalence
class of the global state* q.

An abstraction relation as in Definition 8 defines for each agent of the MIS,
which local states are equivalent and therefore can be condensed to one abstract
state. Note that this definition does not say anything about how to define the
equivalence, because this depends on the concrete system that is model checked.
Therefore these relations have to be handcrafted when modeling a system.

Using the definition of a MIS and Definition 8 we can now specify the
abstraction of a system:

Definition 9. *For a MIS* $S = (\text{Agt}, Act, \mathcal{I}n)$, *an abstraction relation* $\equiv$ *for* S
and a set of favored *agents* $A \subseteq \text{Agt}$ *we define the* abstraction *of* S *with respect
to* $\equiv$ *and* A *as the MIS*

$$S^A_{\equiv} := (\text{Agt}', Act, \mathcal{I}n)$$

where $\text{Agt}' := \{a'_1, \ldots, a'_k\}$ *and* $a'_i = (St'_i, d'_i, out'_i, in'_i, o'_i, \Pi'_i, \pi'_i)$ *with*

i) $St'_i := \{[q]_{\equiv_i} \mid q \in St_i\}$

ii) $d'_i([q]_{\equiv_i}) := \begin{cases} \bigcap_{q' \in [q]_{\equiv_i}} d_i(q') & \text{for } a_i \in A \\ \bigcup_{q' \in [q]_{\equiv_i}} d_i(q') & \text{for } a_i \notin A \end{cases}$

iii) $out'_i([q]_{\equiv_i}, \alpha) := \bigcup\limits_{q' \in [q]_{\equiv_i}} out_i(q', \alpha)$

iv) $in'_i([q]_{\equiv_i}, \gamma_1, \ldots, \gamma_{k-1}) := \bigcup\limits_{q' \in [q]_{\equiv_i}} in_i(q', \gamma_1, \ldots, \gamma_{k-1})$

$v)$ $o'_i([q]_{\equiv_i}, \alpha, \gamma) := \bigcup\limits_{q' \in [q]_{\equiv_i}} \{[q'']_{\equiv_i} \mid q'' \in o_i(q', \alpha, \gamma)\}$

$vi)$ $\Pi'_i := \Pi_i \cap \{p_i \mid \forall q \in \pi_i(p_i): \forall q' \in [q]_{\equiv_i}: q' \in \pi_i(p_i)\}$

$vii)$ $\pi'_i(p_i) := \{[q]_{\equiv_i} \mid q \in \pi_i(p_i)\}$

for all $q \in St_i$, $\alpha \in Act$, $\gamma, \gamma_1, \ldots, \gamma_k \in \mathcal{I}n$ and $p_i \in \Pi'_i$.

Note that there might be $i \in \{1, \ldots, k\}$ and $q \in St_i$ such that $d'_i([q]_{\equiv_i}) = \emptyset$. As this would paralyse the system we will from now on assume that the abstraction relation is chosen in such a way that this does not happen.

Formula i) defines a partition of the local state space by using the handcrafted equivalence relation of this agent. We reduce all equivalent states to just one. Function ii) then computes for this element the available actions by giving agents in A fewer choices and the opponents more choices than before. Due to this construction if a property $\langle\langle A \rangle\rangle \varphi$ (with φ propositional) holds in the abstract system it also holds in the concrete one, since we restricted the actions of the protagonists and extended the set of actions of the antagonists. The possible influences of these actions concerning the environment are calculated by the resulting function iii). It takes for the action α the union of all resulting influence symbols of all states in the equivalence class, i.e., collecting all influence symbols that are an outcome of executing action α in each state q' of the equivalence class $[q]_{\equiv_i}$. Taking the union is motivated by the fact that executing the same action in equivalent local states results in an equivalent influence on the environment. iv) is defined the same way: We just use the union of in_i for each state in the equivalence class. Moreover, the out_i- and in_i-functions are of the same type for the protagonists as well as the antagonists because they do not introduce deliberate choices by the agents but instead introduce nondeterminism which will – as we will see in Section 5 – always work against the formula which is to be verified. The local transition function v) has to be modified to cope with equivalence classes: It gets as input an abstract state, an action and one (nondeterministically chosen) influence symbol. The output is the set of all equivalence classes that are successors. To determine this we unfold both equivalence classes and check whether there is a connection between a concrete state of the first equivalence class to another concrete state of the second equivalence class.

Finally, we have to define how to label the abstract states (cf. vi) and vii)). We do this by assigning a proposition to an abstract state if all concrete states in the equivalence class are labeled with that proposition. If a proposition only holds in some states of the class we remove it from set of propositions. This ensures that if a proposition is true in an abstract state it is also true in all concrete ones.

In the next section we describe how to evaluate whether a formula holds in a system.

5   The Model Checking Algorithm

Our algorithm takes as input a MIS S, a set $init$ of global states of S (the initial states), an ATL formula φ and for each $\psi \in \mathrm{qsf}(\varphi)$ an abstraction relation $\equiv_\psi$.

The algorithm either returns true or it returns unknown but it will never return false. If it returns true it is guaranteed that $S, q \models \varphi$ for all $q \in init$. But if it returns unknown we do not know whether S satisfies φ or not.

This behaviour is due to the way model checking is done here: Several abstractions of S (generated out of the abstraction relations $\equiv_\psi$) are used each to model check a part of φ. And as usual with handcrafted abstractions there can be false negatives. The important point is that there are no false positives, i.e. if the abstractions fulfill φ then so does the concrete system.

Before we can present the algorithm we need the technical notion of a pseudo-MIS which will be used in it.

Definition 10. *A* pseudo-MIS *is a MIS together with a set Π of global propositions (which is disjoint to each set of local propositions) and a global labeling function $\pi : St \to \mathcal{P}(\Pi)$. Note that every MIS can be viewed as a pseudo-MIS with $\Pi = \emptyset$.*

The algorithm now works as follows. Details about efficiently implementing some of the steps are given in the proof of Theorem 1.

Algorithm $modelcheck(S, init, \varphi, (\equiv_\psi)_{\psi \in \mathsf{qsf}(\varphi)})$:
Let $\varphi = \lambda(\theta_1, \ldots, \theta_n, \ell_1, \ldots, \ell_m)$ where

- λ is a monotone Boolean formula, i.e. λ is composed of conjunctions and disjunctions only,
- $\theta_1, \ldots, \theta_n$ are arbitrary ATL formulae each beginning with a quantifier or a negation directly followed by a quantifier, i.e. each θ_i is of the form $\langle\langle B \rangle\rangle \theta_i'$ or $\neg\langle\langle B \rangle\rangle \theta_i'$ (in the latter case we will still write $\equiv_{\theta_i}$ and $[\![\theta_i]\!]$ instead of $\equiv_{\langle\langle B\rangle\rangle\theta_i'}$ and $[\![\langle\langle B\rangle\rangle\theta_i']\!]$), and
- $\ell_1, \ldots, \ell_m$ are literals, i.e. atomic propositions or negations of atomic propositions.

1) For all $i \in \{1, \ldots, n\}$ do:
   i) Set $W_i := label(\theta_i, \equiv_{\theta_i})$.
   ii) Set $S := S(w_i, W_i)$, i.e. S is from now on viewed as a pseudo-MIS, a new global proposition w_i is introduced in S and it is labeled exactly in the states in W_i.
2) If $S, s \models \lambda(w_1, \ldots, w_n, \ell_1, \ldots, \ell_m)$ for all $s \in init$ then return true. Otherwise return unknown.
   Note that for this step the algorithm only has to locally check the labeling of the states $s \in init$ as $\lambda(w_1, \ldots, w_n, \ell_1, \ldots, \ell_m)$ is an entirely propositional formula.

Algorithm $label(\psi, \equiv)$:
Let $\psi = \neg^\psi \langle\langle A \rangle\rangle \mathbf{Y} \lambda(\theta_1, \ldots, \theta_n, \ell_1, \ldots, \ell_m)$ where

- $\neg^\psi$ is $\neg$ if ψ begins with a negation and it is the empty string elsewise,
- $\mathbf{Y} \in \{\mathbf{X}, \mathbf{G}, \mathbf{U}\}$,

- λ is a monotone Boolean formula,
- $\theta_1, \ldots, \theta_n$ are arbitrary ATL formulae each beginning with a quantifier or a negation directly followed by a quantifier, and
- $\ell_1, \ldots, \ell_m$ are literals.

1) Construct the abstraction

$$S' := \begin{cases} S_{\equiv}^{[\![\psi]\!]} & \text{if } \psi \text{ does not begin with a negation} \\ S_{\equiv}^{\mathrm{Agt}\setminus[\![\psi]\!]} & \text{if } \psi \text{ does begin with a negation} \end{cases}$$

We will view S' as a pseudo-MIS in the following steps.

2) For all $i \in \{1, \ldots, n\}$ do:
   i) Set $W_i := \{[q]_{\equiv} \mid \forall q' \in [q]_{\equiv} : q' \in label(\theta_i, \equiv_{\theta_i})\}$.
   ii) Set $S' := S'(w_i, W_i)$.

3) Compute the set W' of global states of S' (note that these are global states of the system abstracted with $\equiv$) satisfying ψ, i.e. $W' :=$

$$\{[q]_{\equiv} \mid S', [q]_{\equiv} \models \neg^{\psi} \langle\langle A \rangle\rangle \mathbf{Y} \lambda(w_1, \ldots, w_n, \ell_1, \ldots, \ell_m)\},$$

by translating S' to a non-deterministic CGS and then using the ATL model checking algorithm from [1, Chapter 4.1]. As already pointed out in Section 3.1 their algorithm is only given for deterministic CGS but can be easily adapted to also handle non-deterministic systems.

There is, however, a caveat here. Because additional non-determinism might be introduced by abstracting the system we have to make sure that the non-determinism works "against the formula" because we want to avoid false positive outputs of our algorithm. This is the reason why we have to interpret the non-determinism as working *for* the agents in A if $\neg^{\psi} = \neg$ and working *against* them otherwise. If we always had it working against them (which seems natural as argued in Section 3.1) then in the former case it could happen that the algorithm comes to the conclusion that $S', [q]_{\equiv} \models \psi$ although $S, q \not\models \psi$ – a false positive. The reason for this would be non-determinism present in S' and absent in S that would presumably prevent agents A to have a winning strategy in S' although they do have one in S.

4) Return $W := \{q \in St \mid [q]_{\equiv} \in W'\}$.

6   Complexity and Soundness of the Algorithm

The following theorem shows that our model checking algorithm runs in time linear in the size of a succinct representation of the concrete system as well as linear in the length of the formula and exponential in the sum of the sizes of the abstract systems. Now, since there is a special abstraction for each modality, the abstractions should be very small and therefore this should be a huge improvement over the *EXPTIME*-completeness of model checking MIS without abstractions.

Theorem 1. *Algorithm modelcheck$(S, init, \varphi, (\equiv_\psi)_{\psi \in \mathsf{qsf}(\varphi)})$ runs in time*

$$O\left(|init| + |S| \cdot |\varphi|\right) \cdot 2^{O\left(\sum\limits_{\psi \in \mathsf{qsf}(\varphi)} \left|S_{\equiv_\psi}^{\llbracket \psi \rrbracket}\right|\right)}$$

where $|S|$ denotes the size of the MIS S in a compact representation. The cardinality of the global state space of S may then be upto $2^{\Theta(|S|)}$.

Proof. The crucial implementation detail is that it is not possible to explicitly enumerate the set returned in step 4 of *label*() because the set may be as large as the global state space St of S. Instead, both *label*() and *modelcheck*() have to save and pass on computed sets of global states in a symbolic way, i.e. by refering to the modular structure of S and to the abstraction relation's equivalence classes. This technique is needed in step 1 of *modelcheck*() and in steps 2i and 4 of *label*().

Also, in step 2i of *label*() it is not possible to check the condition for each $[q]_\equiv \in St'$ by enumerating through all $q' \in [q]_\equiv$ because a single equivalence class may already be as large as the global state space. Hence, the algorithm has to construct the equivalence relation $\equiv' := \equiv \cap \equiv_{\theta_i}$ (which is a refinement of both $\equiv$ and $\equiv_{\theta_i}$) and compute W_i as the set $\{[q]_\equiv \mid \forall [q']_{\equiv'} \subseteq [q]_\equiv : [q']_{\equiv'} \subseteq label(\theta_i, \equiv_{\theta_i})\}$. This can be done in time $O(|S_\equiv^{\llbracket \psi \rrbracket}| \cdot |S_{\equiv_{\theta_i}}^{\llbracket \theta_i \rrbracket}|)$.

Step 3 of *label*() runs in time $2^{O\left(|S_\equiv^{\llbracket \psi \rrbracket}|\right)} \cdot O(|\psi|)$ because the translation to a CGS may involve an exponential blow-up in the system size. All other steps are easy to implement – when keeping in mind the symbolic handling of state sets.

Finally, *label*() is executed at most $|\varphi|$ times. Altogether this gives the claimed upper bound on the runtime.

The following theorem shows that our algorithm is sound. It is, however, not complete because, as usual for abstraction techniques, the capability of the algorithm to show the truth of a formula depends on choosing a suitable abstraction. It should, anyhow, be possible to find good abstractions since it is possible to define a specific abstraction for each strategic operator. Of course that problem could be overcome by an automatic abstraction refinement technique but this, on the other hand, would make a provable upper bound on the runtime in the form of Theorem 1 impossible.

Theorem 2. *Algorithm modelcheck is sound, i.e. if modelcheck$(S, init, \varphi, (\equiv_\psi)_{\psi \in \mathsf{qsf}(\varphi)})$ outputs* true *then $S, q \models \varphi$ for all $q \in init$.*

Proof. (Sketch) First note that if we skipped step 1 of the *label*() algorithm and simply ran the algorithm without constructing any abstractions we would exactly run the bottom-up, subformula labeling, model checking algorithm from [1, Chapter 4.1].

Hence we only have to argue why the abstractions do not lead the algorithm to produce more positive answers than without them. The crucial observation is that for each modality $\langle\langle A \rangle\rangle \mathbf{Y}$ the aspects which are of an existentially quantifying nature, i.e. the actions available to agents A, can only be restricted by an abstraction but never extended and for the aspects of universally quantifying nature, i.e. the actions available to agents $\text{Agt} \setminus A$ as well as the non-deterministic branching of the system, it is the other way around. Thus it is ensured that if a formula $\langle\langle A \rangle\rangle \mathbf{Y} \varphi$ is true in an abstraction it is also true in the original system.

Furthermore, for formulae of the form $\neg\langle\langle A \rangle\rangle \mathbf{Y} \varphi$ the abstraction is constructed the other way around, i.e. extended choices for A and restricted choices for $\text{Agt} \setminus A$, to ensure that if the agents A do not have a winning strategy in the abstraction then neither do they have one in the original system.

The non-determinism, however, is extended even in this case. As already discussed in step 3 of the algorithm we therefore have to change the meaning of the non-determinism to be of existential rather than of universal nature. The sacrifice we have to make is that if the original system is already non-deterministic and this non-determinism ensures some property $\neg\langle\langle A \rangle\rangle \mathbf{Y} \varphi$ then the algorithm will return unknown.

7   Communicating Agents Example

Consider the example of the six agents again (Example 1 and Example 2). We will now apply the model checking algorithm to the example using the formula

$$S, \mathsf{q} \models \langle\langle A \rangle\rangle (\top \mathbf{U} \mathsf{known}_{\mathsf{a}_4})$$

with $A = \{a_1, a_2, a_3, a_4\}$ and q is the global state in which only a_1 knows the message (cf. Example 2). The formula φ describes the following question: "Is it possible for team A to always ensure that a_4 will know the message eventually?" The algorithm takes the formula φ and constructs for all quantifier subformulae an abstract system by using the specific abstraction relation for that quantifier. The multiset $\mathrm{qsf}(\varphi)$ of quantified subformulae consists just of the formula φ. Therefore, we have to define only one abstraction for φ.

Before we give the abstraction relation we note that b_2 is not necessary for the property we want to verify and therefore we can temporarily delete it from the system. As abstraction for φ we do not abstract the agents a_i at all and for agent b_1 we use the equivalence relation given by the following partition of its local state space:

$$S_i \ := \{(R, N) \mid \emptyset \neq R \subseteq \{r_1, \ldots, r_i\}, n_i \in N\} \setminus \bigcup_{j=1}^{i-1} S_j \quad \text{for } i = 1, \ldots, 3$$
$$S_{\text{rest}} := \{(R, N) \mid (R, N) \notin S_1 \cup \cdots \cup S_3\}$$

Now, the agents a_i remain unchanged and the abstracted agent b_1 looks like the following:

$$b_1' = (St_{b_1}', d_{b_1}', out_{b_1}', in_{b_1}, o_{b_1}', \Pi_{b_1}, \pi_{b_1}')$$

where

- $St_{b_1}' = \{S_1, S_2, S_3, S_{\text{rest}}\}$
- $\pi_{b_1}' : S_i \ \mapsto \{\mathsf{known}_{\mathsf{b}_1}\} \quad \text{for } i = 1, \ldots, 3$
  $\qquad\quad S_{\text{rest}} \mapsto \{\mathsf{known}_{\mathsf{b}_1}, \mathsf{unknown}_{\mathsf{b}_1}\}$

- $d'_{b_1}(S_i)$ $= \{\text{send}_x \mid x \in \{a_{i+1}, \dots, a_4\}\}$ for $i = 1, \dots, 3$
  $d'_{b_1}(S_{\text{rest}}) = \{\text{send}_x \mid x \in \{a_1, \dots, a_4\}\} \cup \{\text{noop}\}$

- $out'_{b_1} : (S_{\text{rest}}, \text{noop}) \mapsto \{\textbf{nothing}\}$
  $\qquad (s, \text{send}_{a_1}) \quad \mapsto \{\textbf{m}_{\textbf{b}_1\textbf{a}_1}\}$
  $\qquad (s, \text{send}_{a_2}) \quad \mapsto \{\textbf{m}_{\textbf{b}_1\textbf{a}_2}\}$
  $\qquad (s, \text{send}_{a_3}) \quad \mapsto \{\textbf{m}_{\textbf{b}_1\textbf{a}_3}\}$
  $\qquad (s, \text{send}_{a_4}) \quad \mapsto \{\textbf{m}_{\textbf{b}_1\textbf{a}_4}\}$
  for all $s \in St'_{b_1}$,

- $o'_{b_1} : (S_{\text{rest}}, \alpha, \textbf{nothing}) \quad \mapsto \{S_{\text{rest}}\}$
  $\qquad (S_{\text{rest}}, \alpha, \{\textbf{m}_{\textbf{a}_\textbf{j}\textbf{b}_1}\}) \quad\mapsto \{S_{\text{rest}}, S_j\}$
  $\qquad (S_i, \text{send}_{a_j}, \textbf{nothing}) \mapsto \{S_{\text{rest}}\}$
  $\qquad (S_i, \text{send}_{a_j}, \{\textbf{m}_{\textbf{a}_{\textbf{j}'}\textbf{b}_1}\}) \mapsto \{S_{j'}\}$
  $\qquad (S_i, \text{send}_{a_j}, \{\textbf{m}_{\textbf{a}_4\textbf{b}_1}\}) \mapsto \{S_{\text{rest}}\}$
  for all $\alpha \in Act$, $\gamma \in \mathcal{I}n$, $i, j' \in \{1, 2, 3\}$ and $j \in \{1, 2, 3, 4\}$.

Now, everything is specified so that the algorithm $modelcheck(S, init, \varphi, (\equiv_\psi)_{\psi \in \text{qsf}(\varphi)})$ can be started. S is the MIS mentioned in Section 2, $init = \{q\}$, φ as above and $(\equiv_\psi)_{\psi \in \text{qsf}(\varphi)}$ contains all abstraction relations for the quantified subformulae. Since the formula φ only consists of one quantifier, by invoking the algorithm $modelcheck()$ we get the quantifier subformulae $\theta_1 := \varphi$. The algorithm takes then φ and computes W_1 by executing the labeling algorithm $label(\varphi, \equiv_\varphi)$. Now, we construct the pseudo-MIS $S'_\varphi := S^{\llbracket \varphi \rrbracket}_{\equiv_\varphi}$ for the favored agents a_1, a_2, a_3, a_4. Step 2i) of the labeling algorithm is skipped since there is no further quantified subformula for φ. This is the moment when the recursion stops and we start to label the states in a bottom-up order. $W_1 := \{[q]_{\equiv_\varphi} \mid S'_\varphi, [q]_{\equiv_\varphi} \models \varphi\}$ is computed by creating the non-deterministic CGS and apply the model checking algorithm for ATL.

Now we are almost finished. In the $modelcheck()$ algorithm we set $S' := S'(w_1, W_1)$. The last step is to evaluate whether $S, s \models \varphi$ holds and we therefore answer with true.

8   Conclusion and Future Work

While in the MAS community model checking agent systems already has attracted some attention there has not been much work on abstraction techniques for reducing the state space. In this paper, we presented a technique to cope with the state explosion problem which opens the way to reduce the state space of a MAS so that model checking might get tractable. Clearly, there cannot be a generic automatizable abstraction technique: Model checking ATL for MIS is *EXPTIME*-complete, therefore in the worst case, there are instances where no abstraction technique at all is applicable.

Consequently we focused on handcrafted abstraction relations and proved that the presented model checking algorithm is sound, i.e., if the algorithm claims that a property holds then it really does. Of course, using abstraction always leads to losing completeness. However, abstraction still has its benefits because without reducing the state space many problems could not be model checked at all. Defining different abstraction relations for each quantifier allows to shrink the state space as needed for each subformula. Usually a MAS consists of more than two teams and the agents are more complex than in our example which increases our speedup factor significantly. In fact, we believe that most real problems carry with them a rich structure which allows the abstraction technique to be successfully applied, especially when using the possibility to use more than one abstraction for a single formula.

We decided to take MIS as the modelling framework and argued that for any framework the modularity is important not only because of the nature of MAS but also due to the ability of reducing the state space by replacing or removing agents that are not necessary when checking a certain property. We therefore introduced a modified version of a MIS and defined an abstraction over it.

The need to have a compact, modular and ground representation was motivated by the idea of an IT ecosystem, i.e., a system composed of a large number of distributed, decentralized, autonomous, interacting, cooperating, organically grown, heterogeneous, and continually evolving subsystems. An example for such a system is a smart city that contains agents for cars, traffic lights, cameras, etc. In such an IT ecosystem, new agents are introduced, other agents are removed and others again are modified. If we nevertheless want to ensure some safety, liveness or fairness properties we need a framework that on the one hand enables theoretical analysis and on the other hand supports modularity.

An IT ecosystem in general is the topic of a large research project consisting of 17 professors and 33 scientists in total collecting knowledge in different research areas: multi-agent systems, organic computing, ambient intelligence, software engineering and embedded systems. Together we try to solve the contradiction of having a continually evolving and highly heterogeneous system on the one side and still controlling this system by ensuring some properties on the other side.

We are currently implementing our abstraction technique in a first prototype and will use it for a concrete, non trivial demonstrator scenario [9]. The application will run on a smartphone and will send properties to be checked to a server that will then model check it. Users will get feedback if the formula holds or if it is unknown and can then decide whether they want to take part in the IT ecosystem. For this implementation it will, of course, be very useful to develop some heuristics and automatic refinement methods to generate abstractions.

For the future, we plan to put some effort in developing parallel model checking methods for this system and using a logic that facilitates the use of probabilities.

Acknowledgments. This work was funded by the NTH Focused Research School for IT Ecosystems. NTH (Niedersächsische Technische Hochschule) is a joint university consisting of Technische Universität Braunschweig, Technische Universität Clausthal, and Leibniz Universität Hannover.

References

1. Alur, R., Henzinger, T.A., Kupferman, O.: Alternating-time temporal logic. J. ACM 49(5), 672–713 (2002)
2. Ball, T., Rajamani, S.: Boolean programs: A model and process for software analysis. Tech. Rep. 2010-14 (2000)
3. Clarke, E.M., Grumberg, O., Jha, S., Lu, Y., Veith, H.: Counterexample-guided abstraction refinement for symbolic model checking. J. ACM 50(5), 752–794 (2003)
4. Clarke, E.M., Grumberg, O., Long, D.E.: Model checking and abstraction. ACM Trans. Program. Lang. Syst. 16(5), 1512–1542 (1994)
5. Clarke, E., Grumberg, O., Peled, D.: Model checking. Springer (1999)
6. Cohen, M., Dam, M., Lomuscio, A., Russo, F.: Abstraction in model checking multi-agent systems. In: AAMAS (2), pp. 945–952 (2009)
7. Das, S., Dill, D.: Successive approximation of abstract transition relations. In: Proceedings of 16th Annual IEEE Symposium on Logic in Computer Science 2001, pp. 51–58. IEEE (2002)
8. Dechesne, F., Orzan, S., Wang, Y.: Refinement of Kripke Models for Dynamics. In: Fitzgerald, J.S., Haxthausen, A.E., Yenigun, H. (eds.) ICTAC 2008. LNCS, vol. 5160, pp. 111–125. Springer, Heidelberg (2008), http://dx.doi.org/10.1007/978-3-540-85762-4_8
9. Deiters, C., Köster, M., Lange, S., Lützel, S., Mokbel, B., Mumme, C., Niebuhr, D. (eds.): DemSy - A Scenario for an Integrated Demonstrator in a SmartCity. Tech. Rep. 2010/01, NTH Focused Research School for IT Ecosystems, Clausthal University of Technology (May 2010), http://www.gbv.de/dms/clausthal/H_BIB/IfI/NTH_CompSciRep/2010-01.pdf
10. Emerson, E., Halpern, J.: "Sometimes" and "not never" revisited: On branching versus linear time temporal logic. In: Proceedings of the Annual ACM Symposium on Principles of Programming Languages, vol. 33(1), pp. 151–178 (1986)
11. Enea, C., Dima, C.: Abstractions of Multi-agent Systems. In: Burkhard, H.-D., Lindemann, G., Verbrugge, R., Varga, L.Z. (eds.) CEEMAS 2007. LNCS (LNAI), vol. 4696, pp. 11–21. Springer, Heidelberg (2007), http://dx.doi.org/10.1007/978-3-540-75254-7_2
12. Halpern, J.Y., Fagin, R.: Modelling knowledge and action in distributed systems. Distributed Computing 3, 159–177 (1989), http://dx.doi.org/10.1007/BF01784885
13. Halpern, J., Fagin, R., Moses, Y., Vardi, M.: Reasoning about knowledge. Handbook of Logic in Artificial Intelligence and Logic Programming 4 (1995)
14. Henzinger, T.A., Jhala, R., Majumdar, R.: Counterexample-Guided Control. In: Baeten, J.C.M., Lenstra, J.K., Parrow, J., Woeginger, G.J. (eds.) ICALP 2003. LNCS, vol. 2719, pp. 886–902. Springer, Heidelberg (2003)
15. Henzinger, T.A., Majumdar, R., Mang, F.Y.C., Raskin, J.-F.: Abstract Interpretation of Game Properties. In: SAS 2000. LNCS, vol. 1824, pp. 220–240. Springer, Heidelberg (2000), http://portal.acm.org/citation.cfm?id=647169.718154
16. Jamroga, W., Ågotnes, T.: Modular interpreted systems: A preliminary report. Tech. Rep. IfI-06-15, Clausthal University of Technology (2006)
17. Jamroga, W., Ågotnes, T.: Modular interpreted systems. In: Durfee, E.H., Yokoo, M., Huhns, M.N., Shehory, O. (eds.) Proceedings of AAMAS 2007, pp. 892–899. ACM Press (2007)
18. Kupferman, O., Vardi, M.Y.: An automata-theoretic approach to modular model checking. ACM Trans. Program. Lang. Syst. 22, 87–128 (2000), http://doi.acm.org/10.1145/345099.345104

19. Kurshan, R.: Computer-aided verification of coordinating processes: the automata-theoretic approach. Princeton Univ. Press (1994)
20. McMillan, K.L.: Applying SAT Methods in Unbounded Symbolic Model Checking. In: Brinksma, E., Larsen, K.G. (eds.) CAV 2002. LNCS, vol. 2404, pp. 250–264. Springer, Heidelberg (2002), http://dx.doi.org/10.1007/3-540-45657-0_19
21. McMillan, K.: Symbolic model checking: An Approach to the State Explosion Problem. Kluwer Academic Publishers Norwell, MA (1993)
22. Wooldridge, M.: Computationally grounded theories of agency. In: Proceedings of the Fourth International Conference on Multi-Agent Systems, ICMAS 2000 (2000), http://doi.ieeecomputersociety.org/10.1109/ICMAS.2000.858426

MAS: Qualitative and Quantitative Reasoning

Ammar Mohammed[1] and Ulrich Furbach[2]

[1] Department of Computer and Information Sciences, ISSR, Cairo University, Egypt
ammar@issr.cu.edu.eg
[2] Universität Koblenz-Landau, Artificial Intelligence Research Group, Koblenz
uli@uni-koblenz.de

Abstract. In a former work, we have presented/implemented a framework for modeling and verifying multi-agent systems, using hybrid automata. To specify properties of those systems, one needs a specification language that brings, at the same level of specification, both the qualitative and quantitative requirements. For this aim, there have been proposed several temporal logics with either event or state based approach. Both approaches have their pros and cons which should not be played off against each other. This paper contributes to present a variant of temporal logics which combines the expressiveness of both approaches. Using this proposed logic, we are able reason about many properties in a concise and intuitive manner. In particular, we concentrate on those types of properties that can be verified using reachability analysis. Hence these properties can be verified directly within our implemented framework.

1 Introduction

A great deal of research has made the concept of Multi-Agent Systems (MAS) more precise by means of logical systems, particularly modal logics [36], which has contributed to develop several programming and verification tools to reason about MAS. Temporal logic, LTL or CTL [33,10], is as a subclass of modal logics which is able to reason about the evolving of systems in time. An important advantage of the use of temporal logics is that they verify systems by means of model checking. The latter is one of the approaches that is recently used in automated planning [29,17]. Several work has integrated temporal logic on the top of certain modal logic to be able to reason about actions with temporal properties (cf. [23,8]).

Temporal logics basically allow us to express and reason about those qualitative properties of systems which focus on the temporal order of the occurrence of events. An example of these properties is to specify that a certain property of interest may eventually occur, or in other words the formula is reached in the model. Temporal logics, however, are insufficient to specify those quantitative temporal requirements which put timing deadlines on the behaviors of specified systems. For example, temporal logic can specify that the $action_1$ is always followed by $action_2$, but it can not reveal how long the period between the two action takes place. Because of their inability to specify such quantitative

L.A. Dennis, O. Boissier, and R.H. Bordini (Eds.): ProMAS 2011, LNCS 7217, pp. 114–132, 2012.

properties, temporal logics have to incorporate explicitly the notation of time. For this aim, there have been proposed several extensions to temporal logics that bind the notation of time to formulas (see [4,9] for a survey). The underlying models of these logics are represented as state transition graphs annotated with time constraints, using either *event* or *state* based approach. The former approach uses the discrete time model of the occurrence of events to reason about systems, while the latter approach uses continuous time model that records the state changes of systems at each point of time. Each approach has advantages over the other. The main advantage of event based approach together with its underlying discrete time model, is its simplicity to express quantitative properties by abstracting lots of details within a model of a system. Intuitively most of the quantitative requirements often occur at the discrete changes of the behavior of systems and hence these requirements can reason about agents carrying out actions in time. This approach, however, can not reason about quantitative properties, which may occur within a particular time interval. For example, it might be desirable to reason about the satisfaction of a certain property of interest within an interval of time, say $10 \leq t \leq 20$. This can not be expressed with events unless the time interval coincides with events on the boundaries of the interval. This limitation can be coped with using the expressive power of state based approach. The latter approach, however, can not directly reason about events, which are used to reason about actions of MAS. Converting from the state based to the event based representation often leads to a significant enlargement of the state space. To specify and hence verify a property based on the occurrence of events, it should be converted into an appropriate state base representation before it is checked by state based quantitative temporal logics tools [37,11]. For example, to specify and verify that it is always the case that $event_1$ is followed by $event_2$ within t time unit— this property is called a bounded response property— a traditional solution to verify this within a model M of a multi-agent system is to translate this specification to a testing transition model A, and then check whether the parallel model of A and M can reach a designated state of A.

Usually any quantitative temporal logic needs an interpretation models of the form labeled timed graph or even more general structure like timed automata [2]. A general model of timed automata is hybrid automata [19] in which one can reason not only about time requirements, but also about quantitative behaviors of systems raised from evolution of continuous actions.

The main contribution of this paper is to propose a novel variant of CTL called Region Computation Tree Logic(RCTL) that extends CTL by incorporating time on states and events in order to reason about both qualitative and quantitative requirements of systems particularly MAS. RCTL encompasses, in the same framework, the expressive power of event and state based approach. The formulas of RCTL are interpreted on tree of regions generated from the transition system of hybrid automata presented in a former work [28]. For the purpose of model checking, we concentrate on those quantitative properties that can be verified using reachability analysis. Hence, we will be able to use a former

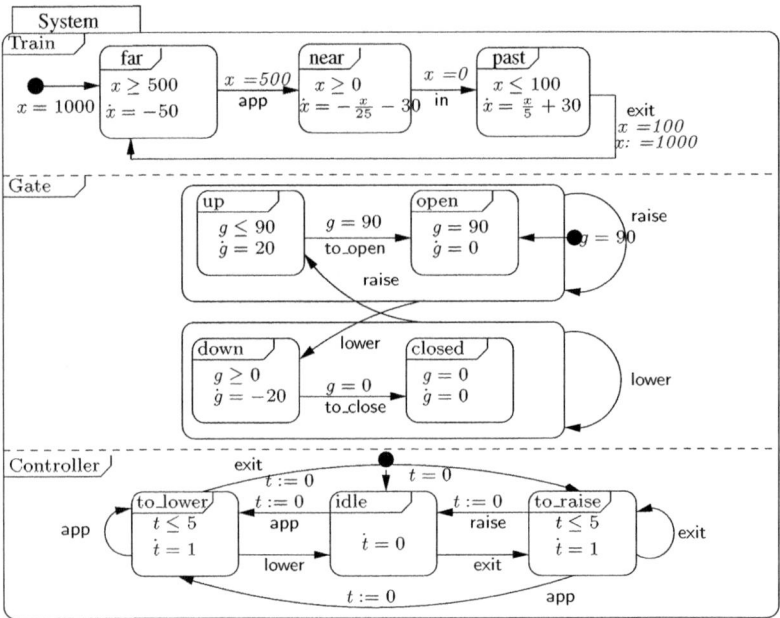

Fig. 1. Specification of the train gate controller as hybrid automata

constraint logic programming approach presented in [28]. In this approach, a model of MAS described as hybrid automata is converted to an equivalent model of constraint logic program. Then requirements are converted to suitable queries that are checked within the constraint logic program.

The rest of this paper is organized as follows. Sec. 2 introduces hybrid automata, which constitute the interpretation model of RCTL. Then syntax and semantics of RCTL are discussed in Sec. 3. Specifications of properties that can be verified by means of reachability analysis are discussed in Sec. 4, before we end up with the conclusion and related work in Sec. 5.

2   Hybrid Automata: Preliminaries

In this section, we briefly review our labeled hybrid automata [28][1], in which we admit the existence of events on transitions, but first we will introduce an illustrative running example that we we use throughout this paper (see [28] for details about the example).

A train gate controller is a reactive multi-agent system consisting of three agent components: the train, the gate, and the controller. In this system, a road is crossing a train track, which is guarded by a gate, which must be lowered to stop the traffic when the train approaches, and raised after a train passed the

---

[1] A MAS scenario from Robobcup has been applied in [35,16].

road. The gate is supervised by a controller that has the task to receive signals from the train and to issue lower or raise signals to the gate. Initially, a train is at a distance of 1000 meters away from the gate and moves at a speed 50 meter per second. At 500 meters, a sensor on the tracks detects the train, sending a signal *app* to the controller. The train slows down, obeying the differential equation $\dot{x} = -\frac{x}{25} - 30$. After a delay of five seconds, which is modeled by the variable t, the controller sends the signal *lower* to the gate, which begins to descend from 90 degrees to 0 degrees at a rate of -20 degrees per second. After crossing the gate, the train accelerates according to the differential equation $\dot{x} = \frac{x}{5} + 30$. A second sensor placed 100 meters past the crossing detects the leaving train, sending a signal *exit* to the controller. After five seconds, the controller raises the gate.

The specification of the previous multi-agent system is graphically illustrated as concurrent hybrid automata in Fig. 1. The variable x represents the distance of the train from the gate. The variable t represents the delay time of the controller, while the position of the gate in radius degrees is represented by the variable g.

2.1   Syntax

Before we proceed in defining the syntax and semantics of our hybrid automata, we first need to define those constraints which may appear as guards on transitions and invariants inside locations of hybrid automata. Additionally need to define those types of constraints which define the possible dynamics in our model.

Definition 1 (Linear Constraints). *Let $\mathbb{X}$ be set of n real variables and $\omega = \sum_{i=1}^{n} a_i \cdot x_i$, with $x_i \in \mathbb{X}$, be a linear combination of variables from $\mathbb{X}$, where $1 \leq i \leq n, a_i \in \mathbb{R}$. A set $\Phi(\mathbb{X})$ of linear constraints over $\mathbb{X}$, with a typical elements φ, is defined by the following syntax:*

$$\varphi ::= \omega \sim b \mid \varphi_1 \wedge \varphi_2 \mid true$$

where $b \in \mathbb{R}$, $\sim \in \{<, \leq, =, >, \geq\}$, and $\varphi_1, \varphi_2 \in \Phi(\mathbb{X})$.

The continuous behaviors of MAS show how physical quantities, e.g. position, temperature and humidity, evolve with respect to time. Those behaviors are usually described by differential equations whose solutions can be described as continuous functions in time. In the following, we define the basic constraints that constitute the continuous dynamics of the variables.

Definition 2 (Dynamical Constraints). *Let $\mathbb{X}$ be a set of n real variables, with a typical element $x \in \mathbb{X}$, and $\dot{\mathbb{X}}$ be set of first derivatives of the variables of $\mathbb{X}$ with a typical element $\dot{x} \in \dot{\mathbb{X}}$. A set $\mathbb{D}(\mathbb{X} \cup \dot{\mathbb{X}})$ of dynamical constraints over $\mathbb{X} \cup \dot{\mathbb{X}}$ with typical element d, is defined inductively by the following syntax:*

$$d ::= \dot{x} \sim c \mid \dot{x} + a \cdot x = c \mid d_1 \wedge d_2 \mid true$$

where $a \neq 0, c \in \mathbb{R}$, $\sim \in \{=, \leq, \geq\}$, $d_1, d_2 \in \mathbb{D}(\mathbb{X} \cup \dot{\mathbb{X}})$.

Having defined the linear and dynamical constraints, we are ready to introduce a hybrid automaton[2].

Definition 3 (Basic Components). *A hybrid automaton is a tuple* $H = (Q, \mathbb{X}, Inv, Flow, E, Jump, Reset, Event, Event_H, q_0, v_0)$ *where:*

- Q *is a finite set of control locations.*
- $\mathbb{X}$ *is an ordered set of n real variables.*
- $Inv : Q \rightarrow \Phi(\mathbb{X})$ *is a function that assigns a linear constraint $Inv(q)$ to each location $q \in Q$.*
- $Flow : Q \rightarrow \mathbb{D}(\mathbb{X} \cup \dot{\mathbb{X}})$ *is a function that assigns a dynamical constraints $Flow(q)$ to each control location $q \in Q$.*
- $E \subseteq Q \times Q$ *is a finite set of transitions among control locations, Conventionally, we write $e = (q_1, q_2)$ for each $e \in E$, where q_1 and $q_2 \in Q$.*
- $Jump : E \rightarrow \Phi(\mathbb{X})$ *is a function that assigns to each transition $e \in E$ a constraints $Jump(e)$, which must hold to fire e.*
- $Reset : E \times \mathbb{X} \rightarrow \mathbb{R}$ *is a mapping, which assigns a real value to each variable on each transition $e \in E$. A reset of a variable $x \in \mathbb{X}$ on a transition $e \in E$ is denoted as $x' = Reset(e, x)$. Conveniently, we write $Reset(e, \mathbb{X})$ to denote the reset of all variables.*
- $Event_H$ *is a finite set of events.*
- $Event : E \rightarrow Event_H$ *is a function that assigns an event $Event(e) \in Event_H$ to each transition $e \in E$. Conventionally, we write this as* $\sigma_1 \xrightarrow[t_1]{Event(e)} \sigma_2$.
- $q_0 \in Q$ *defines the initial location of the automaton.*
- v_0 *defines the initial values of the variables $\mathbb{X}$.*

An example of a hybrid automaton is *train* automaton described in Fig. 1. The *train* has *far*, *near*, and *past* as its control location. The invariant at location *far* is described as $x \geq 500$. The flow of location *far* is given as $\dot{x} = -50$. The jump condition between location *far* and *near* is given as $x = 500$. The variable x is reset to the value 1000 when the control jump from location *past* to *near*. *app* is the event that fires when the control goes from location *far* to *near*.

2.2   Semantics

A hybrid automaton can exactly be in one of its control locations at each stage of its computation. But knowing the present control location is not enough to determine which of the outgoing transitions can be taken next, at all. A snapshot of the current state of the computation should also keep in mind the present valuation of the continuous variables. To begin formalizing the semantics of a hybrid automaton, we need to define the concept of a *state* and to show how control evolves from one state to another. But first we need to define how continuous variables evolve.

---

[2] Each automaton represents an agent.

Definition 4 (Evaluation of Linear Constraints). *Let $\varphi \in \phi(\mathbb{X})$ be a constraints and $v \in \mathbb{R}^n$ be the valuation of the variables $\mathbb{X}$, then we write*

$$v \models \varphi,$$

if v satisfies the constraint φ, which is defined inductively as

$$\varphi = true.$$
$$\varphi = \sum_{i=1}^{n} a_i \cdot x_i \sim c \quad \text{iff} \quad \sum_{i=1}^{n} a_i \cdot v_i \sim c \; holds.$$
$$\varphi_1 \wedge \varphi_2 \quad\quad\quad\; \text{iff} \quad v \models \varphi_1 \; and \; v \models \varphi_2.$$

where v_i is the valuation of the ith components of v

Definition 5 (Evaluation of Dynamical Constraints). *Let $d \in \mathbb{D}(\mathbb{X} \cup \dot{\mathbb{X}})$ be a dynamical constriants and $f : \mathbb{R}^{\geq 0} \to \mathbb{R}^n$ be a differentiable function, then we write*

$$f \models_* d$$

if f satisfies the dynamical constraint d, which is defined inductively as

$$d = true.$$
$$d = \dot{x} \sim c \quad\quad\quad\quad \text{iff} \quad f'(t) \sim c \; holds.$$
$$d = \dot{x} + a \cdot x \sim c \quad \text{iff} \quad f'(t) + a \cdot f(t) \sim c \; holds.$$
$$d = d_1 \wedge d_2 \quad\quad\quad \text{iff} \quad f \models_* d_1 \; and \; f \models_* d_2.$$

where $f'(t)$ is the differentiation of the function f for $t \in \mathbb{R}^{\geq 0}$.

Definition 6 (State). *At any instant of time $t \in \mathbb{R}^{\geq 0}$, a state of a hybrid automaton is given by $\sigma_i = \langle q_i, v, t \rangle$, where $q_i \in Q$ is a control location, v is the valuation of the real variables. A state $\sigma_i = \langle q_i, v, t \rangle$ is admissible iff $v \models Inv(q_i)$.*

The semantics of a hybrid automaton is defined in terms of a labeled transition system between states. Transitions between states are generally categorized into two kinds of transitions: continuous transitions, capturing the continuous evolution of states, and discrete transitions, capturing the changes of location. We will define the semantics of hybrid automaton more formally.

Definition 7 (Operational Semantics). *A transition rule between two admissible states $\sigma_1 = \langle q_1, v_1, t_1 \rangle$ and $\sigma_2 = \langle q_2, v_2, t_2 \rangle$ is*

Discrete transition *iff $e = (q_1, q_2) \in E$, $t_1 = t_2$ and $v_1 \models Jump(e)$, and $v_2 \models Inv(q_2)$, such that v_2 is the valuations coming from $Reset(e, \mathbb{X})$. In this case the event $Event(e)$ occurs. Conventionally, we write this as $\sigma_1 \xrightarrow[t_1]{Event(e)} \sigma_2$.*

Continuous(Delay) transition *iff $q_1 = q_2$, $(t_2 - t_1) > 0$ is the duration of time passed at location q_1, there exists a differentiable function f with $f \models_* Flow(q_1)$ and $f(t_1) = v_1$ and $f(t_2) = v_2$, and for all $t \in [t_1, t_2]$, $f(t) \models Inv(q_1)$.*

An execution of a hybrid automaton corresponds to a sequence of transitions from one state to another. For this purpose, we define the valid run as follows:

Definition 8 (Run: micro level). *A path $\rho = \sigma_1\sigma_2\sigma_3, \ldots$, of a hybrid automaton H is a finite or infinite sequence of admissible states, where the transition from a state σ_i to a state σ_{i+1}, for all $i \geq 1$, is related either by a discrete or continuous transition. A set of all possible paths of A is denoted as $\Pi(H)$. A run of H is a path ρ starting with the initial state σ_0.*

It should be noted that the continuous change of states in a path ρ generates an infinite number of reachable states. Therefore, state-space exploration techniques require a symbolic representation way for representing these infinite states appropriately. One way to do so is to use mathematical intervals. We call this symbolic mathematical interval *region*, which is defined as follows:

Definition 9 (Region). *Given a path $\rho \in \Pi(H)$, a sub-sequence of admissible states $\Gamma = (\sigma_{i+1} \cdots \sigma_{i+m}) \subseteq \rho$ is called a region, if for all states σ_{i+j} with $1 \leq j \leq m$, it holds $q_{i+j} = q$ and for the states σ_i and σ_{i+m+1} with respective locations q_i and q_{i+m+1}, then it must hold $q_i \neq q$ and $q_{i+m+1} \neq q$. Conventionally, a region Γ is written as $\Gamma = \langle q, V, T \rangle$, where $t_{i+1} \leq T \leq t_{i+m}$ is the interval of continuous time, and V is the tuple of intervals valuations of the variables during the time interval T.*

A run of a hybrid automaton can be re-phrased in terms of reached regions, where the change from one region to another is fired by using a discrete step.

Definition 10 (Run: macro level). *A run of hybrid automaton H is $\rho_H = \Gamma_0, a_1, \Gamma_1, a_2, \ldots$, a sequence of (possibly infinite) regions, where a transition from a region Γ_i to a region Γ_{i+1}, written as $\Gamma_i \xrightarrow[t_{i+1}]{a_{i+1}} \Gamma_{i+1}$, is enabled, if there is $\sigma_i \xrightarrow[t_{i+1}]{a_{i+1}} \sigma_{i+1}$, where $\sigma_i \in \Gamma_i$, $\sigma_{i+1} \in \Gamma_{i+1}$ and $a_{i+1} \in Event$ is the generated event before the control goes to the region Γ_{i+1}. Γ_0 is the initial region obtained from a start state σ_0 by means of continuous transitions.*

The operational semantics are the basis for verification of a hybrid automaton. In particular, model checking of a hybrid automaton is defined as the reachability analysis of its underlying transition system. The most useful question to ask about hybrid automata is the reachability of a given state. We define the reachability of a region and state as follows.

Definition 11 (Reachability). *A region Γ_i is called reachable in a run ρ_H, if $\Gamma_i \in \rho_H$. Consequently, a state σ_j is called reachable, if there is a reached region Γ_i such that $\sigma_j \in \Gamma_i$*

2.3   Parallel Composition

The parallel composition of hybrid automata can be used to specify larger systems (MAS), where a hybrid automaton is given for each part of the system and communication between the different parts may occur via shared variables and synchronization labels. The transitions from the different automata are interleaved, unless they share the same synchronization label. In this case, they are synchronized on transitions. As a result of the parallel composition, a new automaton called composed automaton is created which captures the behavior of the entire system. The composed automaton is, in turn, given to a model checker that checks the reachability of a certain state. In [28], we showed how to construct the composition *on-the-fly*— i.e., during the verification phase—, in which the composition of hybrid automata H_1 and H_2 can be defined in terms of synchronized or interleaved regions of the regions produced from run of both H_1 and H_2. As a result of the composition procedure, compound regions are constructed, which consist of a conjunction of a region $\Gamma_1 = \langle q_1, V_1, T \rangle$ from H_1 and another region $\Gamma_2 = \langle q_2, V_2, T \rangle$ from H_2. Therefore, each compound region takes the form $\Lambda = \langle (q_1, V_1), (q_2, V_2), T \rangle$ (shortly written as $\Lambda = \langle \Gamma_1, \Gamma_2, T \rangle$), which represents the reached region at both control locations q_1 and q_2 the during a time interval T.

Definition 12 (Composed Run). *A run of composed automata is the sequence* $\sum_{H_1 \circ H_2} = \Lambda_0, a_1, \Lambda_1, a_2, ...$ *of compound regions, where a transition between compound regions* $\Lambda_1 = \langle \Gamma_1, \gamma_1, T_1 \rangle$ *and* $\Lambda_2 = \langle \Gamma_2, \gamma_2, T_2 \rangle$ *(written as* $\Lambda_1 \xrightarrow{a}_t \Lambda_2$*) is enabled, if one of the following holds:*

- $a \in Event_{H_1} \cap Event_{H_2}$ *is a joint event,* $\Gamma_1 \xrightarrow{a}_t \Gamma_2$*, and* $\gamma_1 \xrightarrow{a}_t \gamma_2$*. In this case , we say that the region* Γ_1 *is synchronized with the region* γ_1*.*
- $a \in Event_{H_1} \setminus Event_{H_2}$ *(respectively* $a \in Event_{H_2} \setminus Event_{H_1}$ *),* $\Gamma_1 \xrightarrow{a}_t \Gamma_2$ *and* $\gamma_1 \to \gamma_2$*, such that both* γ_1 *and* γ_2 *have the same control location—i.e. they relate to each other using a continuous transition.*

To illustrate the previous procedure, consider the hybird automata in Fig. 1. There is a synchronized region between the region obtained from location *far* and from location *idle* in the automata train and controller respectively. Both regions are synchronized using the joint event *app*. Therefore, the synchronized region can be described as $\langle (far, X), (idle, T_1), T \rangle \xrightarrow{app}_t \langle (near, X), (to\_lower, T_1), TT \rangle$ where X and T_1 are the continuous valuations of the variable of the automata train and controller respectively. On the other hand, the region obtained from location *far* and from location *open*, in the automata train and gate respectively, relates to each other using disjoint event *app*. Therefore the obtained region can be described as $\langle (far, X), (open, G), T \rangle \xrightarrow{app}_t \langle (near, X), (open, G), TT \rangle$.

3   Region Computation Tree Logic (RCTL)

This section primarily focuses on the definition of the region computation tree logic (RCTL), which extends the qualitative temporal logic of CTL with time on states, events, and constraints of variables. RCTL combines, in the same level of specifications, qualitative together with quantitative requirements. The formulas of RCTL are interpreted over the possible regions obtained from the run of hybrid automata. As described previously, a region can be seen as a sequence of states separated by transition points. Each transition point marks the instantaneous exit from region Γ_{i-1} and the entrance into region Γ_i, and corresponds to the occurrence of a particular event. Therefore, we see regions constituting the essence of RCTL, such that RCTL can be viewed as a state based quantitative temporal logics in a sense that regions capture the changes of states, and as event based quantitative temporal logics in a sense that events mark the instantaneous exist from region to another. Thus, RCTL brings together, in the same framework, the advantages of both approaches. In the following we show the syntax and semantics of RCTL, but first we define timed variables and its valuation function.

Definition 13 (Timed-variables). *Let* $\mathbb{T}$ *be a set of non-negative real variables called* timed-variables, *and* $\Phi(\mathbb{T})$ *be a set of linear constraints over* $\mathbb{T}$. *The valuation* ξ *of the timed-variables* $\mathbb{T}$ *is a function* $\xi : \mathbb{T} \to \mathbb{R}^{\geq 0}$. *Given* $\pi \in \Phi(\mathbb{T})$, *we write* $\xi \models \pi$, *if* ξ *satisfies the constraint* π.

3.1   Syntax of RCTL

Let $\mathbb{X}$ be a set of real variables, $\mathbb{T}$ be a set of non-negative real variables disjoint from $\mathbb{X}$, $\Phi(\mathbb{X})$ and $\Phi(\mathbb{T})$ be two sets of linear constraints with free variables from $\mathbb{X}$ and $\mathbb{T}$ respectively, L be a set of atomic propositions denoting the locations, and *Event* be a set of atomic propositions denoting events disjoint from L.

Definition 14 (Formulas of RCTL). *The formula* Ψ *of RCTL are inductively defined as*

$$\Psi ::= p \mid a \mid \phi \mid y.\Psi \mid \pi \mid \neg\Psi \mid \Psi_1 \wedge \Psi_2 \mid \exists(\Psi_1 U \Psi_2) \mid \forall(\Psi_1 U \Psi_2)$$

for $y \in \mathbb{T}$, $p \in L$, $a \in Event$, $\phi \in \Phi(\mathbb{X})$, $\pi \in \Phi(\mathbb{T})$, *and* Ψ_1, Ψ_2 *are RCTL formulas.*

Before giving the semantics of RCTL, we introduce some common notations. $\exists\Diamond\Psi$ is equivalent to $\exists(true\ U\Psi)$, $\forall\Diamond\Psi$ is eqivalent to $\forall(true\ U\Psi)$, $\exists\Diamond\Psi$ is equivalent to $\exists(true\ U\Psi)$, and $\forall\Diamond\Psi$ is equivalent to $\forall(true\ U\Psi)$

3.2   Semantics of RCTL

We will interpret the formulas of RCTL over the set of all possible regions generated from possible runs of hybrid automata. Let a region Γ take the form $\Gamma = (q, V, T)$, with $\delta(\Gamma) = q$ is its location, and V and T are the interval of valuations and time respectively, in which the region is admissible. If there is a transition from a region Γ_1 to a region Γ_2, then an event a occurs at some timing point t, written as $\Gamma_1 \xrightarrow{a}_{t} \Gamma_2$. A sub-region $\beta \subseteq \Gamma$, with $\beta \neq \emptyset$ means that $\beta = (q, V', T')$ with $T' \subseteq T$ and $V' \subseteq V$. A state $\sigma \in \Gamma$ means that $\sigma = (q, v, t)$, with $v \in V$ and $t \in T$. σ satisfies a constraint $\phi \in \Phi(\mathbb{X})$, written as $\sigma \models \varphi$, iff $v \models \varphi$. In the following, we show the semantics of RCTL formulas on the set of all possible runs Π_H.

Definition 15 (Semantics). *Let Ψ is a RCTL formula, H be a hybrid automaton, Π_H be the possible runs of H with a region $\Gamma = (q, V, T) \in \Pi_H$, and ξ is a valuation function of timed-variables. The satisfaction relation $\langle \Pi_H, \Gamma \rangle \overset{T}{\underset{\xi}{\vDash}} \Psi$, which means that Ψ is satisfied in the region Γ within the time interval (duration) T for some valuation function ξ, is defined inductively as follows:*

- $\langle \Pi_H, \Gamma \rangle \overset{T}{\underset{\xi}{\vDash}} p$ iff $p = \delta(\Gamma)$.

- $\langle \Pi_H, \Gamma \rangle \overset{T}{\underset{\xi}{\vDash}} a$ iff   *there is Γ' and $t' \in T$ with $\Gamma \xrightarrow[t']{a} \Gamma'$.*

- $\langle \Pi_H, \Gamma \rangle \overset{T}{\underset{\xi}{\vDash}} \phi$ iff   *there is $\beta \subseteq \Gamma$, for each $\sigma_k \in \beta, \sigma_k \vDash \phi$.*

- $\langle \Pi_H, \Gamma \rangle \overset{T}{\underset{\xi}{\vDash}} y.\Psi$ iff   *there is $t \in T$ such that $\xi(y) = t$ and $\langle \Pi_H, \Gamma \rangle \overset{T:=t}{\underset{\xi}{\vDash}} \Psi$.*

- $\langle \Pi_H, \Gamma \rangle \overset{T}{\underset{\xi}{\vDash}} \pi$ iff $\xi \vDash \pi$.

- $\langle \Pi_H, \Gamma \rangle \overset{T}{\underset{\xi}{\vDash}} \neg\Psi$ iff $\langle \Pi_H, \Gamma \rangle \overset{T}{\underset{\xi}{\nvDash}} \Psi$.

- $\langle \Pi_H, \Gamma \rangle \overset{T}{\underset{\xi}{\vDash}} \Psi_1 \wedge \Psi_2$ iff $\langle \Pi_H, \Gamma \rangle \overset{T}{\underset{\xi}{\vDash}} \Psi_1$ and $(\Pi_H, \Gamma) \overset{T}{\underset{\xi}{\vDash}} \Psi_2$.

- $\langle \Pi_H, \Gamma \rangle \overset{T}{\underset{\xi}{\vDash}} \exists(\Psi_1 U \Psi_2)$ iff *there is a run $\Pi \in \Pi_H, \Pi = \Gamma_0, \Gamma_1, \cdots,$ with $\Gamma = \Gamma_0$,*

for some $j \geq 0$, $\langle \Pi_H, \Gamma_j \rangle \overset{T_j}{\underset{\xi}{\vDash}} \Psi_2$, and $\langle \Pi_H, \Gamma_k \rangle \overset{T_k}{\underset{\xi}{\vDash}} \Psi_1$ for $0 \leq k < j$.

- $\langle \Pi_H, \Gamma \rangle \overset{T}{\underset{\xi}{\vDash}} \forall(\Psi_1 U \Psi_2)$ iff *for every run $\Pi \in \Pi_H, \Pi = \Gamma_0, \Gamma_1, \cdots,$ with $\Gamma = \Gamma_0$,*

for some $j \geq 0$, $\langle \Pi_H, \Gamma_j \rangle \overset{T_j}{\underset{\xi}{\vDash}} \Psi_2$, and $\langle \Pi_H, \Gamma_k \rangle \overset{T_k}{\underset{\xi}{\vDash}} \Psi_1$ for $0 \leq k < j$.

The quantifiers $\forall$, and $\exists$, in the previous semantics, are called paths quantifiers. The variable y in the formula $y.\Psi$ holds the time at which Ψ is satisfied. $y := t$ means that the variable y is set to the value t. $\langle \Pi_H, \Gamma \rangle \overset{T:=t}{\underset{\xi}{\vDash}} \Psi$ means that the formula Ψ is satisfied in the region Γ when the time T is restricted to the time point t. In case Ψ represents an atomic proposition from the set *Events*, then $y.\Psi$ binds the time at which the event has occurred. This can be used to specify various quantitative properties, such as time bound response properties as we will see in what follows. However, if Ψ represents a constraint formula, then $y.\Psi$ evaluates the time interval at which the constraint Ψ is satisfied. This allows to specify quantitative properties, which could not be specified using events.

Definition 16 (Satisfiability). *Let H be hybrid automaton with initial state init and Π_H as its possible runs. We say that H satisfies the RCTL formula Ψ from init, written as $(H, init) \vDash \Psi$, iff $(\Pi_H, \Gamma_0) \vDash \Psi$, where Γ_0 is the initial region of Π_H.*

4   Model Checking as Reachability

In the context of hybrid automata, the term model checking usually refers to reachability analysis. This is done by computing first the reachable states of the model under consideration and then searching for states that satisfy or contradict a given property. Like the classical way to compute the reachability of states, our work performs a state-space exploration of a model starting from initial states and spreading the reachability information along control locations and transitions until fixed regions can be reached. This method is in general undecidable. However, we have implemented a simple-decision algorithm, which computes the reached regions of a given hybrid automaton [7].

For the purpose of verification by means of model checking, we need to describe the properties. Generally, the qualitative properties are often classified into reachability, safety and liveness properties. However, when the time becomes a critical factor to react in the environment, then the concept of safety and liveness properties should be refined. In what follows these types of properties will be reviewed with their specifications by means of RCTL. For the purpose of model checking, these properties will be encoded into suitable queries in Constraint logic program (CLP), which follow the outline of CLP model presented in [28]. However, in order to put model checking within our framework, we will concentrate only the reachability requirements. Indeed, many properties of interest can be specified as a form of reachability, as we will see in the sequel.

4.1   Reachability Requirements

The reachability of a property Ψ means that there is a possibility to reach a state where Ψ holds. In other words, the reachability of the property Ψ asserts that starting from an initial state, is there a region along a run in which Ψ is satisfiable. This can be specified in RCTL as follows $init \rightarrow \exists \Diamond \Psi$, where $init$ is the predicate characterizing the set of initial states and is defined as conjunctions of atomic propositions from L and constraints from $\Phi(\mathbb{X})$. It is worth mentioning that checking reachability for hybrid automata is generally undecidable. However, under various constraints of hybrid automata the reachability is decidable. In particular, the decidability result has been proven for for certain classes of hybrid automata including timed and initialized rectangular automata [21].

In terms of the CLP, the reachability of a certain region that satisfies the formula Ψ is done by performing forward reachability analysis from the system's initial state, and then checking whether the conjunction of Ψ with the possible reached regions is satisfied. Assuming for example $init$ has been assigned to the set of initial states, the following is the CLP query to check the safety requirements (see [28] for a concrete example).

```
?- reachable(init,Reached),
      member(Ψ₁,Reached),φ.
```

In the previous query, the formula Ψ is rewritten as a conjunction of two formulas Ψ_1 and ϕ, where $\phi \in (\Phi(\mathbb{X}) \cup \Phi(\mathbb{T}))$ is an atomic the constraint appearing in the formula Ψ. Indeed, any RCTL formula can be rewritten as $\Psi = \Psi_1 \wedge \phi$, if necessary ϕ can be set to true making that conjuct trivial.

To demonstrate the reachability of a formula in a concrete example, let us return to the train gate controller example described Fig. 1. Supposing one wants to check the possibility of reaching a region whose state satisfies that the *train* is at *near* within distance less than 10 *meters* and the *gate* is *closed*. First the initial state of the systems is given by:

$$init : train.far \wedge gate.open \wedge controller.idel \wedge x = 1000 \wedge g = 0 \wedge z = 0.$$

The intended formula is specified as

$$init \rightarrow \neg \exists \Diamond (x \leq 10 \wedge train.near \wedge gate.closed)$$

As shown, the set of atomic propositions L describes the possible locations of hybrid automata. Since locations of different automata may have the same names, we should identify them somehow. To do this, we will refer to each atomic proposition with the form $A.q$ meaning that the automaton A is at location q, as it has been shown in the previous specification.

CLP of the previous formula can be verified by asking the following query:

```
?-reachable((far,[1000]),(open,[0]),(idle,[0]),Reached),
      member((near,close,_,Time,_,X,),Reached), X $=< 10.
```

The successful answer to this query indicates reachability of the specified formula.

A safety property states that *something bad must never happen*. The bad thing represents a critical property that should never occur. Let Ψ represent this critical property, then the safety property is specified as $init :\rightarrow \forall \Box \neg \Psi$. A safety property can be reduced to a reachability property, which can be specified as $init :\rightarrow \neg \exists \Diamond \Psi$. The previous specification asserts that after executing the initial state $init$, the requirement characterized by Ψ will not be reached.

$$init :\rightarrow \neg \exists \Diamond \Psi.$$

It is often that in certain cases we may be interested in the reachability of a certain property either before or after a time deadline has expired called *Time bounded reachability*. For example, the possibility of a formula Ψ to be reached within the bounded time α is specified in RCTL as $init \rightarrow \exists \Diamond (t.\Psi \wedge t \leq \alpha)$. Demonstrating this by the previous example with $\alpha = 19$, We are going to check the reachability of the previous example within 19 sece.

```
?-reachable((far,[1000]),(open,[0]),(idle,[0]),Reached),
    member((near,close,_,Time,_,X,),Reached),
    X $=< 10, Time $=<19.
```

4.2 Quantitative Requirements

As it is known that a safety property asserts what may or may not occur, but do not require that anything ever does happen. In the train gate example described in [28], closing the gate permanently can maintain the safety of the system, but it is unacceptable for the waiting cars or pedestrians in front of the gate. For this reason, the liveness property is needed to specify such requirements, which asserts that some property of interest will always occur. It should be noted that these type of properties can not be falsified in bounded time. Since the occurrence of some state does not say how long it will take for this state to occur, we can not sure that the liveness property is violated. For this reason, these types of properties are not strong enough in the context of quantitative time properties. Here one would like to see a time bound when the good state occurs. This leads to the next kind of properties.

Bounded Response Properties. A bounded response property is one of the most important classes of quantitative requirements used to specify many important applications. It asserts that something will happen within a certain limit of time. A typical application of bounded response property is the specification of worst case performance; that is the specification of an upper bound α on the termination of a system S: if started at time t, then S is guaranteed to reach a final state no later than $\alpha + t$ unit time. For example, specifying that every request will be acknowledged within 3 seconds in communication protocols.

A bounded response property between two events $event_1$ and $event_2$ is specified in RCTL as the formula $init \rightarrow \forall\Box(t_1.event_1 \rightarrow \forall\Diamond(t_2.event_2 \wedge t_2 \leq \alpha+t_1))$. This formula states that whenever there is a request $event_1$ occurs at time t_1, then it is followed by a response $event_2$, at time t_2, such that t_2 is at most $\alpha+t_1$. It should be mentioned that this property can be falsified within time bound. Therefore this property can be specified as a kind of safety requirement represented as reachability. For this reason, proving the previous property means proving that it is not possible to reach a state where $event_2$ is not reached from $event_1$ within $t_2 \leq \alpha + t_1$. In other words, starting from $event_1$, finding a reachable state satisfies $event_2$, within α time bound, is sufficient to check the reachability of the property. In terms of the CLP, the previous property can be encoded into the following steps: First, we get all possible reachable states from $event_1$ within $t_1 + \alpha$ as L. Second, we check that reachability of $event_2$ has not been occurred. A positive answer of the reachability indicates a negative answer to the original problem, and vice versa. The following is a CLP query encoding the previous specification:

```
?- reachable(Ψ₀,Reached),
   reached_from(L,event₁,Reached),
   reached_within(Target, α,L),
   \+ member((_,..,_,event₂),Target)
```

We should say that the traditional way to verify this kind of properties using any quantitative time model- checkers—like UPPAAL [11] and Hytech [22]–is to translate that property to what is called a testing automata A, and then check whether the parallel composition of the underlying model together with A can reach a designated violation state. As we said earlier, the reason behind this translation is that there is no direct use of events in the model. The use of events is limited to construct only the parallel composition of automata. In contrast to our adopted approach, the direct use of events with the model allows us to avoid this translation process.

Specifying quantitative properties by means of time of events are not satisfactory in some cases. Suppose for example that one needs to specify that a part of a certain region can be reached in a particular time bound interval. To do so, we present the bounded invariance properties.

Bounded Invariance Properties. Like the bounded response property, bounded invariance property is one of the most important classes of quantitative timing requirements. It asserts that once an event has been triggered, a certain condition will continuously hold for a certain amount of time. It is often used to specify that something will not happen for a certain period of time. In RCTL this can be specified formally as $init \rightarrow \forall\Box(t_1.event \rightarrow \forall\Box(t_2.\Psi \wedge t_2 \leq \alpha + t_1))$, where α is the duration at which the formula Ψ must be continuously held. For instance, whenever the train approaches the gate, the distance of the train is always larger than 100 meters for the duration of 20 time units. The property $\Psi = X > 100$ in this case represents the distance of the train, and *app* is the triggered event.

Generally, the bounded invariance property can be checked as a safety property. Starting from the time t_1 of the occurence of event , finding a non-reachable violating state for the formula Ψ, within α time bound is sufficient to check the reachability of the property. This can be encoded into CLP as the following

```
?- reachable(Ψ₀,Reached),
   reached_from(L,event,Reached),
   reached_within(Target, α,L),
   member((_,..,X,_,Target), X$≤100.
```

A satisfactory solution to the previous query violates the original property.

The way used to specify the bounded invariance properties can be used to specify what is the so-called *minimal event separation* [20] too, i.e no $event_2$ can occur earlier than α time units after an occurrence of $event_1$. This property can be specified as

$$init \rightarrow \forall\Box(t_1.event_1 \rightarrow \forall\Box(t_2 < t_1 + \alpha \rightarrow \neg t_2.event_2)).$$

5 Conclusion and Related Work

This paper introduced the quantitative temporal logic RCTL that extends the well known temporal logic CTL in order to reason about those qualitative and quantitative properties of MAS that occurs as a result of performing continuous actions over time. We used hybrid automata as interpretation model of RCTL. The formulas of RCTL are interpreted on the possible regions produced form the run of hybrid automata. With regions, RCTL combines the expressive power of both state based and event based quantitative temporal logics, which have been proposed already to extend the qualitative temporal logics. The paper showed how to specify and reason about important properties that can be automatically verified by means of reachability analysis. Furthermore, the paper showed how to encode these properties into suitable queries implemented with constraints logic programming.

Reasoning about MAS by means of hybrid automata or timed automata have been approached by several works, for example [13,14,16,27,24]. These works, however, provide no mean to reason about the quantitative properties in terms of any quantitative temporal logic.

There exist several quantitative temporal logics that can be used to reason about MAS. One can distinguish those temporal logics based on various parameters including the type of computational models; that is linear or computational view of time, the type of accessibility of time; that is whether the time is implicit or explicit in the temporal logics. We classify those works into event or based approach. Examples, of those works, which follow the event based approach, are are *Timed Propositional Temporal Logic* (TPTL) [5], and *Explicit Clock Temporal Logic* [18,34,30] for linear time logics, and *Real-Time Computation Tree Logic* (RTCTL) [15] for computation tree time logic. Examples of state based logics are *Metric Temporal logic* (MTL) [26] and *Metric Interval Temporal Logic* (MITL)[3] for linear time with dense semantics, and *Timed Computation Tree Logic* (TCTL) [1], and *Integrator Computation Tree Logic* (ICTL) [6] for computation tree time. The proposed RCTL in this paper tries to combine the expressiveness of both approaches

The idea of combining event based and state based approach is certainly not new. Several works, like [12,25], motivated their approach by arguing, as we do, that pure state-based or event-based formalisms lack expressiveness in important respects. These works however do not take in consideration the quantitative aspects systems.

Similar to our work, Platzer in [31] introduces a dynamic logic extension for hybrid programs, which are uniform operational model for hybrid systems. The resulting dynamic logic is called differential dynamic logic and constitutes a natural specification and verification logic for hybrid systems. A further extension of his wok is the integration of temporal properties in [32]. This extension provides modalities for quantifying over trace of hybrid systems. As a means for verification, Platzer introduces a sequent calculus for his differential temporal to verify temporal statements about traces of hybrid program. This is done by reducing temporal statements about traces of hybrid program to non-temporal

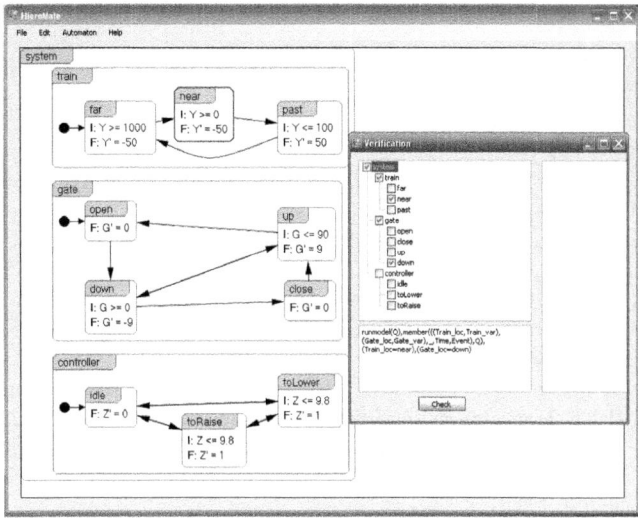

Fig. 2. A tool for modeling and Verification based on CLP

formulas. In contrast to our work, his work does not support the specification and verification of the quantitative time requirements of hybrid Systems.

The process of specifying and verifying certain requirements within a model need converting the both the model and the requirements into a constraints logic program, which is definitely a tedious and undesirable work. The direct use of logic to build a model is often claimed to be an obstacle for systems engineering. Therefore, in [35], a tool environment *HieroMate* has been built (see Fig. 2) with a constraint logic programming core that allows us to specify and hence verify multi-agent systems. With *HieroMate* the process of specifying a certain model is done in the form of graphical state transition diagram annotated with mathematical formalisms, which in turn can be verified directly. As ongoing work, we plan to enrich *HiroMate* with the various kinds of requirements that we discussed in Sec. 4. To do so, we will represent the RCTL formulae in a graphical user interface and let *HieroMate* translates these formulae into an input language to CLP system. The validation of such translation process will be discussed as well.

As a further work, since CLP is a suitable framework, where we can reason not only about the time behaviors of multi-agent systems, bout also about their knowledge, then the combination of both worlds is subjected to a future work.

In another spectrum of future work, we are currently investigating the complexity of RCTL. We will study the undecidability result of RCTL and try to provide fragments of RCTL which are decidable.

References

1. Alur, R., Courcoubetis, C., Dill, D.: Model-checking in dense real-time. Inf. Comput. 104(1), 2–34 (1993)
2. Alur, R., Dill, D.: A Theory of Timed Automata. Theoretical Computer Science 126(2), 183–235 (1994)
3. Alur, R., Feder, T., Henzinger, T.A.: The benefits of relaxing punctuality. J. ACM 43(1), 116–146 (1996)
4. Alur, R., Henzinger, T.: Logics and Models of Real Time: A Survey. In: Huizing, C., de Bakker, J.W., Rozenberg, G., de Roever, W.-P. (eds.) REX 1991. LNCS, vol. 600, pp. 74–106. Springer, Heidelberg (1992)
5. Alur, R., Henzinger, T.: A really temporal logic. Journal of the ACM (JACM) 41(1), 203 (1994)
6. Alur, R., Henzinger, T.A., Ho, P.-H.: Automatic symbolic verification of embedded systems. IEEE Transactions on Software Engineering 22(3), 181–201 (1996)
7. Ammar, A.M.: Hybrid Multi-agent Systems: Modeling, Specification and Verification. Doctoral dessertation, Department of Computer Science, University of Koblenz-landau (2010)
8. Bacchus, F., Kabanza, F.: Using temporal logics to express search control knowledge for planning. Artificial Intelligence 116(1-2), 123–191 (2000)
9. Bellini, P., Mattolini, R., Nesi, P.: Temporal logics for real-time system specification. ACM Comput. Surv. 32(1), 12–42 (2000)
10. Ben-Ari, M., Pnueli, A., Manna, Z.: The temporal logic of branching time. Acta Informatica 20(3), 207–226 (1983)
11. Bengtsson, J., Larsen, K., Larsson, F., Pettersson, P., Yi, W.: Uppaal—a tool suite for automatic verification of real-time systems. In: Proceedings of the DIMACS/SYCON Workshop on Hybrid Systems III: Verification and Control, pp. 232–243. Springer-Verlag New York, Inc., Secaucus (1996)
12. Chaki, S., Clarke, E., Ouaknine, J., Sharygina, N., Sinha, N.: Concurrent software verification with states, events, and deadlocks. Formal Aspects of Computing 17, 461–483 (2005), 10.1007/s00165-005-0071-z
13. Egerstedt, M.: Behavior Based Robotics Using Hybrid Automata. In: Lynch, N.A., Krogh, B.H. (eds.) HSCC 2000. LNCS, vol. 1790, pp. 103–116. Springer, Heidelberg (2000)
14. El Fallah-Seghrouchni, A., Degirmenciyan-Cartault, I., Marc, F.: Framework for Multi-agent Planning Based on Hybrid Automata. In: Mařík, V., Müller, J.P., Pěchouček, M. (eds.) CEEMAS 2003. LNCS (LNAI), vol. 2691, pp. 226–235. Springer, Heidelberg (2003)
15. Emerson, E.A., Mok, A.K., Sistla, A.P., Srinivasan, J.: Quantitative temporal reasoning. Real-Time Syst. 4(4), 331–352 (1992)
16. Furbach, U., Murray, J., Schmidsberger, F., Stolzenburg, F.: Hybrid Multiagent Systems with Timed Synchronization – Specification and Model Checking. In: Dastani, M., El Fallah Seghrouchni, A., Ricci, A., Winikoff, M. (eds.) ProMAS 2007. LNCS (LNAI), vol. 4908, pp. 205–220. Springer, Heidelberg (2008)
17. Giunchiglia, F., Traverso, P.: Planning as Model Checking. In: Biundo, S., Fox, M. (eds.) ECP 1999. LNCS, vol. 1809, pp. 1–20. Springer, Heidelberg (2000)
18. Harel, E., Lichtenstein, O., Pnueli, A.: Explicit clock temporal logic. In: Proceedings of Fifth Annual IEEE Symposium on Logic in Computer Science, Philadelphia, Pennsylvania, USA, June 4-7, pp. 402–413. IEEE Computer Society (1990)

19. Henzinger, T.: The theory of hybrid automata. In: Proceedings of the 11th Annual Symposium on Logic in Computer Science, New Brunswick, NJ, pp. 278–292. IEEE Computer Society Press (1996)

20. Henzinger, T.A., Ho, P.-H., Wong-Toi, H.: A User Guide to HyTech. In: Brinksma, E., Steffen, B., Cleaveland, W.R., Larsen, K.G., Margaria, T. (eds.) TACAS 1995. LNCS, vol. 1019, pp. 41–71. Springer, Heidelberg (1995)

21. Henzinger, T., Kopke, P., Puri, A., Varaiya, P.: What's Decidable about Hybrid Automata? Journal of Computer and System Sciences 57(1), 94–124 (1998)

22. Henzinger, T.A., Ho, P.-H., Wong-Toi, H.: Hytech: A Model Checker for Hybrid Systems. In: Grumberg, O. (ed.) CAV 1997. LNCS, vol. 1254, pp. 460–463. Springer, Heidelberg (1997)

23. Hindriks, K.V., van der Hoek, W., van Riemsdijk, M.B.: Agent programming with temporally extended goals. In: Proceedings of the 8th International Conference on Autonomous Agents and Multiagent Systems, AAMAS 2009, Richland, SC, vol. 1, pp. 137–144. International Foundation for Autonomous Agents and Multiagent Systems (2009)

24. Hutzler, G., Klaudel, H., Wang, D.Y.: Towards Timed Automata and Multi-agent Systems. In: Hinchey, M.G., Rash, J.L., Truszkowski, W.F., Rouff, C.A. (eds.) FAABS 2004. LNCS (LNAI), vol. 3228, pp. 161–172. Springer, Heidelberg (2004)

25. Kindler, E., Vesper, T.: ESTL: A Temporal Logic for Events and States. In: Desel, J., Silva, M. (eds.) ICATPN 1998. LNCS, vol. 1420, pp. 365–384. Springer, Heidelberg (1998)

26. Koymans, R.: Specifying real-time properties with metric temporal logic. Real-Time Systems 2(4), 255–299 (1990)

27. Mohammed, A., Furbach, U.: Modeling multi-agent logistic process system using hybrid automata. In: Ultes-Nitsche, U., Moldt, D., Augusto, J.C. (eds.) Proceedings of the 7th International Workshop on Modelling, Simulation, Verification and Validation of Enterprise Information Systems, MSVVEIS 2008, Barcelona, Spain, pp. 141–149. INSTICC Press (2008); Held in conjunction with 10th International Conference on Enterprise Information Systems (ICEIS 2008)

28. Mohammed, A., Furbach, U.: Multi-Agent Systems: Modeling and Verification Using Hybrid Automata. In: Braubach, L., Briot, J.-P., Thangarajah, J. (eds.) Pro-MAS 2009. LNCS (LNAI), vol. 5919, pp. 49–66. Springer, Heidelberg (2010)

29. Nau, D., Ghallab, M., Traverso, P.: Automated Planning: Theory & Practice. Morgan Kaufmann Publishers Inc., San Francisco (2004)

30. Ostroff, J., Wonham, W.: A framework for real-time discrete event control. IEEE Transactions on Automatic Control 35(4), 386–397 (1990)

31. Platzer, A.: Differential Logic for Reasoning About Hybrid Systems. In: Bemporad, A., Bicchi, A., Buttazzo, G. (eds.) HSCC 2007. LNCS, vol. 4416, pp. 746–749. Springer, Heidelberg (2007)

32. Platzer, A.: A Temporal Dynamic Logic for Verifying Hybrid System Invariants. In: Artemov, S., Nerode, A. (eds.) LFCS 2007. LNCS, vol. 4514, pp. 457–471. Springer, Heidelberg (2007)

33. Pnueli, A.: The temporal logic of programs. In: 18th Annual Symposium on Foundations of Computer Science 1977, pp. 46–57 (1977)

34. Pnueli, A., Harel, E.: Applications of Temporal Logic to the Specification of Real-Time Systems. In: Joseph, M. (ed.) FTRTFT 1988. LNCS, vol. 331, pp. 84–98. Springer, Heidelberg (1988)

35. Schwarz, C., Mohammed, A., Stolzenburg, F.: A tool environment for specifying and verifying multi-agent systems. In: Filipe, J., Fred, A., Sharp, B. (eds.) Proceedings of the 2nd International Conference on Agents and Artificial Intelligence, vol. 2, pp. 323–326. INSTICC Press (2010)
36. Van Benthem, J., ter Meulen, A. (eds.): Handbook of Logic and language. Elsevier (1997)
37. Yovine, S.: Kronos: A verification tool for real-time systems. International Journal on Software Tools for Technology Transfer (STTT) 1(1), 123–133 (1997)

State Space Reduction
for Model Checking Agent Programs

Sung-Shik T.Q. Jongmans[1], Koen V. Hindriks[2], and M. Birna van Riemsdijk[2]

[1] Centrum Wiskunde & Informatica, Amsterdam, The Netherlands
[2] Delft University of Technology, Delft, The Netherlands

Abstract. State space reduction techniques have been developed to increase the efficiency of model checking in the context of imperative programming languages. Unfortunately, these techniques cannot straightforwardly be applied to agents: the nature of states in the two programming paradigms differs too much for this to be possible. To resolve this, we adapt core definitions on which existing reduction algorithms are based to agents. Moreover, the framework that we introduce is such that different reduction algorithms can be defined in terms of the same relations. This is beneficial because it enables the reuse of code and reduces computation time when different techniques are used simultaneously. Specifically, we adapt and combine two known techniques: property-based slicing and partial order reduction. We exemplify our work with the GOAL agent programming language, and implement the theory that we present for GOAL. Several experiments with this implementation show that performance is in line with known results from traditional model checking.

1 Introduction

Model checking techniques for the verification of programs have traditionally been developed in the context of *imperative* programming languages (IPL). Ideally, for model checking programs written in *agent* programming languages (APL), one would take the technology and tools developed for IPLs, and apply them to agent programs without too much alteration. Unfortunately, this is sometimes an INEFFICIENT solution, and sometimes even IMPOSSIBLE:

INEFFICIENT — In [11], we show that it can be beneficial to develop new model checkers tailored to the verification of an APL rather than reusing existing tools for agent verification. The reason is that APL-tailored model checkers can reuse the APL's standard interpreter for fast generation of states. Consequently, there is no need to encode the agent program to lower-level code serving as input to an existing tool, which typically blows up the state space.

IMPOSSIBLE — In this paper, we argue that *state space reduction techniques*,[1] henceforth simply *reduction techniques*, known from traditional model

---

[1] State space reduction techniques combat the *state space explosion problem* (common to both IPL and APL model checking). This is the problem that systems to be verified are typically huge in terms of their *state space*, rendering model checking such systems often beyond our reach: it takes too many resources to finish verification.

L.A. Dennis, O. Boissier, and R.H. Bordini (Eds.): ProMAS 2011, LNCS 7217, pp. 133–151, 2012.

checking cannot be applied directly in an agent context. The reason is that (dependencies between) states and transitions in the transition system of an imperative program differ fundamentally from those of an agent program.

Our main contribution is the redefinition, for agents, of concepts at the heart of existing reduction algorithms with a novel framework that brings together different techniques in a unifying way: we show that both *property-based slicing* (PBS) and *partial order reduction* (POR) can be defined in terms of the same relations using our framework. This enables a shared code base and runtime synergy: computations carried out for one algorithm can be reused by the other. We use the GOAL agent language [6] as running example throughout the paper.

The remainder is organised as follows. Section 2 provides background on model checking and GOAL. In Sect. 3, we argue why existing reduction techniques cannot straightforwardly be applied to agents, and introduce our framework. In Sect. 4, we define PBS and POR algorithms in terms of this framework. Section 5 discusses our implementation. Finally, Sect. 6 discusses related work with respect to reduction techniques in agent verification, and concludes the paper.

2   Preliminaries

Model Checking. Model checking [4] is a technique for automatically establishing whether a program P satisfies a property φ. Usually, φ is expressed in a *temporal logic*, a formalism for describing change over time. In this paper, we consider *linear temporal logic* (LTL) [4]. An LTL formula, denoted by ϕ or φ (if φ is a property to be model checked), is built from a set of propositions $\mathcal{P}$, the boolean connectives, and the temporal operators $\bigcirc$ (next), $\mathcal{U}$ (weak until), and $\mathcal{R}$ (strong release). We denote the set of all LTL formulas by $\mathcal{L}$. An LTL formula is interpreted over an infinite sequence of states, which we call a *computation*, denoted by π. Let $i \geq 0$ be an index of π, and let $\models$ be LTL's entailment relation. Purely propositional (sub)formulas are interpreted with respect to the i-th state on π, denoted by π_i, using a *valuation function* $\mathcal{V}$. Such a function maps a state to the set of propositions in $\mathcal{P}$ that are true in it. Temporal (sub)formulas are interpreted with respect to the (infinite) postfix of π starting in the i-th state:

$$\pi, i \models \bigcirc \phi \quad \text{iff} \quad \pi, i+1 \models \phi$$
$$\pi, i \models \phi \, \mathcal{U} \, \phi' \quad \text{iff} \quad \exists_{k \geq i}(\pi, k \models \phi' \text{ and } \forall_{i \leq j < k}(\pi, j \models \phi))$$
$$\pi, i \models \phi \, \mathcal{R} \, \phi' \quad \text{iff} \quad \pi, i \models \neg(\neg \phi \, \mathcal{U} \neg \phi') \qquad (\text{note that } \mathcal{R} \text{ is the dual of } \mathcal{U})$$

In model checking, the program P is represented by its *transition system* $\mathcal{T} = \langle M, \mu_0, \longrightarrow \rangle$ in which M is a finite *set of states*, $\mu_0 \in M$ is the *initial state*, and $\longrightarrow \subseteq M \times M$ is a *transition relation* connecting states. A *path* π through $\mathcal{T}$ is an infinite sequence of states $\pi_0 \pi_1 \cdots$ such that for all $i \geq 0$: $\pi_i, \pi_{i+1} \in M$ and $\pi_i \longrightarrow \pi_{i+1}$. A computation π of P is a path through its transition system that starts in μ_0, i.e. $\pi_0 = \mu_0$. We denote the set of all computations of P by $\mathbf{\Pi}$. The model checking problem for P and φ, given a valuation function $\mathcal{V}$, can now be formulated more formally as follows: determine for all $\pi \in \mathbf{\Pi}$ whether $\pi, 0 \models \varphi$.

In that case, we say that P *satisfies* φ. Otherwise, if there exists a $\pi \in \Pi$ such that $\pi, 0 \models \neg\varphi$, P is said to *violate* φ, and π is called a *counterexample*.

Various approaches to model checking exist. In this paper, we assume *NDFS explicit-state automata-theoretic LTL model checking* [4], because the implementation we discuss in Sect. 5 extends [11] in which this approach is also taken.[2] In this approach, every $\pi \in \Pi$ is checked for satisfaction of $\neg\varphi$ in *negation normal form* (NNF). If such a computation is found, the model checker immediately halts, and reports it as a counterexample. Otherwise, the model checker terminates after investigating all computations, reporting that $\neg\varphi$ is not satisfied by any computation, i.e. φ is satisfied by all computations. Thus, instead of determining if all computations satisfy φ, in fact one determines whether there exists a counterexample. Henceforth, we assume all LTL formulas in NNF.

An important optimisation that the sketched approach allows for is *on-the-fly exploration*: the transition system of the program under investigation is generated *during* execution of the model checking algorithm instead of *before* it. Consequently, if a counterexample is quickly found and the model checker terminates, no resources have been spent on the generation of parts of the transition system whose inspection has turned out unnecessary. Importantly, the reduction algorithms discussed next are compatible with on-the-fly model checking.

GOAL. The GOAL agent programming language [6] facilitates programming of *rational agents* (i.e. agents that pursue their goals) at the cognitive level: agents choose their actions by reasoning about their *beliefs* and *goals*, which are expressed in some knowledge representation language $\mathcal{L}_X$ (e.g. Prolog). The beliefs that a GOAL agent has at some point in time are stored in its *belief base*, denoted by Σ. Similarly, the goals of a GOAL agent are stored in its *goal base*, denoted by Γ. Goals are *declarative*: they specify *what* the desired state of the world is instead of *how* this state may be brought about. Together, the belief and goal base of an agent constitute its *mental state*, denoted by $\mu = \langle \Sigma, \Gamma \rangle$.[3]

A GOAL agent derives its choice of action from its mental state, hence it needs a mechanism to inspect it. To this end, agents evaluate *mental state conditions* (MSC). An MSC, denoted by ψ, is a boolean expression about the beliefs and goals of an agent, according to the following syntax:

$$\chi ::= \text{any well-formed formula from } \mathcal{L}_X$$
$$\psi ::= \mathbf{bel}(\chi) \mid \mathbf{goal}(\chi) \mid \neg\psi \mid \psi \wedge \psi$$

The semantics of MSCs is defined by the entailment relation $\models_{\text{MS}}$ [6]. Informally, if μ is a mental state then $\mu \models_{\text{MS}} \mathbf{bel}(\chi)$ is true if χ is believed by the agent; similarly, $\mu \models_{\text{MS}} \mathbf{goal}(\chi)$ is true if χ is a goal of the agent. The set of all MSCs, denoted by $\mathcal{L}_{\text{MS}}$, is called the *language of mental state conditions*.

---

[2] Another well-known approach is *symbolic model checking* using *binary decision diagrams* (BDD) [4,13]. This approach is based on an abstraction technique different from the techniques discussed here and is out of scope of this work.

[3] Although we do not discuss knowledge, our implementation is able to deal with this; in contrast, modules [6], percepts, and beliefs about dynamic environments that evolve independently of the agent's acting are at present beyond our scope.

```
1. main: socksAgent{
2.   beliefs{
3.     bothSocksOn :- wearing(sock,left),
4.                    wearing(sock,right).
5.   }
6.   goals{
7.     wearing(sock,left). wearing(sock,right).
8.   }
9.   program{
10.     if     goal(wearing(sock,left))
11.        then putOn(sock,left).
12.     if     goal(wearing(sock,right))
13.        then putOn(sock,right).
14.   }
15.   action-specs{
16.     putOn(S,X){
17.       pre{ not(wearing(S,X)) }
18.       post{ wearing(S,X) }
19. } } }
```

$\mu_0 \qquad\qquad\qquad \mu_1$

t_0

$t_2 \qquad\qquad\qquad t_1$

t_3

$\mu_2 \qquad\qquad\qquad \mu_3$

$$\mu_0 = \left\langle \emptyset, \left\{ \begin{array}{l} \texttt{wearing(sock,left),} \\ \texttt{wearing(sock,right)} \end{array} \right\} \right\rangle$$

$$\mu_1 = \left\langle \begin{array}{l} \{\texttt{wearing(sock,left)}\}, \\ \{\texttt{wearing(sock,right)}\} \end{array} \right\rangle$$

$$\mu_2 = \left\langle \begin{array}{l} \{\texttt{wearing(sock,right)}\}, \\ \{\texttt{wearing(sock,left)}\} \end{array} \right\rangle$$

$$\mu_3 = \left\langle \left\{ \begin{array}{l} \texttt{wearing(sock,left),} \\ \texttt{wearing(sock,right)} \end{array} \right\}, \emptyset \right\rangle$$

Fig. 1. Example agent. On the left, its source code; on the right, its transition system.

MSCs are used in the definition of *action rules*. An action rule, denoted by ρ, is a statement of the form **if** ψ **then** α in which α is an *action*. An action rule may be read as "if ψ is true, then the agent may consider performing α". In that case, the action rule is said to be *applicable*. The effects that performance of an action have on the mental state of an agent are formalised by the *mental state transformer*, denoted by $\mathcal{M}$. The mental state transformer maps an action and a mental state to a *successor mental state*. $\mathcal{M}$ need not be defined for all mental state–action pairs $\langle \mu, \alpha \rangle$: if $\mathcal{M}$ is undefined for μ and α, this means that α cannot be performed in μ. A precise definition of $\mathcal{M}$ is given in [6].

Let μ be a mental state, and let $\rho = $ **if** ψ **then** α be an action rule. If ρ is applicable in μ (i.e. $\mu \models_{\text{MS}} \psi$) and $\mathcal{M}(\alpha, \mu)$ is defined, then α is called an *option* in μ. During each reasoning cycle, a GOAL agent determines its options given its current mental state and set of action rules, and chooses and performs one of them non-deterministically. This is formalised by an *operational semantics*. Let **if** ψ **then** α be an action rule, and let μ be a mental state. Then, the transition relation $\longrightarrow$ is the smallest relation induced by the following transition rule:

$$\frac{\mu \models_{\text{MS}} \psi \qquad \mathcal{M}(\alpha, \mu) \text{ is defined}}{\mu \longrightarrow \mathcal{M}(\alpha, \mu)}$$

The transition relation $\longrightarrow$ is subsequently used to define the transition system $\mathcal{T} = \langle M, \mu_0, \longrightarrow \rangle$ of a GOAL agent, in which we assume that M is a finite[4] set of mental states and that μ_0 is the initial mental state of the agent.

Example 1. The source code and transition system of a simple example GOAL agent, whose task is to put on two socks, appears in Fig. 1. We use this agent, called socksAgent, as a running example throughout this paper.

For model checking GOAL agents, we instantiate the set of LTL propositions $\mathcal{P}$ with the language of mental state conditions $\mathcal{L}_{\text{MS}}$. The valuation function $\mathcal{V}$

---

[4] Finiteness is not imposed by GOAL, but a model checking termination requirement.

in this case maps every mental state μ to the MSCs that are true in it, i.e. $\mathcal{V}(\mu) = \{\psi \in \mathcal{L}_{MS} \mid \mu \models_{MS} \psi\}$. This allows us to formulate and verify properties about the evolution of beliefs and goals of a GOAL agent during its execution.

A final remark on terminology. Although we illustrate our techniques with GOAL, they can be applied to other agent languages as well. Therefore, when we write "mental state" in what follows, we do not refer exclusively to a state of a GOAL agent, but rather to a state of an agent written in some BDI-based APL.

3   Operations on Mental States

The aim of reduction techniques is to remove sets of transitions from the transition system that do not affect the truth value of the property under investigation. In our framework, we identify such sets of transitions by classifying them in terms of *operations*. Informally, we may think of an operation, denoted by τ, as a function that transforms states μ to other states μ'. In that case, τ is said to be *applied* to μ. More specifically, we characterise an operation in terms of the CHANGES that it brings about, and the STATEMENT in the source code from which it can be induced. Below, let $\mathcal{T} = \langle M, \mu_0, \longrightarrow \rangle$ be the transition system of some agent program P, and let $t = \langle \mu, \mu' \rangle \in \longrightarrow$ be a transition.

CHANGES — Grouping individual transitions in $\mathcal{T}$ according to the changes that they bring about enables us to express that the order in which two operations can be applied is without consequence (relevant in POR). To formalise this notion, let $\mathsf{Ch}(t)$ denote the change between μ and μ'.

STATEMENT — Characterising operations by statements allows us to remove sets of transitions from $\mathcal{T}$ by deleting statements from P's source code. This enables us, for instance, to reduce $\mathcal{T}$ by performing static analysis of the program text alone (relevant in PBS). To formalise this notion, let $\mathsf{St}(t)$ denote the set of statements in P's source code from which t can be induced.

Example 2. In case of GOAL, $\mathsf{Ch}(t)$ denotes the beliefs and goals to be added and deleted to get from μ to μ', and $\mathsf{St}(t)$ denotes the action rules that induce t. Applied, for instance, to transition $t_0 = \langle \mu_0, \mu_1 \rangle$ of socksAgent in Fig. 1 yields: $\mathsf{Ch}(t_0) = \langle \Sigma + \{\texttt{wearing(sock,left)}\} - \emptyset, \Gamma + \emptyset - \{\texttt{wearing(sock,left)}\}\rangle$ and $\mathsf{St}(t_0) = \{\texttt{if goal(wearing(sock,left)) then putOn(sock,left)}\}$.

We now define an operation τ formally.

Definition 1. *An operation is a pair* $\tau = \langle T, s \rangle$ *in which s is a statement and* $T \subseteq \longrightarrow$ *is the largest set such that for all $t, t' \in T$:* $\mathsf{Ch}(t) = \mathsf{Ch}(t')$ *and* $s \in \mathsf{St}(t)$.

Example 3. We identify the following operations of socksAgent in Fig. 1 (with t_i, $0 \leq i \leq 3$, as defined in Fig. 1):

$$\tau_0 = \langle\{t_0, t_3\}, \texttt{if goal(wearing(sock,left)) then putOn(sock,left)}\rangle$$
$$\tau_1 = \langle\{t_1, t_2\}, \texttt{if goal(wearing(sock,right)) then putOn(sock,right)}\rangle$$

We use the following notation and definitions. The set of all possible operations is denoted by Ω_τ. If $\tau = \langle T, s \rangle$ is an operation, then we use $\mathsf{Tran}(\tau)$ and $\mathsf{Stat}(\tau)$ as a shorthand for, respectively, T and s. We call $\mathsf{Stat}(\tau)$ the statement that *induces* τ, and say that τ is *enabled* in a state μ if there exists a μ' such that $\langle \mu, \mu' \rangle \in \mathsf{Tran}(\tau)$; we write $\tau(\mu)$ as a shorthand for μ'. The set of all enabled operations in μ is denoted by $\mathsf{En}(\mu)$, i.e. $\mathsf{En}(\mu) = \{ \tau \in \Omega_\tau \mid \tau \text{ is enabled in } \mu \}$. The set of all operations $\mathsf{Ops}(s)$ that a statement s can induce is called its *operation class*, defined as $\mathsf{Ops}(s) = \{ \tau \in \Omega_\tau \mid \mathsf{Stat}(\tau) = s \}$. Finally, for brevity, we write $\mathsf{Ch}(\tau)$ to denote the change brought about by any $t \in \mathsf{Tran}(\tau)$, and write $\mathsf{Ch}(s)$ to denote the set at least having $\bigcup_{\tau \in \mathsf{Ops}(s)} \mathsf{Ch}(\tau)$ as a subset.

3.1   Variable Assignments versus Mental States

State space reduction techniques have originally been developed for use with transition systems whose states are characterised by variables and their values, henceforth called *variable assignment*. By carefully analysing which variables change by applying operations on states (i.e. when moving from one state to the next), relations on operations essential to the application of reduction algorithms can be computed. For instance, one can determine whether enabledness of an operation τ' is affected by the application of an operation τ, by comparing the variables that τ mutates and τ' accesses. We call the sets of variables an operation τ accesses and mutates its *read set*, denoted by $\mathsf{Read}(\tau)$, and its *write set*, denoted by $\mathsf{Write}(\tau)$, respectively. These sets are not used only for determining whether enabledness of operations depends on the application of (other) operations, but also to determine if the application of an operation influences the truth value of LTL formulas. Importantly, analyses based on read and write sets can be done by inspection of the source code alone: the read and write set of an operation τ can be determined straightforwardly by inspecting the variables occurring in the statement that induces τ, i.e. $\mathsf{Stat}(\tau)$. This is of great value, because it allows for *off-line computation* of (most of the) reduction algorithms. This means that the computation of these algorithms does not depend on information that is available only during model checking. Because processing information that is available only at runtime (i.e., while we run the actual model checking algorithm that searches for a counterexample) is likely to be more expensive (e.g., because subroutines of the algorithm need be computed for each state in a transition system), off-line algorithms reduce the overhead at runtime to a minimum.

Example 4. Suppose two operations $\tau, \tau' \in \Omega_\tau$ such that $\mathsf{Stat}(\tau) = [x := x + 1]$ and $\mathsf{Stat}(\tau') = [y := z + 42]$ are enabled simultaneously in some variable assignment ν, e.g. because they belong to different concurrent processes (and x, y, z are shared variables). Then: $\mathsf{Read}(\tau) = \mathsf{Write}(\tau) = \{x\}$ and $\mathsf{Read}(\tau') = \{z\}$ and $\mathsf{Write}(\tau') = \{y\}$. Because $\mathsf{Read}(\tau) \cap \mathsf{Write}(\tau') = \mathsf{Write}(\tau) \cap \mathsf{Read}(\tau') = \emptyset$, application of τ cannot cause τ' to become disabled and vice versa.

When model checking agent programs, however, states are *not* characterised by variable–value pairs, but by mental attitudes, which are very different: how and which mental attitudes change over time is not stated explicitly in the program text, e.g. due to underspecification. We elaborate on this in Sect. 3.2. Hence, in agent verification, we cannot use directly the analysis techniques known from traditional model checking to compute the relations essential to the application of reduction algorithms: the gap between variable assignments and mental states need be bridged. Specifically, to be able to reuse existing reduction algorithms for agents, we need to answer (in the next subsection) the following questions:

1. What are the elements constituting read and write sets when dealing with mental states of agents, which are not composed of variable–value pairs?
2. Given a definition of read and write sets for mental states of agents, can we still compute them off-line?

3.2   Read Sets and Write Sets for Mental States

Ad 1. We aim at a definition of read and write sets for mental states that is sufficiently generic in the sense that these definitions should accommodate multiple APLs. This is nontrivial, because mental states look different in each APL, i.e. the mental attitudes constituting a mental state vary between different languages. To this end, we introduce the notion of an APL-specific *condition language*, denoted by $\mathcal{L}_K$, whose elements are *conditions*, denoted by κ. Informally, the idea is that the read set of an operation τ contains those conditions that *must* be true for τ to be enabled, while τ's write set contains those conditions whose truth value changes due to application of τ. Thus, $\mathsf{Read}(\tau) \subseteq \mathcal{L}_K$ and $\mathsf{Write}(\tau) \subseteq \mathcal{L}_K$. The only requirement that $\mathcal{L}_K$ must satisfy is that it should have the set of propositions $\mathcal{P}$ as a subset, i.e. $\mathcal{P} \subseteq \mathcal{L}_K$: this allows us to determine, by means of write set analysis, whether a transition can affect the truth value of a property. Apart from that, $\mathcal{L}_K$ can be tailored completely to the needs of the APL.

Example 5. In the context of GOAL, the condition language equals the language of MSCs, i.e. $\mathcal{L}_K = \mathcal{L}_{MS}$ (recall that $\mathcal{P} - \mathcal{L}_{MS}$ for GOAL).

Next, to accommodate formal definitions, we assume an entailment relation $\models_K$, relating (mental) states to conditions that are true in them, and a function $\mathcal{I}$ mapping a mental state μ to the subset of $\mathcal{L}_K$ that is true in μ, i.e. $\mathcal{I}(\mu) = \{ \kappa \in \mathcal{L}_K \mid \mu \models_K \kappa \}$. Read and write sets are then defined formally as follows.

Definition 2. *Let τ be an operation. Then:*

$$
\begin{aligned}
\mathsf{Read}(\tau) \;&=\; \{ \kappa \in \mathcal{L}_K \mid \text{there exist states } \mu, \mu' \text{ s.t. } \tau \in \mathsf{En}(\mu), \tau \notin \mathsf{En}(\mu') \\
&\qquad\qquad \text{and } \kappa \in \mathcal{I}(\mu) \text{ and } \mathcal{I}(\mu') = \mathcal{I}(\mu) \backslash \{\kappa\} \} \\
\mathsf{Write}^+(\tau) \;&=\; \textstyle\bigcup_{\langle \mu,\mu' \rangle \in \mathsf{Tran}(\tau)} \mathcal{I}(\mu') \backslash \mathcal{I}(\mu) \\
\mathsf{Write}^-(\tau) \;&=\; \textstyle\bigcup_{\langle \mu,\mu' \rangle \in \mathsf{Tran}(\tau)} \mathcal{I}(\mu) \backslash \mathcal{I}(\mu') \\
\mathsf{Write}(\tau) \;&=\; \mathsf{Write}^+(\tau) \cup \mathsf{Write}^-(\tau)
\end{aligned}
$$

We call $\mathsf{Write}^+(\tau)$ and $\mathsf{Write}^-(\tau)$ the positive and negative write sets of τ; $\mathsf{Write}(\tau)$ is sometimes referred to as τ's total write set.

We use the distinction between positive and negative write sets in Sect. 3.3. The distinction is important, because it allows us, for instance, to state that some transition τ can enable a transition τ': in that case, the *positive* write set of τ coincides with the read set of τ'. Conversely, if τ's *negative* write set does *not* coincide with the read set of τ', τ cannot disable τ'. Note that "not disabling" is different from "enabling", and in general, Write^+ and Write^- are not each other's complement: $\mathcal{L}_K \setminus \mathsf{Write}^+(\tau) \neq \mathsf{Write}^-(\tau)$ and $\mathcal{L}_K \setminus \mathsf{Write}^-(\tau) \neq \mathsf{Write}^+(\tau)$.

Example 6. Consider operation τ_0 of `socksAgent`, defined in Ex. 3. For convenience, we restrict this example to the MSC set {`goal(wearing(sock,left))`, `goal(wearing(sock,right))`, `bel(bothSocksOn)`} $\subset \mathcal{L}_{\mathrm{MS}}$. Now, the positive write set of τ_0 equals {`bel(bothSocksOn)`},[5] while both its read set and negative write set equal {`goal(wearing(sock,left))`}. From this, we can deduce that τ_0 disables itself, while it has no effect on enabledness or disabledness of τ_1.

Ad 2. As outlined in Sect. 3.1, off-line computation of read and write sets is important, because it reduces the resource consumption of reduction algorithms at runtime. For imperative programming languages, as shown in Ex. 4, this can be done easily. Unfortunately, in case of agent programs, the situation is more complex: conditions from $\mathcal{L}_K$ often do not occur explicitly in the agent's source code, and cannot be simply extracted from it without further analysis.

Example 7. Consider the read and write sets of operation τ_0 of `socksAgent` given in Ex. 6. While τ_0's read set can be determined straightforwardly from the action rule `if goal(wearing(sock,left)) then putOn(sock,left)`, this is not the case for its write set for two reasons. First, the removal of the goal `wearing(sock,left)` occurs automatically due to GOAL's semantics, and is not specified explicitly in the program text. Second, the derivation of `bothSocksOn` using the Prolog rule in the belief base (see Fig. 1) cannot be detected by inspection of this action rule alone.

Switching to a more general perspective, we must deal with two issues when computing read and write sets for GOAL agents. First, not all beliefs and goals that an operation adds or deletes can be derived from the source code of a GOAL agent, making it difficult to determine which MSCs incur a change of truth value. Second, as changing the belief base by an operation also changes the consequences that can be derived from Prolog rules, we need an algorithm to approximate these. The issue is that this algorithm must run on only the source code and that the content of the belief base at runtime is unknown.

Thus, we may need to derive read and write sets with more complex analysis techniques. Unfortunately, it may be impossible to compute *precise* read and write sets using the source code alone due to underspecification of the agent or

---

[5] One may observe that only t_3, and not t_0, makes `bel(bothSocksOn)` true, even though t_0 and t_3 induce the same change. This shows that an operation can make different MSCs true or false, depending on the mental state to which we apply it. In general, if a write set of an operation τ contains an MSC ψ, there exists at least one mental state μ such that application of τ to μ changes the truth value of ψ.

the occurrences of uninstantiated variables combined with Prolog-style reasoning as sketched in the previous example. There are two ways to resolve these issues: acquire sufficient information by generating the entire transition system, or use *approximation techniques*. We prefer the latter, because the former is incompatible with on-the-fly model checking. We stress that approximation is unnecessary in an IPL context, because there, read and write sets can be obtained with straightforward source code inspection.

The key property any approximation technique for read and write sets must satisfy is that of *over*-approximation: to ensure that model checking with reduction algorithms yields the same results as without, approximate read and write sets (denoted here in $\mathfrak{font}$) need to over-approximate the precise sets. Formally:

Property 1. Let s be a statement. For all $\tau \in \mathsf{Ops}(s)$: $\mathsf{Read}(\tau) \subseteq \mathfrak{Read}(s)$ and $\mathsf{Write}^+(\tau) \subseteq \mathfrak{Write}^+(s)$ and $\mathsf{Write}^-(\tau) \subseteq \mathfrak{Write}^-(s)$ and $\mathsf{Write}(\tau) \subseteq \mathfrak{Write}(s)$.

Intuitively, over-approximation of read and write sets is required because these sets are used to determine dependencies between operations: the less dependencies present, the more reduction can be obtained. Thus, if all operations depend on each other, no reduction is gained. By over-approximating, dependencies that actually do not exist are nevertheless assumed. Although this may cause reduction algorithms to be less effective, correctness is assured. Henceforth, we assume all sets $\mathfrak{Read}$ and $\mathfrak{Write}$ to satisfy Property 1 (e.g. in the proof of Lemma 1).

3.3 Relations on Operations

Next, we use read and write sets to define relations on operations known from existing literature [4] on reduction techniques (see Table 1), and used by the algorithms in Sect. 4. Our contribution is that we define each relation not only in terms of precise read and write sets, but also in terms of their approximate counterparts. The resulting *approximate relations* can be computed before the transition system is generated (instead of during its generation), i.e. off-line. This reduces computational overhead of reduction algorithms at runtime to a minimum, and ensures compatibility with on-the-fly model checking. We prove lemmas to show how the precise and approximate relations relate to each other.

Table 1. Formal definition of relations on operations and statements

Relation	Precise (for operations τ, τ')	Approximate (for statements s, s')
Visibility	$\mathsf{Vis}(\tau, \phi)$ iff $Props(\phi) \cap \mathsf{Write}(\tau) \neq \emptyset$	$\mathfrak{Vis}(s, \phi)$ iff $Props(\phi) \cap \mathfrak{Write}(s) \neq \emptyset$
Enables	$\mathsf{Enables}(\tau, \tau')$ iff $\mathsf{Read}(\tau') \cap \mathsf{Write}^+(\tau) \neq \emptyset$	$\mathfrak{Enables}(s, s')$ iff $\mathfrak{Read}(s') \cap \mathfrak{Write}^+(s) \neq \emptyset$
Independence	$\mathsf{Indep}(\tau, \tau')$ iff $H^{en}_{\mathsf{Indep}}(\tau, \tau')$ and $H^{comm}_{\mathsf{Indep}}(\tau, \tau')$	$\mathfrak{Indep}(s, s')$ iff $H^{en}_{\mathfrak{Indep}}(s, s')$ and $H^{comm}_{\mathfrak{Indep}}(s, s')$

The first relation we discuss is the *visibility relation* Vis. Let τ be an operation, and let ϕ be an LTL formula. Then, $\mathsf{Vis}(\tau, \phi)$ states that application of τ can affect the truth value of ϕ; the formal definition can be found in Table 1. Because Vis is defined in terms of precise write sets, which typically cannot be computed off-line (see Sect. 3.2), we introduce the *approximate visibility relation* $\mathfrak{Vis}$, which is an approximation of Vis defined in terms of approximate write sets (see Table 1). Relations Vis and $\mathfrak{Vis}$ are related by the following lemma.

Lemma 1. *Let s be statement, let τ be an operation such that $\mathsf{Stat}(\tau) = s$, and let ϕ be an LTL formula. If $\mathsf{Vis}(\tau, \phi)$, then $\mathfrak{Vis}(s, \phi)$.*

Proof. By definition of Vis in Table 1, $Props(\phi) \cap \mathsf{Write}(\tau) \neq \emptyset$. Also, because $\mathfrak{Write}$ satisfies Property 1, $\mathfrak{Write}(s) \subseteq \mathsf{Write}(\tau)$. Hence, $Props(\phi) \cap \mathfrak{Write}(s) \neq \emptyset$. The lemma then follows from the definition of $\mathfrak{Vis}$ in Table 1. □

Thus, $\mathfrak{Vis}(s, \phi)$ is true if s induces an operation τ whose application affects the truth value of ϕ, as such over-approximating the relation Vis.

The second relation we discuss is the *enables relation* Enables. Let τ, τ' be operations. Then, $\mathsf{Enables}(\tau, \tau')$ states that application of τ to some state μ can cause τ' to become enabled, i.e. τ is enabled in μ while τ' is not, but in the state that results from applying τ to μ, τ' *is* enabled. The formal definition (in terms of precise read and write sets) occurs in Table 1, together with the definition of the *approximate enables relation* $\mathfrak{Enables}$ (in terms of approximate read and write sets). Relations Enables and $\mathfrak{Enables}$ are related by the following lemma, whose proof is analogous to that of Lemma 1 (omitted for reasons of space).

Lemma 2. *Let s, s' be statements, and let τ, τ' be operations such that $\mathsf{Stat}(\tau) = s$ and $\mathsf{Stat}(\tau') = s'$. If $\mathsf{Enables}(\tau, \tau')$, then $\mathfrak{Enables}(s, s')$.*

Thus, $\mathfrak{Enables}(s, s')$ is true if s induces an operation τ whose application can enable an operation τ' induced by s', over-approximating the relation Enables.

The third relation we discuss is the *independence relation* Indep. Let τ, τ' be operations. Then, $\mathsf{Indep}(\tau, \tau')$ is true if the *independence conditions* in the left column of Table 2 hold for each state μ of the transition system: ENABLEDNESS states that independent operations cannot *disable* each other, while COMMUTATIVITY states that applying independent operations in either order results in the same state. In practice, checking the independence conditions in each state would be too much a computational burden. Therefore, as usual [4], Indep is defined heuristically (see Table 1 and the middle column of Table 2).

We approximate ENABLEDNESS with condition H_{Indep}^{en} given in Table 2, which is guaranteed to be true if ENABLEDNESS is true. The intuition behind it is that if an operation τ does not disable an operation τ', then τ cannot make a condition κ on which enabledness of τ' depends (i.e. $\kappa \in \mathsf{Read}(\tau')$) false. Similarly, COMMUTATIVITY is approximated with $H_{\mathsf{Indep}}^{comm}$ in Table 2. The intuition behind $H_{\mathsf{Indep}}^{comm}$ is that if the orders in which operations τ and τ' can be applied both lead to the same state, the changes that they bring about are disjoint, i.e. τ does not (partially) undo changes brought about by τ' and vice versa.

Definitions of H_{Indep}^{en} and $H_{\mathsf{Indep}}^{comm}$ (similar to those in [4]) are in terms of operations instead of statements: to be able to compute independences before actual

Table 2. Independence conditions, definitions, and heuristics

Condition	Heuristic	Approximate heuristic
ENABLEDNESS : $\tau \in \mathsf{En}(\tau'(\mu))$	$H^{en}_{\mathsf{Indep}}(\tau, \tau')$: $\mathsf{Read}(\tau') \cap \mathsf{Write}^-(\tau) = \emptyset$	$H^{en}_{\mathfrak{Indep}}(s, s')$: $\mathfrak{Read}(s') \cap \mathfrak{Write}^-(s) = \emptyset$
COMMUTATIVITY : $\tau(\tau'(\mu)) = \tau'(\tau(\mu))$	$H^{comm}_{\mathsf{Indep}}(\tau, \tau')$: $\mathsf{Ch}(\tau) \cap \mathsf{Ch}(\tau') = \emptyset$	$H^{comm}_{\mathfrak{Indep}}(s, s')$: $\mathsf{Ch}(s) \cap \mathsf{Ch}(s') = \emptyset$

model checking, we require the latter. Therefore, as before, we introduce the
approximate independence relation $\mathfrak{Indep}$, in whose definition (see Table 1) the
precise heuristics have been replaced by their approximate counterparts $H^{en}_{\mathfrak{Indep}}$
and $H^{comm}_{\mathfrak{Indep}}$ (see the right column of Table 2). Relations Indep and $\mathfrak{Indep}$ are
related by the following lemma; its proof is analogous to that of Lemma 1.

Lemma 3. *Let s, s' be statements, and let τ, τ' be operations such that* $\mathsf{Stat}(\tau) = s$ *and* $\mathsf{Stat}(\tau') = s'$. *If* $\mathfrak{Indep}(s, s')$, *then* $\mathsf{Indep}(\tau, \tau')$.

We use $\mathsf{Dep}(\tau, \tau')$ (and $\mathfrak{Dep}(s, s')$) as a shorthand for "$\mathsf{Indep}(\tau, \tau')$ is false" (and
"$\mathfrak{Indep}(s, s')$ is false"), and call τ, τ' (and s, s') *dependent*.

4   State Space Reduction

In a nutshell, the idea of state space reduction is as follows. Let $\mathcal{T} = \langle M, \mu_0, \longrightarrow \rangle$
be the *complete* transition system. The aim of reduction techniques is to find a
reduced transition system $\widehat{\mathcal{T}} = \langle \widehat{M}, \mu_0, \widehat{\longrightarrow} \rangle$ such that $\widehat{M} \subseteq M$ and $\widehat{\longrightarrow} \subseteq \longrightarrow$.
The idea is that $\widehat{M}$ and $\widehat{\longrightarrow}$ may be *significantly smaller* than M and $\longrightarrow$,
and that investigating $\widehat{\mathcal{T}}$ will require fewer resources (time and memory) than
inspection of $\mathcal{T}$ would. To ensure that model checking $\widehat{\mathcal{T}}$ for φ yields the same
results as model checking $\mathcal{T}$, henceforth referred to as *correctness*, $\widehat{\mathcal{T}}$ should be
both SOUND and COMPLETE with respect to $\mathcal{T}$ and φ [7]. Let $\mathit{\Pi}$ be the set of
computations in $\mathcal{T}$, and let $\widehat{\mathit{\Pi}}$ be the set of computations in $\widehat{\mathcal{T}}$. Then:

SOUND — If $\boldsymbol{\pi} \in \mathit{\Pi}$ s.t. $\boldsymbol{\pi} \models \neg\varphi$, then there exists a $\widehat{\boldsymbol{\pi}} \in \widehat{\mathit{\Pi}}$ s.t. $\widehat{\boldsymbol{\pi}} \models \neg\varphi$.
COMPLETE — If $\widehat{\boldsymbol{\pi}} \in \widehat{\mathit{\Pi}}$ s.t. $\widehat{\boldsymbol{\pi}} \models \neg\varphi$, then there exists a $\boldsymbol{\pi} \in \mathit{\Pi}$ s.t. $\boldsymbol{\pi} \models \neg\varphi$.

In the remainder, we describe and define two reduction techniques, PBS and
POR, in terms of the relations given in Sect. 3.3. We stress that these techniques
by themselves and the ideas behind them are not new: both have extensively
been studied in the context of imperative languages. Their coherent definition
for agents in terms of the same relations, however, is a contribution of ours. This
requires the following efforts. With respect to PBS, we redefine data structures
used in traditional PBS in terms of relations given in Sect. 3.3. With respect
to POR, we can straightforwardly apply the existing *ample set method*, which
is already defined in terms of relations similar to those of Sect. 3.3; a novelty,
however, is the introduction of a heuristic that generalises SPIN's [4].

4.1 Property-Based Slicing

The aim of *property-based slicing* (PBS) is to remove statements from the source code of the system to be verified that do not *influence* the (negated) property $\neg\varphi$. Removal of such statements may cause certain states and transitions to be eliminated from the transition system, thus yielding a reduction. A PBS algorithm is run *before* generation of the transition system commences (and *without* the need for generation of the complete transition system). The challenge of PBS is to remove as much code as possible while preserving correctness.

PBS algorithms represent the source code of the system under verification as a graph [15]. Such a graph makes explicit how execution of one statement can influence the execution of other statements as well as the property to be checked. Moreover, it enables the formulation of the PBS problem as a graph reachability problem. In our PBS algorithm, we use *influence graphs*. Informally, the influence graph with respect to a set of statements S (by which some program P is defined) and a (negated) property $\neg\varphi$ is a graph whose vertices are statements and $\neg\varphi$, and whose edges are elements of the visibility and enables relation.

Definition 3. *Let S be the set of statements by which some program P is defined, and let $\neg\varphi$ be a negated property. The influence graph $\mathcal{G}(S, \neg\varphi) = \langle \mathcal{N}, \mathcal{E} \rangle$ is a digraph with $\mathcal{N} = S \cup \{\neg\varphi\}$ and $\mathcal{E} = \{\langle s, \neg\varphi \rangle \in S \times \{\neg\varphi\} \mid \mathfrak{Vis}(s, \neg\varphi)\} \cup \{\langle s, s' \rangle \in S \times S \mid \mathfrak{Enables}(s, s')\}$.*

The first line of the definition of $\mathcal{E}$ represents the notion of *direct influence* on $\neg\varphi$: every edge $\langle s, \neg\varphi \rangle$ indicates that there exists an operation $\tau \in \mathsf{Ops}(s)$ that can influence the truth value of a proposition in $\neg\varphi$. The second line of $\mathcal{E}$'s definition represents the notion of *indirect influence* on $\neg\varphi$: every edge $\langle s, s' \rangle$ indicates that there exist operations $\tau \in \mathsf{Ops}(s)$ and $\tau' \in \mathsf{Ops}(s')$ such that τ can enable τ'. If s' influences $\neg\varphi$ (directly or indirectly), s influences $\neg\varphi$ indirectly.

Closely related to influence is the notion of *routes*. A route through an influence graph is a finite sequence of vertices $s_0 \cdots s_n \neg\varphi$, abbreviated $s_0 \rightsquigarrow \neg\varphi$, such that every statement occurs only once on a route, i.e. if $i \neq j$ then $s_i \neq s_j$ for all $0 \leq i, j \leq n$, and every route ends in $\neg\varphi$. The set of all routes through an influence graph $\mathcal{G}(S, \neg\varphi)$ is denoted by $Routes(\mathcal{G}(S, \neg\varphi))$. The idea central to our PBS algorithm is that every statement that is *not* on any route through the influence graph $\mathcal{G}(S, \neg\varphi)$ can safely be removed from the source code: these statements have no influence on the truth value of $\neg\varphi$. The algorithm takes a set of statements S as input, and computes a reduced set of statements $\widehat{S}$ by constructing an influence graph and computing routes. To determine if a route exists, the algorithm starts at a vertex s, and explores the influence graph until the vertex $\neg\varphi$ is reached, or no more reachable yet unexplored vertices are left.[6]

Existing PBS algorithms work in roughly the same way: the program is represented as a graph, reducing the PBS problem to graph reachability analysis. A key difference is that in our approach, the connection between operations and

---

[6] Several optimisations may be implemented. For instance, if a depth-first exploration strategy is applied, all vertices on the depth-first stack at the moment $\neg\varphi$ is reached also have a route to $\neg\varphi$, making additional searches for these statements unnecessary.

statements is made very explicit,[7] allowing for a rigid proof of correctness. We have not found similar explicit connections in the existing literature on PBS.

Theorem 1. *Our PBS algorithm preserves soundness and completeness.*

Proof (Sketch). We adopt the premise that if a computation π satisfies $\neg\varphi$, i.e. $\pi \models \neg\varphi$, then an operation that influences $\neg\varphi$ is applied during π's generation.

SOUNDNESS *If $\pi \models \neg\varphi$ and by our premise, there exists a computation π' such that $\pi' \models \neg\varphi$ and that is generated exclusively by applying influential operations. Hence, as the algorithm retains all statements that can induce influential operations, π' is also a computation in the reduced transition system.*
COMPLETENESS *Because the algorithm does not introduce new statements to the set S, no new transitions are introduced either.* □

We note that the adopted premise in the previous proof is *false* if $\neg\varphi$ (in NNF) contains $\bigcirc$ or $\mathcal{R}$ operators: $\bigcirc \phi$ can be true without application of an influential operation if ϕ is already true in the current state, while $\phi \mathcal{R} \phi'$ can be true if ϕ' is true from the current state onwards without an influential operation ever being applied (i.e. ϕ never becomes true). Thus, the PBS algorithm is only applicable if $\neg\varphi$ is in the $\{\bigcirc, \mathcal{R}\}$-free fragment of LTL.

4.2   Partial Order Reduction

Next, we present a *partial order reduction* (POR) algorithm in terms of the relations of Sect. 3.3. POR algorithms try to exploit the observation that the various orders in which certain events can take place are irrelevant with respect to a certain property. Once such a situation is identified, a POR algorithm forces the model checker to choose only one *representative* order and to disregard all the others. While a PBS algorithm is applied prior to the generation of the reduced transition system, a POR algorithm is run *during* its generation (and *without* the need for generation of the complete transition system first).

There are various approaches to POR. Here, we focus on the *ample set method* [4] as it fits the relations of Sect. 3.3 seamlessly. The idea is to construct a reduced transition system by selecting only a subset of all enabled operations in each state (and disregarding the other enabled operations). To preserve correctness, such a subset, called an *ample set* and denoted by $\mathsf{Ample}(\mu)$, must satisfy the following:

C0 (Emptiness) $\mathsf{Ample}(\mu) = \emptyset$ iff $\mathsf{En}(\mu) = \emptyset$.
C1 (Ample Decomposition) In the complete transition system, on any path starting from some state μ, an operation dependent on an operation from $\mathsf{Ample}(\mu)$ cannot appear before some operation from $\mathsf{Ample}(\mu)$ is executed.
C2 (Invisibility) If $\mathsf{En}(\mu) \neq \mathsf{Ample}(\mu)$, all operations in $\mathsf{Ample}(\mu)$ are visible.

---

[7] The visibility and enables relations ($\mathfrak{Vis}$ and $\mathfrak{Enables}$) are defined in terms of read and write sets on statements ($\mathfrak{Read}$ and $\mathfrak{Write}$), which are related to read and write sets on operations (Read and Write) by Property 1, which are defined in terms of individual transitions of the transition system.

C3 (Cycle Closing) If a cycle contains a state in which an operation τ is enabled, then it also contains a state μ such that $\tau \in \mathsf{Ample}(\mu)$.

Details about these conditions are given in [4].

Let μ be a state. A naive implementation of the ample set method would be to check for all subsets of $\mathsf{En}(\mu)$ whether the four conditions are satisfied, and then pick one such subset as ample set. The problem with such an implementation, however, is that checking **C1** is computationally just as hard as the model checking problem for the complete transition system [4]. Therefore, in practice, rather than checking **C1** for an arbitrary subset of enabled operations, a heuristic approach that finds a set of operations that is *guaranteed* to satisfy **C1** is used. We call such a set a *candidate set*. Such an approach does not always lead to an ample set that yields the greatest reduction possible, but can be effective nevertheless. Once candidate sets are chosen, they need only be checked for **C0**, **C2**, and **C3**, which are easy to compute. Our idea for choosing candidate sets is to first select a subset of S, denoted by $\widehat{S}$, which satisfies the following:

Property 2. Let S be the set of statements defining a program. Then, for all $s' \in \widehat{S}$, there does not exist a $s \in S \setminus \widehat{S}$ s.t. (i) $\mathfrak{Dep}(s, s')$ and (ii) $\mathfrak{Enables}(s, s')$.

Once a set $\widehat{S}$ satisfying Property 2 is found, the set of all enabled operations in a state μ that can be induced by a statement $s \in \widehat{S}$ is selected as a candidate set C, i.e. $C = \mathsf{En}(\mu) \cap \bigcup_{s \in \widehat{S}} \mathsf{Ops}(s)$. It is guaranteed that C satisfies **C1**.

Lemma 4. *If $\widehat{S}$ satisfies Property 2, $C = \mathsf{En}(\mu) \cap \bigcup_{s \in \widehat{S}} \mathsf{Ops}(s)$ satisfies **C1**.*

*Proof (Sketch). There are two situations in which **C1** may be violated, which differ by whether τ is induced by a statement s' outside $\widehat{S}$ or in it. In the former case, if $s' \notin \widehat{S}$, there exists a statement in $\widehat{S}$ on which s' depends (because τ is dependent on an operation in C). This situation is covered by condition (i) of Property 2. In the latter case, if $s' \in \widehat{S}$, then τ is not enabled in the current state (because $\tau \notin C$). Hence, there exists another statement s that enables s'. If $s \notin \widehat{S}$, then $\mathfrak{Enables}(s, s')$, hence this situation is covered by condition (ii) of Property 2. Otherwise, if $s \in \widehat{S}$, the previous argument can be applied inductively.* □

In practice, the challenge is finding suitable sets $\widehat{S}$ as efficiently as possible. A straightforward approach is iterating over all elements in the power set of S, and checking Property 2 for each $\widehat{S} \in 2^S$. However, as this requires time exponential in the number of statements, this is not a good idea. Instead, we let the search for sets $\widehat{S}$ be guided by the definition of $\mathfrak{Dep}$: we search for sets $\widehat{S}$ that are guaranteed to satisfy (i) of Property 2. This search can be done in time linear in the number of statements $|S|$ and the size of $\mathfrak{Dep}$, and yields at most $|S|$ sets $\widehat{S}$ instead of $2^{|S|}$ for which (ii) of Property 2 need be checked. The idea is to regard the relation $\mathfrak{Dep}$ as a graph whose vertices are statements and whose edges are elements of the relation. Because every edge is an element of $\mathfrak{Dep}$, each statement belonging to a set $\widehat{S}$ cannot have edges to statements outside $\widehat{S}$: a set $\widehat{S}$ satisfying (i) of Property 2 corresponds to a *connected component* in the graph, which can be found with a depth-first search [9]. Such a search runs in time linear in the number of vertices and edges. As there cannot be more connected components than vertices, this approach yields at most $|S|$ sets $\widehat{S}$. The previous comprises the key difference with SPIN's POR implementation: in SPIN, sets $\widehat{S}$ satisfying Property 2 are always singletons. We have generalised this with an approach that reduces the problem to finding connected components. Note that our approach's applicability is not limited to agents, but extends to, for instance, SPIN as well.

The POR algorithm is run each time successors of a state μ are required during model checking. It first computes sets of operations satisfying **C1** as outlined above and then performs simple checks for **C0**, **C2** (using $\mathfrak{Vis}$), and **C3**. If no set satisfying all conditions can be found, all successors in μ are returned. Like all POR algorithms, the algorithm described is applicable only if the property under investigation is in the *stuttering invariant* subset of LTL: it may not contain $\bigcirc$ operators. Also, it is compatible with on-the-fly model checking, provided the remarks made in [8] are taken into account.

Theorem 2. *Our POR algorithm preserves soundness and completeness.*

Proof (Sketch). The algorithm is, essentially, the algorithm in [4] with a different approach to generating **C1**. *Soundness and completeness thus follow from the ample set method's correctness as proven in Sect. 10.6 of [4] and Lemma 4.* □

5   Implementation and Experience

We have implemented the algorithms discussed in the previous section as extensions to the *interpreter-based* GOAL model checker introduced in [11]. The idea of the interpreter-based approach to agent verification is to implement model checking algorithms on top of an existing agent interpreter. An alternative approach is to encode the semantics of the agent language in a format that an existing model checker can process and to use this existing model checker for actual verification. Interpreter-based model checking, however, has been shown to consume less resources and offers immediate language support without the need for complex translations [11].

With respect to the implementation of reduction techniques, the interpreter-based approach has another benefit: the model checking algorithms implemented on top of the existing agent interpreter can easily be extended with implementations of reduction algorithms. In contrast, if existing model checkers are used for agent verification, such extensions are likely to be less straightforward to implement. As a result, one is bound to use reduction techniques that ship with the existing model checker, but that are not tailored to the agent language that the agent program is written in. It has been shown [2] that generic reduction algorithms may not work well on translated agent programs.

The PBS and POR algorithm discussed are defined in terms of the same relations on operations. From a software engineering point of view, the implementation of these techniques benefits from this in two ways: SHARED-CODE-BASE and RUNTIME-SYNERGY.[8]

---

[8] Note we address the recommendation of [14] that research in state space reduction should not only focus on new techniques, but also on combining existing ones.

SHARED-CODE-BASE — We implemented a library for analysis of action rules and computation of the visibility, enables, and (in)dependence relation. The implementations of the PBS and POR algorithms both use this library.

RUNTIME-SYNERGY — Computation of the visibility, enables, and dependence relation occurs at most once each verification run. Subsequently, the PBS and POR implementations can both use the results of these computations; no duplicate calculations are performed.

To investigate whether our PBS and POR algorithms are able to significantly reduce resource consumption, we have carried out several small experiments involving non-deterministic single-agent systems. In what we call the *blender experiments*, we have investigated an agent whose task is to put bananas and oranges into a blender to make juice. In the *blocks counter experiments*, the subject of verification is an agent that breaks down towers of blocks, while counting to some natural number. Finally, in the *wumpus experiments*, we have model checked agents that must navigate through an unknown maze in search of a heap of gold, while avoiding bottomless pits and a vicious cave animal: the wumpus. With these experiments, we aim at investigating whether PBS and POR algorithms for agent languages like GOAL have the same potential as in traditional model checking. Below, we give a synopsis; details appear in [10].

With respect to PBS, the blender and blocks counter experiments show that the reduction can be significant: the measured decrease of the state space ranged from 75% to 99%, the reduction in runtime (including PBS computation) ranged from 43% to 97%, and the measured reduction in memory consumption (including PBS computation) ranged from 25% to 88%. However, in the wumpus experiment, a reduction in resource consumption was not achieved: in fact, the entire verification procedure took longer to finish with PBS enabled than without PBS, although the difference was less than three seconds for the most complex wumpus agent. The reason is that a wumpus agent's tasks (exploring the cave, grabbing the gold, hunting the wumpus) all influence each other, i.e. all action rules are on a route in the influence graph. Consequently, no action rules are removed by the PBS algorithm, hence no reduction is obtained, despite the spending of resources on its computation. A prerequisite for the PBS algorithm to yield a reduction is, thus, that the property under investigation concerns a task of the agent that is not influenced by its other tasks. This prerequisite is satisfied by the agents in the other two experiments: putting bananas in a blender does not influence putting oranges in a blender (and vice versa), and deconstructing a tower does not influence counting (and vice versa).

Similar to the PBS results, our blender and blocks counter experiments with POR show that this technique can yield significant reductions, particularly if the agent under consideration is (i) *loosely coupled*, meaning that there are few dependencies between the different tasks that it needs to carry out (the case in the blocks counter experiments),[9] or (ii) significantly underspecified (the case in the

---

[9] This is a stronger requirement than the PBS prerequisite regarding influence, because influence is a directed relation (e.g. A can influence B, while B does not influence A), while dependence is undirected (e.g. A depends on B iff B depends on A).

blender experiments). While the former has already been pointed out in existing POR literature, the latter seems specific to the application of POR to agents, as underspecification in imperative languages is rare. Using POR, the measured reduction of the state space ranged from 59% to over 99%, the reduction in runtime (including POR computation) ranged from 34% to 98%, and the measured reduction in memory consumption (including POR computation) ranged from 8% to 50%. As the agents in the wumpus experiments are neither loosely coupled nor underspecified, no reduction is obtained using POR. We speculate that nondeterministic agent programs are, in general, tighter coupled than concurrent imperative systems. Therefore, POR may be less often applicable in an agent context than in traditional model checking. Further investigations are, however, necessary to confirm or disprove this conjecture.

6 Related Work and Conclusion

Related Work. Both PBS and POR have extensively been studied in traditional model checking. An extensive survey with many references is given in [14]. Here, we focus on state space reduction techniques for agent model checking.

To the best of our knowledge, PBS has been studied in an agent context only by Bordini et al. [2,3], who have designed a PBS algorithm for AgentSpeak systems. Their algorithm is based on earlier work on slicing logic programs [16], because *plans* in AgentSpeak are similar to guarded clauses in logic programming. The algorithm of Bordini et al. slices AgentSpeak programs by removing such plans from agents, and is, like other PBS algorithms, based on a graph representation of the program. An important difference between Bordini et al. and our work is that we have defined our PBS algorithm generically, i.e. not tailored to any specific APL. However, we do not consider our effort a generalisation of Bordini et al., because we have not based our PBS algorithm on [16] or [2,3]. Instead, we see our work as a second and independent attempt to applying PBS to agents; it would be interesting to instantiate our framework for AgentSpeak, and compare the performance of the algorithm of Bordini et al. to ours.

To the best of our knowledge, POR has only been studied in an agent context by Lomuscio et al. [12]. While both our work and the work of Lomuscio et al. are based on the ample set method and applied in a context in which a depth-first strategy is used for the generation of the transition system, our approach differs in a number of ways. Most notably, [12] focuses on the verification of *models* of agent-based systems, while we consider verification of actual agent *programs*. Other work in the latter direction is the AIL framework [5] and its model checker AJPF [1]; a comparison between the aforementioned interpreter-based model checker for GOAL and AJPF appears in [11].

Conclusion. We have introduced a framework, based on operations on mental states of agents, that facilitates the definition and implementation of the existing PBS and POR techniques in a unifying way. We have argued that existing state space reduction algorithms do not fit agent programs seamlessly due to the different nature of mental states (compared to variable assignments), and proposed a solution. The resulting definition of read and write sets for agents is the heart of our framework. With these and the relations defined in terms of them, in principle, we can readily reuse existing reduction algorithms. Nevertheless, we have also advanced the theory of PBS and POR to some extent: with respect to PBS, we have a very explicit connection between the algorithm and the transition system (absent in previous contributions), while with respect to POR, we have introduced an alternative heuristic to be used for ample set computation (Property 2). Finally, by defining two different techniques in terms of the same relations, we gain implementation benefits: shared code-base and runtime synergy.

We identify three directions for future work: (i) expanding our experience with both techniques to gain a better understanding of when their application can be beneficial and to what extent, (ii) instantiating the framework for multi-agent systems, and (iii) extending the framework to open systems.

References

1. Bordini, R., Dennis, L., Farwer, B., Fisher, M.: Automated Verification of Multi-Agent Programs. In: Proceedings of ASE, pp. 69–78 (2008)
2. Bordini, R., Fisher, M., Visser, W., Wooldridge, M.: State-Space Reduction Techniques in Agent Verification. In: Proceedings of AAMAS, pp. 896–903 (2004)
3. Bordini, R., Fisher, M., Wooldridge, M., Visser, W.: Property-based Slicing for Agent Verification. Journal of Logic and Computation 19(6), 1385–1425 (2009)
4. Clarke, E., Grumberg, O., Peled, D.: Model Checking. The MIT Press (2000)
5. Dennis, L.A., Farwer, B., Bordini, R.H., Fisher, M., Wooldridge, M.J.: A Common Semantic Basis for BDI Languages. In: Dastani, M., El Fallah Seghrouchni, A., Ricci, A., Winikoff, M. (eds.) ProMAS 2007. LNCS (LNAI), vol. 4908, pp. 124–139. Springer, Heidelberg (2008)
6. Hindriks, K.: Programming Rational Agents in GOAL. In: El Fallah Seghrouchni, A., Dix, J., Dastani, M., Bordini, R. (eds.) Multi-Agent Programming, pp. 119–157. Springer (2009)
7. Holzmann, G.: The SPIN Model Checker. Addison-Wesley (2003)
8. Holzmann, G., Peled, D., Yannakakis, M.: On Nested Depth First Search. In: Grégoire, J.C., Holzmann, G., Peled, D. (eds.) The SPIN Verification System, DIMACS, vol. 32, pp. 23–31. American Mathematical Society (1997)
9. Hopcroft, J., Tarjan, R.: Efficient Algorithms for Graph Manipulation. Tech. Rep. STAN-CS-71-207, Stanford University (1971)
10. Jongmans, S.-S.T.Q.: Model Checking Goal Agents. Master's thesis, Delft University of Technology (2010)
11. Jongmans, S.-S.T.Q., Hindriks, K.V., van Riemsdijk, M.B.: Model Checking Agent Programs by Using the Program Interpreter. In: Dix, J., Leite, J., Governatori, G., Jamroga, W. (eds.) CLIMA XI. LNCS, vol. 6245, pp. 219–237. Springer, Heidelberg (2010)
12. Lomuscio, A., Penczek, W., Qu, H.: Partial Order Reductions for Model Checking Temporal-epistemic Logics over Interleaved Multi-agent Systems. Fundamenta Informaticae 101(1-2), 71–90 (2010)

13. Lomuscio, A., Raimondi, F.: MCMAS: A Model Checker for Multi-agent Systems. In: Hermanns, H., Palsberg, J. (eds.) TACAS 2006. LNCS, vol. 3920, pp. 450–454. Springer, Heidelberg (2006)
14. Pelánek, R.: Fighting State Space Explosion: Review and Evaluation. In: Cofer, D., Fantechi, A. (eds.) FMICS 2008. LNCS, vol. 5596, pp. 37–52. Springer, Heidelberg (2009)
15. Tip, F.: A Survey of Program Slicing Techniques. Tech. Rep. CS-R9438, Centrum Wiskunde & Informatica (1994)
16. Zhao, J., Cheng, J., Ushijima, K.: Literal Dependence Net and Its Use in Concurrent Logic Programming Environment. In: Proceedings of Workshop on Parallel Logic Programming, pp. 127–141 (1994)

Part IV

Multi-Agent Programming
Contest

The Multi-agent Programming Contest 2011: A Résumé

Tristan Behrens[1], Michael Köster[1], Federico Schlesinger[1],
Jürgen Dix[1], and Jomi F. Hübner[2]

[1] Department of Informatics, Clausthal University of Technology,
Julius-Albert-Str. 4, Clausthal-Zellerfeld 38678, Germany
{dix,behrens}@in.tu-clausthal.de,
{michael.koester,federico.schlesinger}@tu-clausthal.de
[2] Department of Automation and Systems Engineering,
Federal University of Santa Catarina,
P.O. Box 476, Florianópolis, SC, 88040-900, Brasil
jomi@das.ufsc.br

Abstract. The Multi-Agent Programming Contest is an annual AI competition aiming at comparing deliberative techniques for problem solving, that are based on formal approaches and computational logics. In 2011 the Contest was held for the seventh time and witnessed the introduction of the new *agents on Mars* scenario. We give an overview of the Contest in general but concentrate on the agents on Mars scenario. We also provide empirical results that we received before, during and after the tournament.

1 Introduction

In this paper, we give a comprehensive overview of the Multi-Agent Programming Contest[1] 2011. The Contest is an annual international event that has started in 2005. In 2011 the competition was organized and held for the seventh time. The Contest is an attempt to stimulate research in the field of programming multi-agent system by 1) identifying key problems, 2) collecting suitable benchmarks, and 3) gathering test cases which require and enforce coordinated action that can serve as milestones for testing multi-agent programming languages, platforms and tools. Research communities in general benefit from competitions that attempt to evaluate different aspects of the systems under consideration and furthermore allow for comparing state of the art systems, act as a driver and catalyst for developments and pose challenging research problems.

In this paper we

- introduce the Contest and its infrastructure,
- present and elaborate on the 2011 scenario,
- introduce the nine teams that took part in the tournament, and
- present results and findings acquired before, during and after the tournament.

---

[1] http://multiagentcontest.org

L.A. Dennis, O. Boissier, and R.H. Bordini (Eds.): ProMAS 2011, LNCS 7217, pp. 155–172, 2012.

2   Related Work

The Multi-Agent Programming Contest has generated several publications over the years [9,10,11,3,1]. Similar contests, competitions and challenges are *Google's AI challenge*[2], the *AI-MAS Winter Olympics*[3], the *Starcraft AI Competition*[4], the *Mario AI Championship*[5], the *ORTS competition*[6], and the *Planning Competition*[7]. Every such competition rests in its own research niche. Our Contest has been designed for problem solving approaches, that are based on formal approaches and computational logics.

3   The Multi-agent Programming Contest

The Contest's main focus lies on developing deliberative techniques for problem solving based on formal approaches and computational logics [7,8]. In the following, we provide a brief overview of the Contest's history. We refer to [2] for a full account on the Contest's history. Since its first manifestation in 2005 we witnessed four distinct phases. The first phase was marked by food gatherers scenario [9]. The goal was to implement a multi-agent system that was populated by agents that were programmed to find and collect food items, which were supposed to be stored in a special depot. 2005 was the only year in which we required from the participants to implement the agents and the environment. In the subsequent edition the organizers provided the environment.

The year 2006 both marked the beginning of the gold miners scenario [10] phase, which ended in 2007, and the introduction of the *MASSim* platform: A platform for executing the Contest tournaments. The overall task of the gold miners scenario was to implement agents that were situated in a grid-like world. This environment is semi accessible, provides agents with local information and assigns each agent a distinct sphere of influence. The tournament consisted of several simulations, whereas in each simulation two teams competed for gold. The team that gathered the highest number of gold items after a fixed number of steps, won the simulation. The core problems of the gold miners scenario were obstacle avoidance, environment exploration and efficient path planning.

The cows and cowboys scenario was used in 2008 to 2010 and has been designed to enforce cooperative behaviors. Again, the environments topology was represented by a grid that contained obstacles. On top of that the environment contained a population of simulated cows. Cows were active entities that were steered by a flocking algorithm. The goal was to arrange agents in a manner that scared cows into special areas, called corrals, in order to get points. While still maintaining the core tasks of environment exploration and path planning, we also made the use of cooperative strategies an obligation.

---

[2] http://aichallenge.org/
[3] http://www.aiolympics.ro/
[4] http://eis.ucsc.edu/StarCraftAICompetition
[5] http://www.marioai.org/
[6] http://skatgame.net/mburo/orts/
[7] http://ipc.icaps-conference.org/

The agents on Mars scenario, which we discuss in this paper, was introduced in 2011 [4]. In short, we have generalized the environment topology to a weighted graph. Agents were expected to cooperatively establish a graph covering while standing their ground in an adversarial setting and reaching achievements.

4   The MASSim Platform

The *MASSim* (*Multi-Agent Systems Simulation*) platform facilitates a testbed environment implemented in Java (see [4] for technical details). Its aim is the fair evaluation of coordination and cooperation approaches via round based game simulations. Individual agents are embodied in a dynamic shared environment that is an open, internet-based simulation platform. *MASSim* decouples the environment from the agent implementation, thus lowering the technical threshold for entering the Contest. Agent-environment connections are facilitated by TCP/IP sockets, which relay simple XML-based messages for agent-environment interaction by means of sensing and acting. Scenarios in general are plug-ins. *MASSim* instantiates such plug-ins and, on top of that, executes whole tournaments, which means scheduling and executing single simulations while maintaining an overview of the performance of the participating agents. *MASSim* also provides means for both online and offline visualization. While the former can be used by the general audience to monitor each simulation, the latter is more useful for the participants to evaluate their strategies after the tournament. *MASSim* can also he highly customized via config files.

Figure 1 summarizes the technical infrastructure of *MASSim*. The platform consists of the following components:

- The **core** is the central component that coordinates the interaction of the other components and implements the tournament scheduler.
- The **simulation plug-in** describes a discrete game and logically contains the environment of the agents. This component is based on a plug-in architecture that allows the implementation and use of new scenarios in a simple and straightforward manner.
- The **agent-server communication component** manages the communication between the server and the agents. The communication relies on the exchange of XML messages of moderate complexity. The agents receive percepts and can act in the environment by encoding their actions as XML messages and relaying them to the server.
- The **teams of agents** connect to the server via TCP/IP, and communicate using the above-mentioned XML-messages.
- The **visualization component** renders each state of the evolution of the environment to a SVG file. The SVG files can then be viewed as videos.
- The **web server** provides the online-monitoring functionality. Participants can use the web interface to monitor the progress of a tournament, including the current tournament results and the ongoing matches and simulations.
- The **scenario monitor** is an application that allows for an online visualization during development and is provided for debugging purposes.

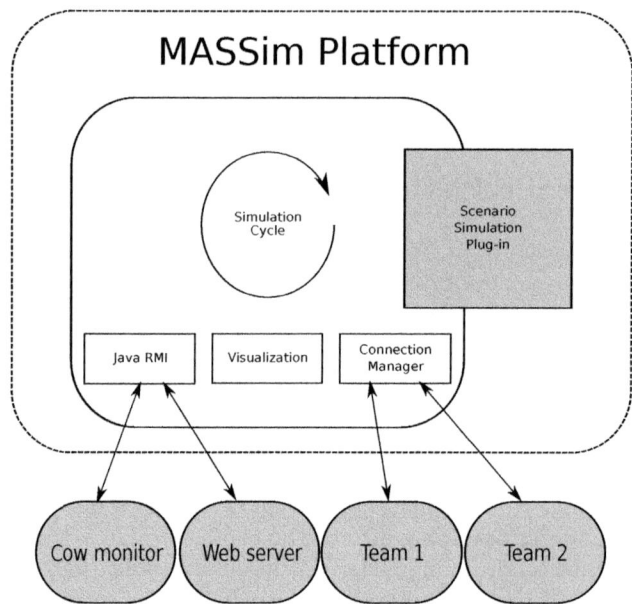

Fig. 1. Schematic view of the *MASSim* architecture

5   MAPC 2011: Agents on Mars

In the following we will focus on three things: Firstly, we give an introduction of the agents on Mars scenario. Secondly, we elaborate on the developing phase. And thirdly, we discuss the tournament itself, while providing a short introduction and comparison of the participating teams and examining the results of the simulations.

The design of the agents on Mars scenario was fueled by a couple of motivating factors. The first one was the desire to increase of complexity by adding more actions. The evolution of the Contest showed a steady erosion of agents' effectoric capabilities. That is, the set of available actions decreased over time, resulting in the fact that the cows and cowboys scenario only featured movement actions. This basically reduced all planning efforts to a path planning problem. Additionally the introduction of roles, that is assigning different sets of available actions to different agents, has been a matter of discussion in the past. The introduction of different roles was expected to yield an increase in complexity and a challenge for team coordination and agent cooperation. Also, adding another dimension for winning beyond fulfilling only a single task, has been a desideratum for some time. And finally, after three manifestations of the cows and cowboys scenario it was rather naturally to come up with a new one, that is the agents on Mars scenario that we introduce now.

5.1   The Scenario

It is now a tradition to accompany the technical description of each scenario with a motivating little story:

In the year 2033 mankind finally populates Mars. While in the beginning the settlers received food and water from transport ships sent from earth shortly afterwards – because of the outer space pirates – sending these ships became too dangerous and expensive. Also, there were rumors going around that somebody actually found water on Mars below the surface. Soon the settlers started to develop autonomous intelligent agents, so-called All Terrain Planetary Vehicles (ATPV), to search for water wells. The World Emperor – enervated by the pirates – decided to strengthen the search for water wells by paying money for certain achievements. Sadly, this resulted in sabotage among the different groups of settlers.

Now, the task of your agents is to find the best water wells and occupy the best zones of Mars. Sometimes they have to sabotage their rivals to achieve their goal (while the opponents will most probably do the same) or to defend themselves. Of course the agents' vehicle pool contains specific vehicles, some of them have special sensors, some of them are faster and some of them have sabotage devices on board.

Last but not least, your team also contains special experts, the repairer agents, that are capable of fixing agents that are disabled. In general, each agent has a special expert knowledge and is thus the only one being able to perform a certain action. So your agents have to find ways to cooperate and coordinate themselves.

The environment's topology is constituted by a weighted graph. Each vertex has a unique identifier and a number that indicates its value. Each edge on the other hand has a number that represents the costs of moving from one of its vertices to the other. These vertex-values are crucial for calculating the value of zones. A zone is a subgraph that is covered by a team of agents according to an coloring algorithm that is based on a domination principle. Several agents can stand on a single vertex. If a set of agents dominates such a vertex by numbers, the vertex gets the color of the dominating team. A previously uncolored vertex that has a majority of neighbors with a specific color, inherits this color as well. Finally, if the overall graph contains a colored subgraph that constitutes a frontier or border, all the nodes that are inside this border is colored as well. This means that agents can color or cover a subgraph that has more vertices than the number of agents. Figure 2 show a screenshot of a relatively small map, depicting, amongst other things, the graph coloring.

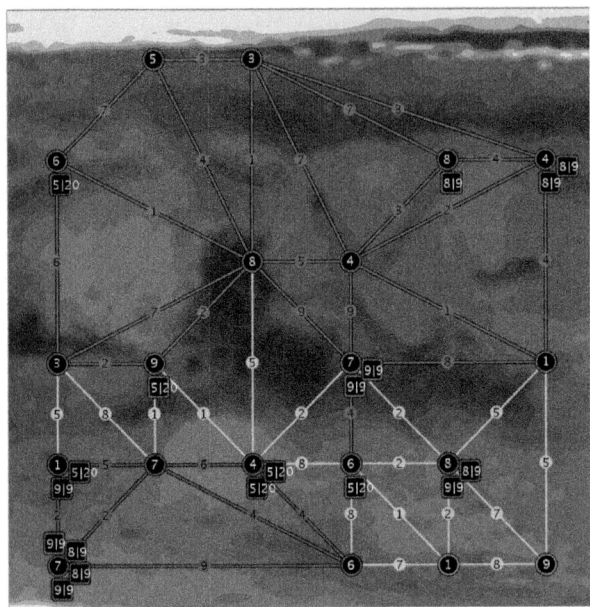

Fig. 2. A screenshot of the agents on Mars scenario

Before elaborating on the agent roles we have to specify the effectoric capabilities of the agents. A, vehicle during the simulation, has a state that is defined by its position on the map, its current energy available for executing actions and its current health. On top of that, each team has a budget for equipping the vehicles during the simulation. These actions[8] are defined by the scenario:

- skip is the nop-action, which does not change the state of the environment,
- recharge increases the current energy of a vehicle by a fixed factor and can be performed at any time without costs,
- attack decreases the health of an opponent, standing on the same vertex, if successfully executed and decreases the current energy of the attacker,
- parry parries an attack and decreases the energy of the defending agent,
- goto moves the vehicle to a neighboring vertex while decreasing its energy by the weight of the traversed edge,
- probe yields the exact value of the vertex the vehicle is standing on and decreases the probing vehicle's energy
- survey yields the exact weights of visible edges while decreasing the energy
- inspect costs energy and yields the internals of all visible opponents,
- buy equips the vehicle with new components, which increase its performance, and cost money, and
- repair repairs a teammate, which again costs energy.

---

[8] Of course, all the actions that cost energy will fail if the vehicle under consideration does not have enough.

We have defined five different roles. Each team consists of two vehicles for each role, that is a total of ten vehicles per team. Each role defines the vehicle's internals and its capabilities. The roles differ in energy, health, strength and visibility range. The effectoric capabilities are as follows:

- **explorer** can skip, move to a vertex, probe a vertex, survey visible edges, buy equipment and recharge its energy,
- **repairer** can skip, move to a vertex, parry an attack, survey visible edges, buy equipment, repair a teammate and recharge its energy,
- **saboteur** can skip, move to a vertex, parry an attack, survey visible edges, buy equipment, attack an opponent and recharge its energy,
- **sentinel** can skip, move to a vertex, parry an attack, survey visible edges, buy equipment and recharge its energy,
- **inspector** can skip, move to a vertex, inspect visible opponents, survey visible edges, buy equipment and recharge its energy.

Achievements are tasks that, if fulfilled, contribute to the teams' budgets. We have defined a set of achievements that includes having zones with fixed values, inspecting a specific number of vehicles, probing a number of vertices, surveying a fixed number of edges and successfully performing and parrying a number of attacks.

In each step, each vehicle is provided with its currently available percepts:

- the state of the simulation, i.e. the current step,
- the state of the team, i.e. the current scores and money,
- the state of itself, i.e. its internals,
- all visible vertices, i.e. identifier and team,
- all visible edges, i.e. their vertices' identifiers,
- all visible vehicles, i.e. their identifier, vertices and team,
- probed vertices, i.e. their identifier and values,
- surveyed edges, i.e. their vertices' identifiers and weights, and
- inspected vehicles, i.e. their identifiers, vertices, teams and internals.

After sending percepts, the server grants some time for deliberation. After that the new state is computed. The simulation state transition is as follows:

1. collect all actions from the agents,
2. let each action fail with a specific probability,
3. execute all remaining `attack` and `parry` actions,
4. determine disabled agents,
5. execute all remaining actions,
6. prepare percepts,
7. deliver the percepts.

The introduction of the agents on Mars scenario was also accompanied by the release of an environment interface that has been developed to be compatible with the *environment interface standard* [6]. This standard allows java based problem solving approaches to make use of a jar-file provided by the organizers that facilitated connecting to and communicating with the *MASSim* server. This is done my mapping the whole communication to Java-method invocations and callbacks.

5.2   Before the Tournament: Designing, Implementing, Testing and Balancing

The preparations for 2011 edition of the Multi-Agent Programming Contest began with the decision to develop a new scenario. The goal was to keep the interest in the Contest fresh, and to try to encourage more use of certain key aspects of MAS-programming, like communication, team coordination, autonomy, reactiveness, et cetera. A lot of effort was required to ensure that the new scenario was interesting, fair, and well balanced, and that it did not compromise the technical quality standards set by the previous Multi-Agent Programming Contest editions.

There were a few phases in the design of the game. After the first brainstorming and discussion among the organizers, a simplistic standalone prototype was developed in which the agents and the execution of the simulation were manually controlled. The prototype featured four teams competing in a single map, and at this stage agents could only execute the actions goto and attack. The topology of the map was, as in the final version, represented by a weighted graph, although completely randomly generated.

One of the most important characteristics that this first prototype allowed us to test was the very goal of the game, i.e., the zone conquering mechanism. Several different approaches to what to consider a *zone* were implemented and compared before we could fine-tune to the chosen algorithm. We believe that it is very important for the participants to be able to watch the simulations in real time and instantly understand what is going on; this was a defining factor in favor of the chosen algorithm: Although it may not seem trivial, it is rather intuitive to visualize. Furthermore, it only relies in the graph's topology and does not make use of the nodes' cartesian coordinates, used for drawing but not intended to be passed to agents.

The scenario was then presented to the community, making the prototype available. We received a lot of fruitful feedback. A newer version of the game introduced the rest of the actions, the different roles for the agents, and the notion of achievements. At this point the new scenario was stable enough to move from the standalone prototype to a *MASSim* implementation. The next phase was about balancing all the parameters that affected the game, like the agents' internals, the costs of actions, and the value of achievements.

For the balancing and testing of the game, not only we relied on feedback from the community, but we also held a course on multi-agent programming at Clausthal University of Technology in which students had to implement fully functional teams to compete among each other[9]. From their matches we got a big insight of things that could be improved. For example, it was pointed out that the energy of agents was rather low, and had to use the recharge action extremely often, especially when moving around. Another very important discovery was that the achievements' score was very high, resulting in a surprisingly large difference in the final score in favor of a team that didn't use the buy action over a team that spent most of the achievement points at the moment of getting

---

[9] One of the two teams was *HempelsSofa*, that took part in the Contest out of competition.

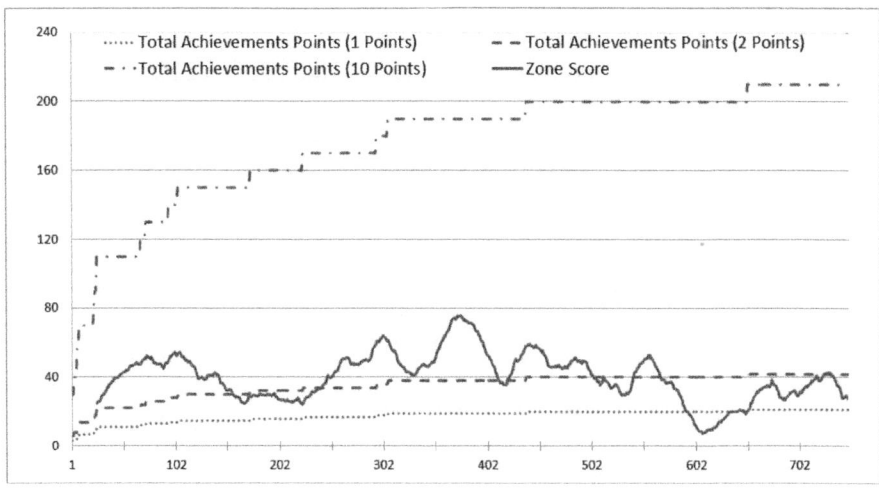

Fig. 3. Balancing zone score with achievement points

them, even when the performance regarding the zone conquering was better for the latter. Figure 3 was extracted from one of these matches. It shows the evolution of the Zone Score for one team, and the points that the team would have earned from achievement points had it not spent them, assuming 10 points per achievement, 2 points per achievement and 1 point per achievement. It can be clearly seen that 10 points per achievement, as was our original approach, seems exaggerated, whereas awarding only 1 point per achievement would appear to have very little influence in the final score. The final decision was to award 2 points per achievement during the tournament. The cost of the buying action was modified accordingly.

Some members of the community raised the issue of fairness. They were concerned that the randomness in the generation of the map and placement of the agents, as well as having four teams competing in the same simulation, could favor one of the teams and not reflex the actual performance. Since we did not have enough time to come up with a good strategy to make this configuration fair and prove its fairness, we rolled back to having only two teams per simulation, in a symmetrical environment with symmetrical placement of agents. Nevertheless, we believe that the idea simulations with more than two teams is worth revising for future editions.

5.3   The Tournament: Participants and Results

In total nine teams from all around the world took part in the tournament (see Table 1). Full introductions of the teams can be found in [5] and in the papers included in this volume.

The *d3lp0r* team from Universidad Nacional del Sur, Argentina, was implemented to show that argumentation via defeasible logic programming can be

Table 1. Participants overview

Team	Affiliation	Language
d3lp0r	Universidad Nacional del Sur, Argentina	Prolog/Python
HactarV2	TU Delft, Netherlands	GOAL
HempelsSofa[9]	Universität Göttingen, Germany	Java
Nargel	Arak University, Iran	Java/JADE
Python-DTU	Technical University of Denmark	Python
Simurgh	Arak University, Iran	Java/JADE
Sorena	Arak University, Iran	JACK
TUB	TU Berlin, Germany	JIAC V
UCD Bogtrotters	University College Dublin, Ireland	AgentFactory

applied in a multi-agent gaming situation. It has been implemented using Python, Prolog and DeLP. The solution is a decentralized architecture, where each agent runs as an individual process and percepts are shared via a broadcasting mechanism with a minimal complexity. This coordination mechanism is facilitated by a perception server that gathers and distributes all relevant percepts. Decision making takes place on an individual agent level and has no centralized characteristics. The team's main strategy is to detect profitable zones based on the data collected about explored vertices and position the agents correctly to maintain, defend and expand the zones.

The *HactarV2* team from TU Delft, Netherlands, was implemented using the GOAL agent-oriented programming language with Prolog as the knowledge representation language. The team follows a decentralized strategy based on an implicit coordination mechanism, where agents predict the actions that other agents perform and base their own choice of actions on that prediction. The agents share all data about the map and opponents with each other, while neither using a centralized information store nor a central coordination manager. The teams main strategy is to firstly compute the zone with the highest value and secondly building and maintaining a swarm of agents around the node with the highest value.

HempelsSofa[9] has been developed at Göttingen University. The team is based on a solution that has been implemented during a course on multi-agent programming, held at Clausthal University of Technology. The agents were developed in Java using a simplified architecture that allows for an explicit mental state and inter agent communication. All agents are executed in a single process and each agent has access to a shared world model that is updated every time and agent perceives something.

Python-DTU from Technical University of Denmark is based on an auction based agreement approach and has been implemented in Python. The solution is decentralized, allowing agents to share percepts through shared data structures and coordinate their actions via distributed algorithms. Agents share all new percepts in order to keep the agents' internal world models identical. In the first ten percent of each simulation the team explores the map and inspects the opponents. After that, a valuable zone is conquered and maintained while letting saboteurs attack and repairers repair. Valuable zone detection is facilitated by firstly selecting the most valuable known vertex and then focussing on vertices around the selected one. Communication and coordination involves placing bids on different goals and then executing an auction-based agreement algorithm.

Team *Nargel* from Arak University, Iran, is a true multi-agent system developed using Java for agent behaviors and JADE for agent communication. The performance of the agents was on a level that did not require any distribution of agents on different machines. The team strategy is based on the intent to conquer zones, while also disturbing the opponent's ones. The disturbing behavior is more successful than the zone making strategy. Agents share their acquired knowledge by means of inter-agent communication only and thus do not have a centralized pool if information. On top of that, intentions are also on an individual agent level, thus resulting in a decentralized coordination approach.

The *Simurgh* team, also from Arak University, made use of Java as an agent implementation language, while using the Gaia methodology for analysis and design. The team uses a decentralized coordination and cooperation mechanism, in which agents share their percepts via a shared communication channel. Agents autonomously generate goals based on their knowledge. Goals in conflict are resolved. Each agent is executed in its own thread and has its own world model. The agents are divided into three groups. The zone holders are responsible for creating and maintaining zones using a scattering algorithm. The world explorers intent to complete their world model quickly. And the repairers strive to repair disabled agents as soon as possible.

Sorena is the third team from Arak University. The developers used the Prometheus methodology for the system specification and the JACK agent platform for actually implementing and executing the agents.

The *TUB* team comes from Berlin Technical University. The team's development has been done by roughly following the JIAC methodology. The team is completely decentralized, while each agent is perfectly capable of performing each role. Usually one agent is responsible for zoning and agents position themselves on the map using a simple voting protocol. Agents share all their percepts, which, although having a high complexity, worked perfectly for the small team. The team makes use of both implicit and explicit coordination. Implicit coordination is considered to be achieved by sharing intentions. Explicit coordination, however, is only used for the collaboration of inspectors and saboteurs. From the beginning each agent follows its own achievement collections strategy. The zone score on the other hand is locally optimized by letting agents move to the next node that improves the zone.

The *UCD Bogtrotters* team from University College Dublin, Ireland, has been implemented using the AF-TeleoReactive and AF-AgentSpeak multi-agent programming languages running on the AgentFactory platform. The overall team strategy involves a leader agent, which assigns tasks to other agents, and platform services for information sharing. Finding zones is facilitated by a simple clustering algorithm. The team combines a set of role dependent strategies and the overall zone creation strategy.

The tournament took place from 5th to 9th of September 2011. Each day every team played against two other teams so that in the end all teams played against all others. We started the tournament each morning at 10 am and finished at around 6 pm. A match between two teams consisted of the 3 same simulations only differing in the size of the graph. For a win the team got 3 points and for a draw 1 point. The results of this year's Contest are depicted in Table 2.

Table 2. Results

Pos.	Team	Score		Difference	Points
1	HactarV2	2,979,591 :	734,185	2,245,406	72
2	Python-DTU	3,468,448 :	745,940	2,722,508	60
3	TUB	2,835,401 :	914,883	1,920,518	57
4	UCDBogtrotters	2,379,663 :	1,459,391	920,272	45
5	HempelsSofa[9]	1,243,262 :	2,185,634	-942,372	36
6	Simurgh	928,893 :	2,219,281	-1,290,388	18
7	Sorena	888,631 :	2,366,805	-1,478,174	15
8	d3lp0r	888,837 :	3,821,088	-2,932,251	15
9	Nargel	765,296 :	1,930,815	-1,165,519	6

The team *HactarV2* did not loose a single match and achieved almost 3 million points. The second-place finisher *Python-DTU* scored half a million points more but lost 3 simulations against *HactarV2* and 1 simulation against *TUB*. Almost on the same level was *TUB*: They lost 3 matches against *HactarV2* and 2 simulations against *Python-DTU*. In the mid-table were *HempelsSofa* and *UCDBogtrotters*. While the latter still had a positive difference the former had already more than 1 million negative points. The reason for that was the low performance on the first day due to a bug in the team's implementation. Finally, the last four teams had a negative score concerning the difference of points. They did not win against the five better placed teams.

5.4   Participants' Team Quality and Stability

In order to analyze the quality and stability of the teams – and to a certain extent also the stability of the platforms – we summed up the number of actions sent by an agent in time (i.e., in two seconds) and the actions that failed due to lack of time. The results are shown in Table 3. Since each team had the opportunity to test the network connection (and especially the network bandwidth) two weeks before in some test matches, these results cannot only give us some hints regarding the overall performance but also some indications concerning the quality and stability of each agent team. Together with the experiments we made throughout the Contest, i.e., checking the network ping and bandwidth, we can conclude the following:

The first three teams *HactarV2*, *Python-DTU* and *TUB* did not have any problems sending actions in the two second time interval. Their network connection was good, but more important – as the Contest results (Tab. 2)

Table 3. Actions not sent in time

Team	Day 1	Day 2	Day 3	Day 4	All
HactarV2	0,67%	0,10%	0%	0%	0,19%
Python-DTU	0%	0,19%	0%	0%	0,05%
TUB	0,03%	0,30%	0,11%	1,08%	0,38%
UCDBogtrotters	39,51%	5,47%	1,55%	0,64%	11,79%
HempelsSofa	8,10%	0,03%	0,08%	4,57%	3,20%
Simurgh	41,14%	42,47%	12,63%	3,03%	24,82%
Sorena	1,85%	6,58%	0,55%	0,37%	2,34%
d3lp0r	29,42%	13,32%	16,79%	0,54%	15,02%
Nargel	6,24%	0,45%	0,91%	1,10%	2,18%

show - their agents were able to process the percepts sent by our server and to provide a useful answer in time.

The *UCDBogtrotters* had some problems (a bug in the code of the agents) on the first day. After fixing it the agents were still too slow sometimes. Additionally, the explorer agents as well as the inspector agents tried to execute the parry-action which was not allowed for these rules. For this reason we argue that the stability was quite okay but the code quality was not perfect.

HempelsSofa had a serious bug at day one and the team performed very bad. The bug was caused by not testing the agent team with the right credentials for the tournament. Afterwards the response time was good. Thus, the quality and stability was okay, but the testing routines failed.

The Iranian teams *Simurgh*, *Nargel* and *Sorena* faced some network bandwidth problems in the test matches. However, they improved there code and/or used some computers from different countries for the real Contest. Nevertheless they did not perform well. The results of *Simurgh* – especially when taking into account that they were only sending 60 percent of actions in time for the first two days – were still okay but the code had some major flaws: The explorers and inspectors tried to execute the *parry*-action which was not allowed for these rules. The stability and code quality of *Nargel* and *Sorena* can be classified as medium since on day 1 respectively day 2 the teams had some connection problems.

d3lp0r finally implemented the communication protocol between the server and the agent teams in the wrong way. Their agents were not able to attack other agents if the name of the opponent was starting with an upper case later. Aside, only at the very last day they were able to send enough actions in time. Thus we infer that both, the code quality as well as the stability was low. The results attest this claim as well.

5.5   Overview of the Teams' Strategies

In this section, we describe the overall behavior of each agent implementing one of the five roles. In order to improve the readability we will combine the data from all matches and describe only the general properties of these roles. Additionally, we will focus on the five teams *HactarV2, Python-DTU, TUB, UCDBogtrotters*

Table 4. HactarV2 vs. Python-DTU – HactarV23 repairer. The buy action has not been performed at all.

Action	Frequency	Success Rate	Overall Rate	Overall Success Rate
buy	-	-	-	-
goto	69 of 69	100,00%	9,20%	9,20%
parry	0 of 2	0,00%	0,27%	0,00%
recharge	646 of 646	100,00%	86,13%	86,13%
repair	8 of 8	100,00%	1,07%	1,07%
skip	0 of 5	0,00%	0,67%	0,00%
survey	20 of 20	100,00%	2,67%	2,67%

and *Simurgh*. For a detailed description of the strategies we refer to the technical report [5] and to the papers of the four teams published in this book. An example for the repairer agent of team *HactarV2* is shown in Tab. 4. The Status can be either "not used" if the action was not used at all or "not allowed" if the action if the action is not allowed to be performed by that particular role. "Action" refers to the name of the action and "Frequency" to the amount of successful and not successful executions. The overall rate tells us how often this action was executed in comparison to all other actions and the last column shows how often this action was used successfully.

In the following, we describe the behavior of each role for each team. Note, that the values describe the percentage of used actions on average, so they do not sum up to 100. However, the values reflect the real values quite accurately.

HactarV2. The explorer used mainly the actions recharge and goto. 55% of all executed actions where the recharge actions (against *Python-DTU* it was even more than 80%) and approximately 30% the goto-action. The survey-action was only used 1-2%. The buy-action was not used once and the probe-action was executed 5%. All actions that were tried to execute were also successfully executed. The **repairer** did not buy anything either and executed goto in 30% of the cases. This action was always successful. The action parry was executed 6% but only one out of four was successful. 53% of all actions were the recharge. repair was used in 8% and survey in 2%. The saboteur used 20% the goto action. parry was not used, survey less than 1% and buy just 1%, attack 41%. and recharge 35%. The sentinel executed the goto-action in 29% the cases. parry (5%), survey (2%) and buy (not used) were almost never used. The recharge-rate was around 64%. The inspector used the action goto in 36% the cases. recharge was done 56% and inspect (4%) and survey (1%) were almost never used. The action buy was not used at all.

In summary, only the saboteur was buying new equipment. Additionally, it was using its special action attack a lot. The other agents were walking around and using their special actions only from time to time.

Python-DTU. The explorer used recharge a lot (85%). And the goto in 10% the cases. The action survey was executed less than 1%. buy was never used and probe in 4 of 100 times. The **repairer** did not use buy and parry.goto was executed 11%, recharge 51%. repair 35% and survey almost never (1%). The saboteur did not use parry or survey and almost never buy (less than 1%). goto (15%) , attack (20%) and recharge (47%) were used more often. The sentinel was mostly only recharging (recharge 77%). buy was not used, parry in 2% the cases and survey just in 4%. The action goto was the second most used action (12%). The inspector was recharging a lot (84%). Otherwise it was running around (goto 12%). inspect (less than 1%), (survey 2%) and buy (0%) were rarely used.

The saboteur was the only one buying new equipment but even this role did not use it a lot. The repairer repaired a lot of agents. All other agents were recharging quite often.

TUB. The explorer used recharge just in 34% the cases. The most often executed action was goto (52%). survey (5%) and probe (7%) were used to analyze the topology. However, the agent did not try to improve its values, i.e., the action buy was never used. The repairer did not execute buy nor parry. Also survey was used in less than 1%. Instead it was trying to repair (29%) other agents. Therefore it had to go the agents (goto 33%) and sometimes to recharge (33%). The saboteur did not try to defend itself (parry was never used), and did not analyze the topology (survey less than 1%). buy was only used in 1% the cases. Instead it tried to find opponents (goto 20%) and attack (32%) them. The recharge-rate was around 36%. The sentinel Did not execute parry or buy and almost never tried to survey (1%). But it was moving a lot goto 54% and recharging (recharge 44%) when necessary. The inspector, finally, was walking around (goto 55%) and recharging (recharge 43%). The inspect-acton was used – as well as survey – less than 1% and buy was not used at all.

The agents of team *TUB* were walking around quite often, the repairer was working very well. The saboteur tried to find and deactivate the opponents. However, the team did not try to improve their agents by buying new things.

UCDBogtrotters. This team had some problems with the connection, so their agents were sending invalid actions (or no actions in time) quite often. The explorer executed recharge in 43% the cases, goto in 23%. survey only 2% as well as probe. The buy-action was never used. parry not allowed but tried to use 7%. The **repairer** bought in less than 1% the cases something. It was going around sometimes (goto 7%) and trying to defend itself (parry 24%). recharge was used 33 of 100 times. The actual repair was executed in 14 out of 100 actions. survey, finally, was almost never used (less than 1%). The saboteur was walking around (goto 27%), trying to attack 14% others. parry was used just in one match but was never successful due to lack of energy. survey was executed in less than 1% the cases. buy only 1%, recharge quite often (24%). The sentinel was not really working (a lot of invalid messages) (goto 11%, parry 8%, survey less than 2%,buy less than 1%, recharge 51%). The inspector was going around (goto 17%) trying to inspect other agents (inspect 3%) but did not buy anything. Also the survey was almost never used (less than 1%). Instead recharge was the main action (42%). However, this agent had some bug because

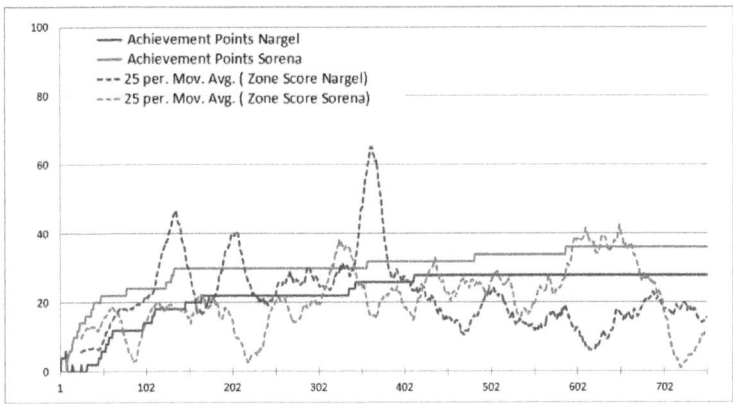

Fig. 4. Sorena against Nargel

it was sending a lot of invalid messages and even tried to parry although it was not allowed for this role.

Simurgh. Since the team *Simurgh* was not sending actions in time for the first two days, we only present the data from the one match against *HactarV2*. The explorer recharged in 17% the cases and was going around a lot (goto 38%). The survey-action was executed 4%. probe in 11 of 100 actions. buy was never used but parry (although not allowed) was tried to use in this match. The repairer did not buy anything either but tried to defend itself (parry 8%). If not attacked it was searching for agents to repair (goto 15%) and repaired them (repair 21%). When energy was missing it was recharging (recharge 32%). Finally, the survey-action was executed in less than 1% the cases. The saboteur did not try to defend itself (parry was not used), and did rarely attack (12%). Aside, the goto (12%) and recharge (16%) were the main actions. survey (less than 1%) and buy (less than 1%) were almost never used. These two agents did not that often send actions in time. The sentinel was just going around (goto 35%), defending itself when necessary (parry 4%), surveying the topology (survey 1%) and recharging sometimes (recharge 39%). buy was not used. Lastly, the inspector walked around (goto 35%) and recharged (recharge 41%) whenever lacking energy. inspect was executed in less than 1% cases. This also hold for survey (1%). The action buy was not used. Additionally, parry was tried to use in 4% the cases although forbidden by the role.

5.6   Two Interesting Matches

To conclude this section, we provide examples of how teams performed during the simulations. We consider two matches, that is *Sorena* against *Nargel* and *HactarV2* versus *Python-DTU*. Again, an exhaustive comparison is beyond the scope of this paper.

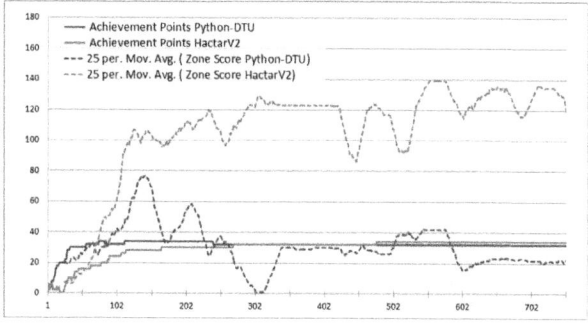

Fig. 5. HactarV2 against Python-DTU

Figure 4 shows a match between Sorena and Nargel. The diagram shows the achievement points and the zones scores of both teams and how these evolve over time. Peaks in the zones scores graph correspond to situation in which team have conquered a very valuable zone. This match is especially interesting because it is the only one in which the achievements points decided the winner.

Figure 5, however, shows a match between HactarV2 and Python-DTU. Both team conquer zones in the first 100 steps. While HactarV2 manages to maintain or even extend its zones over time, Python-DTU fails to do so. On the other hand, both teams gather and maintain their achievement points without problems. HactarV2, does not buy any items, nut Python-DTU does.

6   Summary, Conclusion and Future Work

This paper was supposed to provide an overview of the Multi-Agent Programming Contest. We have introduced the Contest in general and provided a historical summary. The Contest went through several phases, whereas the agents on Mars scenario currently marks the latest one. We provided a brief but adequate elaboration on this scenario, which was followed by an evaluation of the 2011 tournament. We have introduced the teams that took part and evaluated their performance.

Of course there exist multiple paths for possible future work. We could focus on improving existing and developing new automatic means for evaluating single simulations, individual matches and whole tournaments. What we have shown in this paper can be considered to be a first serious approximation of such facilities.

Also, it would be interesting to assess if it would be beneficial to steer the Contest into a more specialized direction in order to strengthen its niche in the research ecology. This includes but is not limited to focussing on the planning aspect of the competition, leaving behind path planning as the main facet of agent deliberation.

On top of that, we could focus on the massive agents direction, with a lot of agents with different roles and thus different capabilities. This would allow us to take into account the scalability of agent-oriented programming platforms.

Additionally it would be worthwhile to focus on agent communication and to evaluate that aspect of the tournament by routing agent-messages through the *MASSim* server for proper evaluation.

References

1. Behrens, T., Dastani, M., Dix, J., Köster, M., Novák, P. (eds.): Special Issue about Multi-Agent-Contest. Annals of Mathematics and Artificial Intelligence, vol. 59. Springer, Netherlands (2010)
2. Behrens, T., Dastani, M., Dix, J., Köster, M., Novák, P.: The multi-agent programming contest from 2005–2010: From collecting gold to herding cows. Annals of Mathematics and Artificial Intelligence 59, 277–311 (2010)
3. Behrens, T.M., Dastani, M., Dix, J., Novák, P.: Agent Contest Competition: 4th Edition. In: Hindriks, K.V., Pokahr, A., Sardina, S. (eds.) ProMAS 2008. LNCS (LNAI), vol. 5442, pp. 211–222. Springer, Heidelberg (2009)
4. Behrens, T., Dix, J., Hübner, J., Köster, M., Schlesinger, F.: Mapc 2011 documentation. Technical Report IfI-12-01, Clausthal University of Technology (to appear, December 2012)
5. Behrens, T., Dix, J., Hübner, J., Köster, M., Schlesinger, F.: Mapc 2011 evaluation and team descriptions. Technical Report IfI-12-02, Clausthal University of Technology (to appear, December 2012)
6. Behrens, T., Hindriks, K., Dix, J.: Towards an environment interface standard for agent platforms. Annals of Mathematics and Artificial Intelligence 61, 3–38 (2011)
7. Bordini, R., Dastani, M., Dix, J., El Fallah Seghrouchni, A. (eds.): Programming Multi Agent Systems: Languages, Platforms and Applications. Multiagent Systems, Artificial Societies and Simulated Organizations, vol. 15. Springer, Berlin (2005)
8. Bordini, R.H., Dastani, M., Dix, J., El Fallah-Seghrouchni, A. (eds.): Multi-Agent Programming: Languages, Tools and Applications. Springer, Berlin (2009)
9. Dastani, M., Dix, J., Novak, P.: The First Contest on Multi-agent Systems Based on Computational Logic. In: Toni, F., Torroni, P. (eds.) CLIMA VI 2005. LNCS (LNAI), vol. 3900, pp. 373–384. Springer, Heidelberg (2006)
10. Dastani, M., Dix, J., Novák, P.: The Second Contest on Multi-Agent Systems Based on Computational Logic. In: Inoue, K., Satoh, K., Toni, F. (eds.) CLIMA VII 2006. LNCS (LNAI), vol. 4371, pp. 266–283. Springer, Heidelberg (2007)
11. Dastani, M., Dix, J., Novák, P.: Agent Contest Competition: 3rd Edition. In: Dastani, M., El Fallah Seghrouchni, A., Ricci, A., Winikoff, M. (eds.) ProMAS 2007. LNCS (LNAI), vol. 4908, pp. 221–240. Springer, Heidelberg (2008)

HactarV2: An Agent Team Strategy Based on Implicit Coordination

Marc Dekker, Pieter Hameete, Michiel Hegemans, Sebastiaan Leysen,
Joris van den Oever, Jeff Smits, and Koen V. Hindriks

Delft University of Technology
Mekelweg 4, 2628 CD Delft, The Netherlands
agent-contest@mmi.tudelft.nl

Abstract. In this paper we report on the design and implementation
of our multi-agent system, called HactarV2, for the Agent Contest 2011.
HactarV2 has been implemented in the agent programming language
GOAL. One of the main challenges of the Agent Contest is to design a
decentralized multi-agent system that is able to strategically compete
with other agent teams. To address this challenge, the strategy of Hac-
tarV2 is based on implicit coordination between agents and there is no
central manager that keeps track of all information. The aim, moreover,
has been to minimize the communication between agents. Communication is used by HactarV2 agents to ensure that each of them maintains
the same map of the environment. The Mars scenario of this year required agents to explore, locate and occupy high valued zones on the
planet Mars. Because initially agents are randomly placed on the map,
in the first phase of the game the agents individually explore the map
and update each other. Agents have different roles and we describe the
strategies used by individual agents per role. In the second phase of the
game, which starts when the agents have located high value nodes on
the map, the agents group together and act as a swarm to maintain and
possibly expand the zone on the map that is occupied by the agents.

1 Introduction

In this paper we report on the design and development of our multi-agent sys-
tem (MAS) called HactarV2 for the 2011 Multi-Agent Contest organized by
Clausthal University of Technology. The HactarV2 MAS has been developed at
Delft University of Technology by the authors, a team of six students and Koen
Hindriks, who supervised the team.

The team name is based on the super computer Hactar from the book "Life,
the Universe and Everything"[1]. Hactar is a computer whose components reflect
the pattern of the whole. After failing its intended purpose it gets pulverized
and scattered through the universe. Still operational, Hactar proceeds to slowly
recombine and become a cloud of particles. It then tries to destroy the universe
only to be thwarted by the main protagonist's terrible cricket skills. We think
that HactarV2 is a fitting name for our MAS because initially all agents are

L.A. Dennis, O. Boissier, and R.H. Bordini (Eds.): ProMAS 2011, LNCS 7217, pp. 173–184, 2012.

scattered all over the map as their positions are randomly allocated and then the agents later during the game recombine into a swarm.

2   System Analysis and Design

During the design and development of our MAS we have used the agile software development approach Scrum [2]. We used the open-source platform iceScrum[3] for managing and maintaining our development process and for collecting all ideas concerning strategy choices, implementation issues and optimization problems. We decided not to use an agent-based development methodology such as Prometheus[4] because the team did not have sufficient experience with any of these methods.

In the design of our MAS we opted for a completely decentralized approach. One of the main reasons for this choice has been the communication overhead that is needed when a central manager would have been introduced. This would have required the MAS to perform multiple reasoning cycles to exchange messages between all agents and a manager agent. Our agents, however, use all available time within a simulation round (2 seconds) to decide which action to take. As a consequence, messages are received only in the next simulation round. Information exchanged between agents thus would possibly be outdated which makes message exchange ineffective. This applies in particular to information about positions and the zone that is occupied by agents but, of course, less so to information about the map itself because the map itself remains the same throughout the game.

Instead of exchanging many messages with a central manager that controls what agents do, we designed our agents to base their decisions mainly on the information that is perceived by the agent itself. This ensures that the information is up-to-date and reduces the need for communication.

Message exchange between agents is used in particular (i) for informing other agents about the structure of the map, (ii) between disabled agents and repairers for requesting a repair, and (iii) between non-saboteur agent to saboteurs for reporting locations of opponent agents. Moreover, an agent will only send these messages if it is sure that the receiving agent does not perceive this information itself.

The main reason for exchanging map information between agents is that they need to have all available map information to ensure adequate performance and to avoid doing probe and survey actions that already have been performed by others. Therefore, information acquired by performing a probe or survey action is broadcast to all other agents. This may require each agent to process up to 90 messages that are received from the other 9 agents per round. Because processing all received map information each round requires extensive updating of the belief base, we have had to pay quite some time to optimizing these updates. The benefit of sharing all map information, however, is that the exploration process can be optimized in terms of speed and efficiency (i.e. avoid duplicating actions that have already been performed) and agents are able to do path finding completely autonomously. A downside of this design, of course, is that all agents have to process the map information which would not have been the case in a centralized design.

Our decentralized design implies that agents make decisions autonomously. One potential issue that may arise in such a setup is that different agents will attempt to achieve the same goals. In order to prevent this, agents have been equipped with the capability to predict what other agents will do. This allows agents to decide who will actually adopt a particular goal. We discuss these capabilities in more detail in Section 4.

2.1 Testing

While developing our MAS, we have put a lot of effort in testing and analyzing test results. We considered testing to be very important as it greatly facilitates the evaluation of various ideas and strategies that we tried during our short development cycles. A great benefit of extensive testing has been that it quickly made us familiar with all the details of the simulation scenario.

We have used various test strategies. Initial testing focused on whether the MAS behavior was coherent. At this stage we used dummy agents as opponents that did nothing during a simulation (performed skips each round). In subsequent stages, when we had a reasonably performing MAS, we tested against the Java teams that were supplied by the organizers. These tests were particularly interesting as they informed us about the way our agents reacted to very different agents. We also performed tests in which our most recent MAS played against older versions in order to verify whether we actually improved our MAS over time. During these tests we observed suboptimal behavior that we believe could only have been found because the strategy of the opposing MAS of our earlier versions was still quite similar. We have also participated in all test matches that were organized by the contest organizers.

One testing tactic that we used while debugging our MAS involved the use of an edited XML configuration file for a simulation which granted our team 2 million seconds to send their actions. This made it easier to pause the agent system and study the state of the MAS at a time when something went wrong. As a result, bugs were found more easily.

In total we have spent roughly 500 man hours on implementing our MAS. Around 200 hours were spent on increasing performance and solving other problems and the remaining time was spent on implementing and debugging the multi-agent strategy.

3   Software Architecture

The HactarV2 MAS has been programmed completely in the agent programming language GOAL [5–7]. All team members were familiar with GOAL because it is being taught as a first year course in the Computer Science curriculum at Delft. In this section, we briefly discuss GOAL and some aspects related to how we structured our code.

3.1 GOAL

GOAL is a logic-based agent programming language. One of its main strengths is that it facilitates the development of high-level strategies for agents. The current version of GOAL uses Prolog to represent the knowledge, beliefs, and goals of an agent. Prolog is a declarative programming language. Prolog programs consist of rules and facts which describe *what* is the case and computation is a form of theorem proving instead of the usual procedural style where a programmer needs to write programs that dictate *how* something is to be computed. Using Prolog, GOAL agents can derive new facts from their beliefs about the environment and the goals they want to achieve. GOAL agents derive their choice of action from their beliefs and goals by means of condition-action rules.

We have found that it is quite important to pay attention to the predicates used to represent the environment in Prolog. This is important to ensure readability of the program code and for performance reasons. For example we had to replace our initial map representation because it decreased the performance of the system to much.[1]

GOAL is distributed with a complete IDE for programming, testing and debugging a multi-agent system. The platform fully supports the Environment Interface Standard [8]. This allowed us to focus completely on the strategic aspects of the contest and we did not have to spent time on lower-level details, such as sending actions to and analyzing the XML files that are received from the simulation server.

The complete system (i.e. MAS and environment interface) was run on a single high end machine. Development on a single machine has been easier. We have considered whether we should distribute the MAS on multiple machines, which is supported by GOAL, mainly for performance reasons. Because our MAS turned out to be efficient enough to run it on a single machine, we have not investigated this possibility any further.

3.2 Agent Structure

GOAL agents execute a classic Observe-Decide-Act (ODA) cycle. At the start of each reasoning cycle of a GOAL agent, all percepts are collected and processed. Our agents start a new cycle after receiving information from the simulation server that a new round has started and first processes all percepts and received messages. The agent then proceeds to decide what to do next using condition-action rules. When the choice is made the selected action is sent to the environment.

GOAL agents are sets of *modules*. There are three types of modules that have a special role, including the event and main module mentioned above and a third module called *init module* for initializing the agent. A programmer, however, can add as many modules as he needs. For example, code related to communication, percept handling, navigation, as well as role specific tasks have been placed in

---

[1] We could trace performance of Prolog queries by means of the logging functionality provided by GOAL.

separate modules. The main benefits of the use of modules are that it significantly reduces the chance of code duplication and that it facilitates multiple programmers to each focus on a specific part of the code while still maintaining a clear overview of the overall structure of the MAS.

Every agent in our MAS has a similar structure. We decided to make one master agent which can handle all different roles. Each agent uses role specific modules while sharing standard modules related to e.g. navigation. The function of our main module is to connect all the smaller sub-modules and jump back and forth between them. Once all the common tasks have been executed the main module checks the role of the agent in question and selects role-specific modules that handle all tasks and decisions that concern that specific role.

The total program code consists of 1758 lines of code spread over 18 files.

4   Strategies, Details and Statistics

The strategy of our MAS distinguishes two phases. In the first phase, discussed mainly in Section 4.1, agents do not yet act as a team. This corresponds to the initial state of the game in which agents are randomly placed on the map. In the second phase, agents act as a team in order to occupy high valued zones on the map. This phase is discussed in Section 4.2. As path planning is quite important in the game, we discuss our approach to finding routes on the map separately in Section 4.3.

4.1   Individual Agent Strategy

At the beginning of a game all agents move and act on their own. Per role a different strategy has been designed. We also designed *defensive* strategies for each role and a buying strategy which we discuss at the end of the section.

The goal of an *explorer* agent at the start of the game is to find the highest valued node on the map. We call this node the *optimum*. This strategy works because the map generator produces maps that have one cluster of higher valued nodes at the center of the map. Once the optimum is found, the name of this node is sent to the other agents and a swarm can be formed to occupy the zone around this node. The first phase ends when the optimum has been found.

The strategy of an explorer for finding the optimum consists of the following rules. First probe current node is unprobed and survey local unsurveyed edges.The agent will now go to a node that has not yet been probed only if it is connected to this and last node and the current node has a lower value then the last. Otherwise the agent will go back to the last visited node. The exception is that if there is a neighboring node which has a higher value than this one, the agent will go there. The agent will also try to go to a neighboring node that is not close to a (potentially) dangerous opponent. If there are no safe nodes, the agent will take a chance and go to a potentially dangerous node anyway. The agent will conclude that the optimum has been found if no move can be made according to the previously outlined rules. This conclusion may not always be right (the algorithm outlined is not perfect) but works pretty well in practice.

Once the optimum has been found, an explorer agent will join the other agents and start swarming as a team around the optimum. It will continue to go to and probe nodes when nearby nodes are found that not yet have been probed. Doing so allows it to find even higher valued nodes than the node that is currently believed to be the optimum. If it finds a new optimum, the agent will inform the other agents.

As a defensive strategy, an explorer basically will try to run away as quickly as possible from nodes it considers to be unsafe. A node is considered to be unsafe if on that node an opponent agent is located that is a saboteur or the role of that agent is unknown. All other nodes are considered to be safe. Explorer agents will only move to safe nodes.

A *sentinel* moves on the map using the same exploration strategy as discussed above. It tries to keep its distance from (potentially) dangerous opponents. After an explorer finds a zone worth defending around the optimum, the sentinel will go there as well, join the other agents, and start swarming around the optimum. We experimented with sentinels that bought a lot of sensors in order to be able to see a large part of the map. But we discarded this strategy for the sentinel because it is very expensive and did not seem to benefit the performance of our MAS.

As a defensive strategy, a sentinel will parry when an opponent saboteur is present on the same node. The idea is that in this way, if the saboteur attacks, our team can gather parry achievements. If the role of an opponent agent is unknown, a repairer will also initially parry. However, when the first parry turned out to be unnecessary, with a 50% chance, a sentinel agent will ignore opponents with unknown roles on the same node. Moreover, in case multiple agents are defending against one opponent saboteur, agents will leave the node with a 50% chance whenever their parry was useless. This 50/50 choice prevents that one opponent saboteur will keep multiple agents busy on a node.

The *inspector* uses the same basic exploration strategy and swarming behavior that most agents use. The main difference is that the priority of an inspector agent is to inspect opponents that have not been inspected yet. After doing so, the information obtained is shared with all other agents. In addition an inspector will repeatedly inspect an opponent saboteur every 50 rounds. This enables the saboteurs from our MAS to keep track of the state of opposing saboteurs.

As a defensive strategy, an inspector will run away if the opponent agent is known to be a saboteur. However, if the opponent agent is unknown, it will move towards it to inspect it.

Agents that are disabled will ask for help from a *repairer* agent. Disabled agents will move towards the repairer that is closest after informing it that the agent wants to be repaired by the repairer. If a repairer is not already committed to another agent, it will also start moving towards the disabled agent that requested for help. Whenever a repairer gets a request to repair another repairer, however, it will drop its current commitment and start to move towards that repairer. A repairer will also drop its current commitment when it gets disabled itself and start moving towards the other repairer. Disabled agents send a path to the repairer they are moving to, to prevent the repairer from having to calculate a path towards the disabled agent and to save time.

Repairers use exactly the same defensive strategy as sentinels.

The *saboteurs* start the match in search and destroy mode. They receive information from all agents that is useful for locating opponent agents. They will move towards a last known location of an opponent agent that is closest to their own position and attack that agent. While testing we found that this often resulted in the opponent having fewer agents available at the start of the game which reduced the effectiveness of our opponent.

Buying can be important during the game but we consider achievement points to be more important. Therefore our buying strategy is designed to keep our achievement points as high as possible and to spend less money than the opponent does. As the amount of money available has quite an impact on the points that are scored each round, we decided to only upgrade our saboteurs.

The upgrading of saboteurs is aimed at ensuring two things: (i) our saboteurs have 1 health point more then the highest strength of any of the opponent saboteurs and (ii) the strength of our saboteurs is equal to the highest number of health points of any of the opponent saboteurs. If both of these goals are realized, then our saboteurs will survive a blow of an opponent saboteur while destroying them in a single hit.

We start buying upgrades for saboteurs immediately so that they are better then our opponents from the start. After that we wait for input from the inspectors about the opponent saboteurs before upgrading further. Very important is that we will always attack opponent agents at our own location before upgrading. This prevents opponent saboteurs from interrupting our agents and also interrupts whatever the opponent agent is doing. As a result our score is lower than that of our opponents in the first 100 or so steps but this investment pays off in the remainder of the match; this effect can be clearly seen in Figure 1.

An assumption we have made is that the opponent team gives higher priority to upgrading saboteurs than to upgrading other roles. But even if this assumption would not be true, the idea is that upgrading of other roles is not that important because our saboteurs cannot be attacked by these roles.

Saboteurs do not have a "defensive" strategy but will always attack because they are designed to be superior to the opponents agents.

4.2   Swarming Strategy

When explorer agents have found the optimum (i.e. the node with highest value) and all other agents have been informed about this, these agents will start moving towards the optimum. Because all map information is shared between agents, the probability that each agent will be able to find a path to the optimum is quite high. If an agent is not able to find such a path, it will continue surveying edges until it finds a path to the optimum. Finding an optimum moves the game to the second phase in our strategy. We call this phase the *swarming* phase.

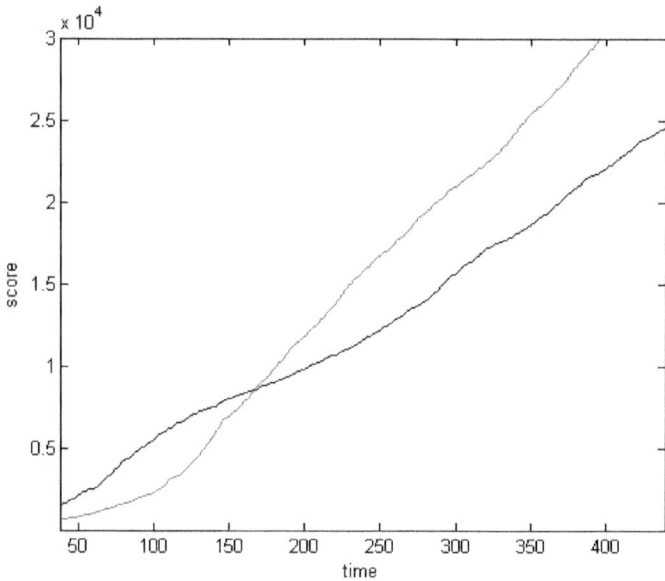

Fig. 1. Scores HactarV2(Gray) vs TUB(Black)

In order to explain the behavior of the agents from this point on that we have called *swarming* we introduce several concepts. An agent that is part of our team is said to be *dependable* if that agent can effectively participate as a team member in the swarming behavior. Other agents can derive (predict) whether an agent can be depended on because the roles of all friendly agents are known and all of our agents use similar code. These facts allow other agents to predict what kind of action another agent will perform in the next round and to derive from that whether that agent will be dependable.

Agents that are located on the same node are ranked and assigned a unique number called the *agent's rank*. This rank is used when multiple agents are predicted to perform the same action. In that case, based on their rank it is decided which agent will perform that action; the other agents will then perform another action. This rank-based mechanism allows agents to divide tasks among themselves without the need for communication while at the same time ensuring that each agent performs a unique action whenever possible.

Another concept we use is that of one agent being *connected* to two other agents. A link between two agents is said to exist if there are at most two edges that connect the nodes on which these agents are located and these nodes are owned by our team. An agent is said to be *connected* if that agent has links with at least two other dependable agents. The nodes that connected agents are located on are called *swarm positions*.

The zone of nodes which is owned by our team and contains the optimum is called the *optimum zone*. All agents maintain a list of nodes that are part of this zone as well as a list of those nodes that are just outside this zone. An agent is said to be inside the optimum zone if the node that the agent is on only has edges to nodes that are part of the optimum zone. An agent is said to be on the edge of the optimum zone if the agent is on a node that is part of the optimum zone that is connected to a node that is not part of that zone.

While moving towards the optimum zone the agents will constantly check if they are already in a swarming position that is part of that zone. If that is not the case, they will continue moving towards the optimum zone. All agents that try to become part of the swarm intend to be within the optimum zone. This means that our MAS will create at most one swarm.

Once an agent has arrived in the optimum zone, the agent will determine the highest valued node directly outside the optimum zone and move towards that node. By using this tactic the swarm will always expand in the direction of the highest valued nodes not yet owned by our MAS. When the agent reaches a position on the edge of the swarm it will consider all nodes it can move to. In addition it will predict to which nodes its connected agents may want to move. Based on this information, an agent can determine without communication if it can make the best move compared to any of the agents it is connected to. If that is the case, an agent will move to expand the zone, and otherwise it will stay on its current node in order to ensure that the agents will still be connected. (To ensure connectedness it is not required that only one agent moves to expand the zone and we can use the agent rank discussed above to determine which agents can move. We do not discuss the rather complicated details here, however.)

If for some reason an agent is no longer connected with agents in the optimum zone, it will start moving back towards the optimum until it reconnects to agents that are part of the swarm. Using this set of rules we obtain a very robust swarm. They allow agents to hook up with the swarm but also allow agents with more urgent tasks to leave without disturbing the swarm area too much.

If our zone is being threatened by opposing agents our saboteurs will defend it. Opponent agents are considered threatening if they are not disabled and located at a node that is just outside the current optimum zone. While a saboteur defends the zone it is no longer considered to be dependable. That way the swarm will not be disrupted by unpredictable movements from the saboteur. If a threatening opponent agent moves away from our current zone before it is attacked, the saboteur will become part of the swarm again. Saboteurs that take part in the swarm will not actively look for or attack opponent agents. This is consistent with our main strategy: to ensure that the MAS occupies the optimum zone and the opponent agents cannot occupy a zone that is worth more points.

Especially when the opposing agents had a very similar strategy that involves capturing nodes with the highest values it is difficult for our agents to occupy and maintain a large optimum zone. In these games the points that are obtained by achievements can determine the difference between winning and losing. Attack and parry achievements yield the most points while the inspect achievement yields the fewest points. Probed and zonescore achievements typically also yield few points except when agents occupy almost the entire map. Therefore, we decided to focus on attack and parry achievements.

4.3   Path Planning

In principle our agents do not plan actions in advance. Agents decide every reasoning cycle which action to perform based on the rules that are part of the agent program. Path planning is an exception to some extent because an agent will compute a path to move from a node A to another node B. So, an agent plans at most n rounds ahead where n is the length of a path that is followed. Following a path, however, can quite easily be disrupted if an alternative action is considered a better option.

The path finding algorithms we have used are based on an implementation of Dijkstra's shortest path algorithm in Prolog that is available on the web [9]. Our agents use seven, slightly different versions of this algorithm. These versions differ from each other in what they aim for. The most basic version simply searches for a path between two nodes A en B. But we also have versions for finding a path to the closest non-probed node or non-surveyed edge. Yet other versions search for a path to the closest repairer or closest opponent agent.

5   Conclusion

We have enjoyed the Agent Contest experience very much. It has also taught us various valuable lessons. Maybe the most important thing that we have learned from participating in the Agent Contest is that the continuous testing of a MAS can greatly help to improve the effectiveness of that MAS. We became particularly aware of this after the initial testing against the dummy agent team (agents that performed skip actions) resulted in basic strategies that also worked against teams developed by other groups.

A second lesson that we have learned is that the design of the structure of an individual agent and the MAS can make a big difference during the development of a MAS. We benefited in particular from the module concept that is supported by GOAL[5, 7]. The strategy associated with each role has been coded in a separate module and there are dedicated modules for functions such as navigation and communication that are shared by agents. This greatly facilitated dividing coding tasks within the team. Maintaining a clear and concise documentation of the system has also been important in this regard. We have documented in particular the *ontology* used and shared by all agents. The ontology documents all predicates used to represent the beliefs, goals, percepts, actions, and knowledge rules of agents and briefly explains the meaning of each predicate and how its parameters should be instantiated. The ontology facilitates keeping track of what everyone is doing and has saved us a lot of time.

We believe that the key strength of our MAS resides in the performance of our saboteur and repairer but also in the manner our agents team up and form quite robust swarms. The buying strategy of our saboteur has also been quite effective. The final contest, however, also demonstrated some points that still can be improved. For example, we observed that sometimes both saboteurs attacked one and the same target and that our swarm sometimes is not as robust as it should be.

Our MAS performed very well and we won the Agent Contest. As mentioned above, the strategy of our saboteurs and repairers proved the key to success. Our saboteurs are aggressive at the start of a game but put on a tight leash when a swarm is formed to ensure that opponent agents cannot get their agents near the high valued nodes. Our repairers make sure that as many agents as possible are active and are able to participate in the swarm.

Mainly because of our buying strategy, we usually start with a lower score than our opponents. This is made up for, however, when the highest valued node is found by our agents and we start to gather more and more achievement points. This is clearly illustrated in Figure 2. In this figure the gray line represents the score of HactarV2 and the black line represents the score of the Python-DTU team. For the first 175 steps HactarV2's score stays below that of Python-DTU's but thereafter HactarV2 takes and keeps the lead.

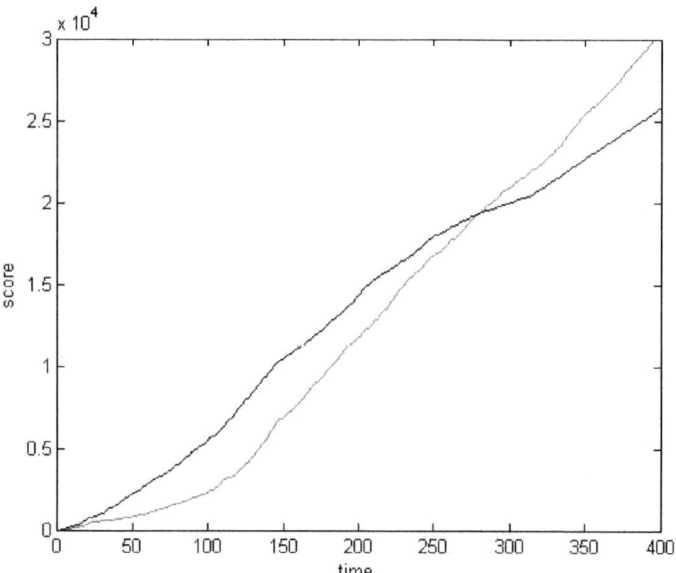

Fig. 2. Scores HactarV2(Gray) vs Python-DTU(Black)

To write our code we used the agent programming language GOAL and the IDE that is distributed with this language. This was the first time that GOAL has been used in the Multi-Agent Programming Contest and we are very satisfied with its performance. We have deviated from some of the guidelines for programming GOAL agents for reasons of efficiency but otherwise GOAL proved to be very suitable for the programming of, for example, the fast and efficient path planning algorithm that we used.

We think that the Mars scenario is a good and interesting scenario. It poses some interesting challenges with respect to coordinating agents. We believe that scaling up the contest by having more agents would create an even bigger challenge. Maybe one quite interesting idea is to be able to earn and dynamically add new agents during the game, for example, based on certain achievements. More pragmatically, as we discussed above, we have found testing to be very important for the success of our MAS and we believe that it is a good idea to start contest wide testing earlier and in phases. In a first phase - which we think should start about a month before the contest - a general test to check for and identify possible problems related to establishing a connection and to communication is advised. Thereafter in the second phase test matches should be organized that allow teams to test their strategies.

We also think that adding local optimums in the map would make the contest more interesting. This would require more complicated strategies for swarming and would provide a bigger challenge for the exploration of the map. Finally, we think it would be a good idea to add an extra achievement that promotes the cooperation of agents. This achievement should not replace the achievement for the area that is controlled but would count the number of agents that share a connection each turn and sum this amount over all turns. This would reward teams whose agents cooperate above teams whose agents move around individually.

References

1. Adams, D.: Life, the Universe and Everything. Harmony Books (1982)
2. Schwaber, K.: Scrum development process. In: Proceedings of the 10th Annual ACM Conference on Object Oriented Programming Systems, Languages, and Applications (OOPSLA), pp. 117–134 (1995)
3. iceScrum. icescrum, free and opensource platform for your agile developments (2009), http://www.icescrum.org/en/
4. Padgham, L., Winikoff, M.: Prometheus: A Methodology for Developing Intelligent Agents. In: Giunchiglia, F., Odell, J.J., Weiss, G. (eds.) AOSE 2002. LNCS, vol. 2585, pp. 174–185. Springer, Heidelberg (2003)
5. Hindriks, K.V.: Programming rational agents in goal. In: Multi-Agent Programming: Languages, Tools and Applications, pp. 119–157. Springer, US (2009)
6. Hindriks, K., de Boer, F.S., van der Hoek, W., Meyer, J.J.C.: Agent Programming with Declarative Goals. In: Castelfranchi, C., Lespérance, Y. (eds.) ATAL 2000. LNCS (LNAI), vol. 1986, pp. 228–243. Springer, Heidelberg (2001)
7. (2011), http://mmi.tudelft.nl/trac/goal
8. Behrens, T., Hindriks, K., Dix, J.: Towards an environment interface standard for agent platforms. Annals of Mathematics and Artificial Intelligence, 1–35 (2010)
9. Barker, C.: LPA Win-Prolog goodies. A WWW collection of Prolog source snippets (1999),
http://colin.barker.pagesperso-orange.fr/lpa/dijkstra.htm

Implementing a Multi-Agent System in Python with an Auction-Based Agreement Approach

Mikko Berggren Ettienne, Steen Vester, and Jørgen Villadsen*

Department of Informatics and Mathematical Modelling
Technical University of Denmark
Richard Petersens Plads, Building 321, DK-2800 Kongens Lyngby, Denmark
jv@imm.dtu.dk

Abstract. We describe the solution used by the Python-DTU team in the Multi-Agent Programming Contest 2011, where the scenario was called Agents on Mars. We present our auction-based agreement algorithm and discuss our chosen strategy and our choice of technology used for implementing the system. Finally, we present an analysis of the results of the competition as well as propose areas of improvement.

1 Introduction

This paper documents our solution to the Multi-Agent Programming Contest 2011 (MAPC) [1,6] as the Python-DTU team.

The aim of MAPC is to stimulate research in the area of Multi-Agent Systems (MAS). It is a returning competition which has been held every year since 2005. The challenge is to solve a cooperative task in a dynamic environment using a multi-agent system. This year's MAPC presented a new scenario called Agents on Mars in which two opposing teams control 10 agents and compete to control "zones" of a graph in a discrete time world.

This year's contest was the 7th edition of MAPC. Every year participants have stated their implementation language/framework and submitted their source code along with a short report describing their solution. In 2005 MAPC was built on a "Food-Gatherers" scenario, 2006-2007 presented a "Goldminers" scenario and 2008-2010 presented a "Cows and Cowboys" scenario. This year again presented a new scenario "Agents on Mars" making it unfeasible to build a solution from earlier year's implementations. Throughout the years many participants have used existing MAS frameworks, in particular Jason [7] and JIAC [8] which are both open source and implemented in Java, while other participants have implemented their own MAS frameworks. Naturally MAS frameworks can be reused in different scenarios and framework experiences from earlier years are worth considering. We participated in the contest in 2009 and 2010 as the Jason-DTU team since we used the Jason platform and its agent-oriented programming language AgentSpeak [4,5]. We performed well but for the contest this year, with the new and more complex scenario, we decided to focus on an

---

* Corresponding author.

L.A. Dennis, O. Boissier, and R.H. Bordini (Eds.): ProMAS 2011, LNCS 7217, pp. 185–196, 2012.

auction-based agreement approach and to implement the multi-agent system in the programming language Python.

Our observation from this and previous years is that because of the complex nature of the scenarios, choosing which strategies to apply poses the greatest challenge. Compared to that, the actual requirements for a supporting framework are not overwhelming which led us to implement our own framework. While Jason had some immediate benefits, e.g. with regards to agent communication, we regularly encountered problems where we would have preferred to have complete control over every aspect of the implementation. Thus our decision to implement our own framework for this year's competition was evident. We chose Python as we think it is in many ways superior with respect to development speed and succinctness compared to Java, C#, C++ and other languages that we have experience with. Furthermore Python supports multiple programming paradigms, including the functional, which proved quite effective for this setting. This is also confirmed by the final implementation which takes up very few lines of code compared to earlier years and yet proved to be very effective.

We used approximately 400 man hours in total for implementing the system and for participating in the official test matches. We discussed agent designs and strategies with other teams during the competitions only.

2   System Analysis and Design

We did not use any multi-agent system methodology because we preferred to have complete knowledge and control of every part of the implementation. We chose a decentralized solution where agents shared percepts through shared data structures and coordinated actions using distributed algorithms. Our agreement based auction algorithm heavily relies on communication and is part of how agents decide on goals. Each agent acts on its own behalf based on its local view of the world.

In the following we describe our decentralized solution to agent cooperation using a distributed auction algorithm.

2.1   The Agreement Problem

Many situations arise where a subset of our agents must cooperate to solve a task. For example, we use most of our agents to survey the graph in the beginning of every match. To do this our agents need to agree on who surveys which parts of the graph. In the same way our saboteurs have to agree on which opponents to attack and our repairers must agree on which of our agents to repair. Some agents might also be more suitable for a goal than others (because of special abilities, shorter distance to goal, etc.). We would like to assign agents in such a way that as many goals as possible are accomplished in as little time as possible, since accomplishing goals quickly gives a higher score. Before assigning goals to agents we start by assigning *benefits* to each goal for each agent, such that the benefit of a goal is high if the goal is important to solve and such that the benefit will be higher the faster the agent can accomplish it (e.g. the shorter the distance from the agent to the goal is, taking the energy of the agent into account). We would then hope to achieve the following properties when designing an algorithm to assign goals to agents:

1. The total benefit of the assigned goals should be as high as possible. Preferably optimal or close to it.
2. The running time of the algorithm should be fast, since we need to assign goals to agents at every time step in the competition and still have time left for other things such as environment perception, information sharing, etc.
3. The algorithm should be distributed between the agents resembling a true multi-agent system.
4. It should not be necessary for the agents to have the same beliefs about the state of the world in order to agree on an assignment.
5. The algorithm should be robust. If it is possible, our agents should be able to agree on an assignment even if some agents break down or some communication channels are broken.

The algorithm described in the following is inspired by [2,3] and achieves this with some compromises while still satisfying every point to some extent.

2.2 Auction Algorithm

To solve the problem we use an auction algorithm in which agents will make bids against each other on the goals that they would like to pursue. The rules of the auction will be designed so we can be sure that the algorithm will terminate in a finite number of rounds and that all agents are assigned to different goals at termination. Also, the assignment will be near optimal in a sense that is defined later in this section.

We assume that there are n agents and at least n different goals, such that there always exists a feasible assignment of a distinct goal to each agent. It is also assumed that the agents are using a network of communication channels where all pairs of agents are not necessarily connected at all times. Though we do assume that the graph of the communication network is connected at all times. When designing an auction each goal i will at a given time t have a *price* denoted $p_i(t)$. Initially, we let $p_i(0) = 0$ for all goals i. The price of a goal will be the highest bid made by an agent on that goal (except when the price is 0). As in a real world auction, agents will now place bids on the goals which give them the largest *net value*. Here we define the net value of agent i for goal j by

$$net\ value_{ij} = benefit_{ij} - p_j$$

which is the benefit the agent will get from the goal minus the price of the goal.

In each bidding round, agents place bids according to their local information about the current prices. If an agent has not currently placed the highest bid on any goal then the agent will place a bid on the goal which maximizes his current net value according to his current knowledge of the prices of the goals.

The highest bid as well as local information about the current prices and current highest bidders of goals are in each round sent to all neighbour agents, i.e. agents to which a communication channel exists. In addition local beliefs are updated according to the prices received from neighbour agents. If several agents have made the same bid for a goal, the agent with the highest index will win the goal. The updated values are then used by the agents to calculate the *net values* for the next bidding round. Thus, in one bidding round at time step t the algorithm works by letting each agent i do the following:

1. Receive the newest prices and owners of all goals. Update the local belief base if there are higher bids on any of the goals that the agent did not already know about. This includes updating the *net values* of the goals. Also, the agent may have lost a goal it owned in the previous round.
2. If the agent is not currently the owner of a goal, it will place a bid on the goal j with the highest *net value* according to its belief base. It does so by setting itself as owner of j and increasing p_j by $\gamma = v_i - w_i + \varepsilon$ where v_i is the net value of j and w_i is the net value of the goal with the second highest net value. ε is a positive number which is a parameter of the algorithm that influences the running time and the quality of the final assignment. Generally speaking, a low value of ε gives high quality assignments but longer running time.

An example run is shown in figure 1 where $\varepsilon = 1$ and goal benefits are integers. This was also the case when we used the algorithm in practice which gave us a very short running time. In practice we simulated a complete communication network topology by using a shared database of bids between the agents.

In general the algorithm terminates when n rounds without new bids occurs, in which case all agents have an assigned goal. In our case with a complete communication network, it can terminate as soon as one round without new bids occurs assuming that no communication channels are broken. For a proof that the algorithm does in fact terminate no matter what choice of $\varepsilon > 0$ and no matter the choice of structure of the connected communication network we refer to [2]. Here it is also proven that the algorithm terminates in $O(\Delta n^2 \lceil \frac{max_{i,j}\{benefit_{ij}\} - min_{i,j}\{benefit_{ij}\}}{\varepsilon} \rceil)$ and that the final assignment obtained by the algorithm is within $n\varepsilon$ of being optimal. Here n is the number of participants and $\Delta \leq n - 1$ is the maximum network diameter, which is the longest distance between two vertices in the communication network, which is practically reduced to 1 when using a shared data structure as we did in practice.

This choice of algorithm gives quite good solutions with respect to maximizing total benefit, the running time was no problem during competition and the computation is completely distributed between the agents. The agents do not need to share beliefs about the world state, but only need to use their local belief base to approximate their own benefits for different goals. Finally, the algorithm will work even if some communication channels break down which should make the solution more robust than a centralized approach in some environments.

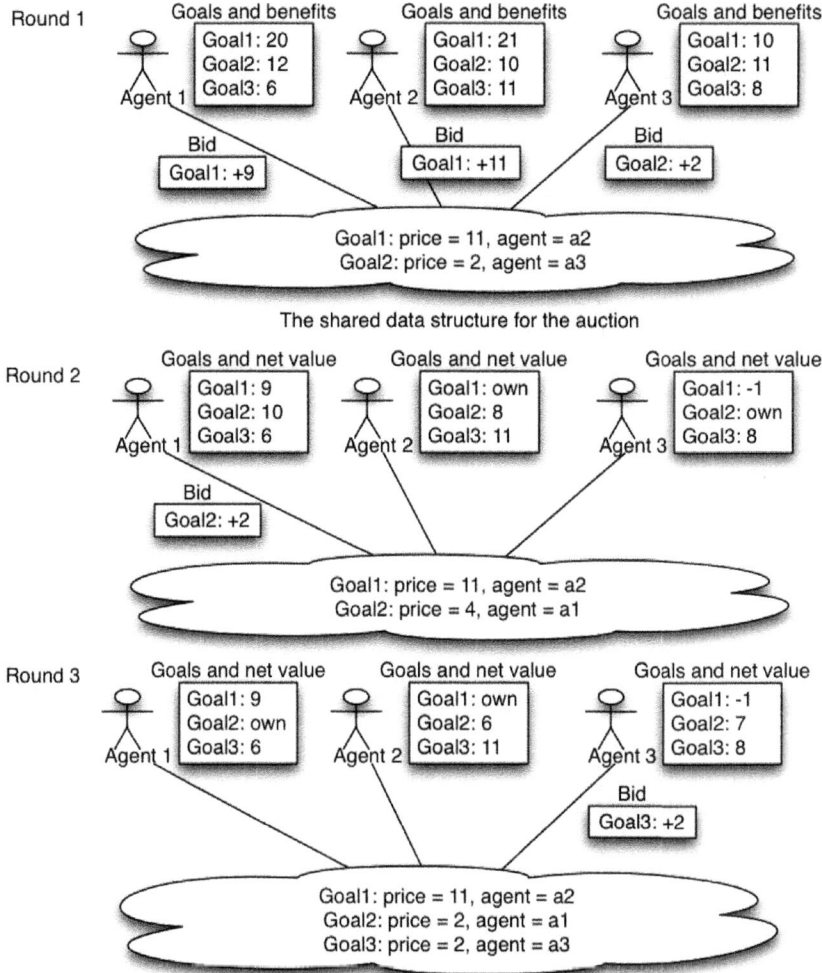

Fig. 1. An example of an auction between three agents. In round 1 the auction data structure is empty before the bidding and thus goal benefits are equal to goal net values. Each agent places a bid on its preferred goal. The bids are calculated as the difference between the two best goals plus ϵ. The data structure stores the highest bid and the corresponding agent for each goal. Both agent 1 and agent 2 bid on goal 1 and agent 1's bid is discarded as it is lower than agent 2's bid. In round 2 the net values have changed as the new bids in the shared data structure are considered. Agent 2 and 3 have not been overbidden, so they won't bid in this round and does now consider themselves owners of the goals they bid on in round 1. However agent 1 overbids agent 3 on goal 2 as the shared data structure shows. Now in round 3 agent 1 has become the owner of goal 2 and agent 3 bids on goal 3 as this is the best goal for it considering the latest bids in the data structure. Now all agents are assigned a goal and the auction ends. We see in this case that we do not get the optimal solution (agent 1 = goal 1, agent 2 = goal 3, agent 4 = goal 2, total benefit = 42) but instead a solution very close to the optimal (total benefit = 41).

3   Software Architecture

The competition is built on the Java MASSim-platform and the Java EISMAS-Sim framework is distributed with the competition files. This framework is based on EIS [9] and abstracts the communication between the server and the agents to simple Java method-calls and call-backs. To utilize this framework we started out with the Java implementation of Python called Jython which in contrast to Python can import Java libraries and classes.

A true multi-agent system allowing distribution of the agents was not enforced by the competition rules. However we took up this challenge as it posed some interesting distribution problems as seen in section 2.1. To support agent communication in our multi-agent system we started out using the Apache ActiveMQ as a messaging server which offers clients for all popular programming languages.

Using the EISMASSim Java framework together with ActiveMQ clients written in Python and glueing it all together with Jython gave some performance issues when exchanging percepts between the agents. We found that each component performed well when tested in a controlled context and thus the issues were with the interaction between the components. We decided to skip Jython, ActiveMQ and EISMASSim and to instead follow a much cleaner Python-only implementation. Even though some work was needed to implement the protocol specific parts which EISMASSim handled, this left us with a more flexible implementation of which we had complete knowledge and control of every part and relieved us from most of the performance issues.

We did not have time to implement our own messaging server with a simple text-based protocol but instead choose to use a set of shared data structures for agent communication. This ensured great performance and was possible because distributing the agents on different computers was not necessary.

3.1   Modeling the Environment

Each agent keeps an internal model of the environment. The environment is trivially modeled as a graph using simple data structures and classes. Every agent is responsible for parsing the messages it receives from the competition server and updating its model accordingly. The agents are also responsible for sending new percepts to the other agents of the team.

Agent positions are represented by a two way mapping allowing retrieval of all agents at a given position, or the position of a given agent. Due to the non-static nature of the agents and their limited visibility range, agents must be removed from this mapping when moving out of the visible area for an agent to avoid inconsistency between the "true" world as represented by the server and the internal world of the agent. The agents also share their percepts of other agents and their own position. However it does happen that an enemy agent moves out of vision for all team agents. In this case we keep the agent in the position mapping allowing inconsistency until it becomes visible again and the mapping is updated. An agent can then use this inconsistent information if it needs to locate the "disappeared" agent. Thus instead of randomly searching in non-visible areas, it can start searching in the area where the agent disappeared.

3.2   Goal Searching

A goal is contained in the abstract type we call Action which is not only used for the agreement auction itself, but also for the agents to carry out the necessary steps to achieve a goal when they have won it in the auction. In our implementation, satisfying a goal implies reaching a specific vertex and then performing some action (in some cases the skip action). The Action type is defined as follows:

```
1  class Action():
2      def __init__(self, goal, type, vertex=None, cost=0, path=[], arg='', length = 0):
3          self.goal = goal
4          self.type = type
5          self.arg = arg
6          self.vertex = vertex
7          self.cost = cost
8          self.path = path
9          self.length = length
```

Here *goal* is the name used to distinguish goals during the auction, *type* is the action the agent must perform when reaching the vertex given in *vertex* and *arg* is a possible argument for the action to be executed. *cost* is subtracted from a constant and the result is used as the goal benefit needed for the auction. The *path* contains a list of vertices the agent must follow to reach the vertex given in *vertex* and *length* is simply the length of this path.

The code below is part of the *get_goals* method which returns a set of Actions. It shows how a saboteur performs a goal search before participating in an agreement auction. The RUNTIME parameter is a constant determining when the team strategy changes from *achievement* to *area controlling* as further described in section 4.

If the current agent is a saboteur and attacking is enabled we check if the team is currently on the *area controlling* strategy in line 5. If this is the case, the agent's knowledge of the currently controlled zone is updated in line 6. Line 7 is a custom best-first search returning a set of Actions. The first parameter is a string to which an opponent name will be appended. This will be given as the goal name to the Action constructor while the second parameter is given as the type. The rest of the Action constructor parameters are given directly from within the search. The third parameter indicates where to start the search from, namely the position of the agent. The fourth parameter is a pointer to a function that determines which vertices are valid goals and which are not. In this case a valid goal is a vertex in the currently controlled zone with a non-disabled opponent agent placed on it. The last parameter indicates that the search can stop when 2 valid goals are found, because only the two saboteurs will bid on these goals. The for-loop on lines 8-9 lowers the found Actions' cost value equally by a constant so great that they will always be chosen over other possible Actions. If less than 2 Actions are found, other Actions are needed, as the agent must be sure to win the auction for at least one goal. To find additional goals another similar search is run, however this time the fourth parameter is a new function pointer. This function will validate every vertex that is not in the currently controlled zone and has a non-disabled agent placed on it.

If the current phase is instead the *achievement* phase, the code jumps from line 5 to line 12 and in this search the currently controlled zone is not computed and thus no vertices will be ignored by the validating function.

```
1   if
2     ...
3   elif self.type == SAB:
4         if DO_ATTACK:
5             if self.runtime > RUNTIME:
6                 self.get_expand()
7                 goals = self.bfs('attack_owned_', ATTACK, start, self.get_opponent_in_owned, 2)
8                 for g in goals:
9                     g.cost = g.cost - 100
10                if len(goals) < 2:
11                    goals.extend(self.bfs('attack_', ATTACK, start, self.get_opponent, 2))
12            else:
13                goals = self.bfs('attack_', ATTACK, start, self.get_opponent, 2)
14        else:
15            goals = self.bfs('survey_', SURVEY, start, self.is_unsurveyed, 10)
```

It might still be the case that less than two Actions have been found. This is handled at a later point in the *get_goals* function. Actions helping area controlling are added if the strategy is *area controlling* and survey actions are added if the strategy is *achievement*. Note that the agent must then have at least 10 different goals as it now possibly auctions against all the other 9 agents. If the agent still has not found enough Actions, ignore actions with low benefit will be added to the Action set until sufficient actions are available.

4   Strategies, Details and Statistics

Considering the complexity of the environment in combination with the nondeterminism introduced by the opposing team's agents, it is clear that classical planning approaches will not suffice for this scenario. We instead let the agents implement a greedy top-level strategy by calculating prioritized sets of goals at each simulation-step. The goals depend on the agent's role, the state of the agent's internal world and how far the simulation has progressed as described in section 3.2. The strategy is greedy as agents does not consider subsequent goals when deciding on a set of goals.

4.1   General Strategy

In the Agents on Mars scenario there are two main ways to earn points. The first is achievement points which are given to a team if they achieve some goals cf. [1]. 2 points were rewarded for reaching an achievement. This means that the team will get 2 points every step for the remainder of the match, unless the points are used to buy special abilities for the agents. It follows that if we are interested in making achievements it makes most sense to do so as early as possible in a match, since this will give us points in every time step for the rest of the match. Another interesting thing is that the number actions required to get achievements in each area increases exponentially. For example, one gets 2 achievement points when the team has done 5 successful attacks, then another 2 after 10 successful attacks, then 20 successful attacks, then 40 successful attacks, then 80 successful attacks, etc. This means that if we are to maximize our earning from achievements, it is probably a good idea to be versatile and good at all the different kinds of achievements. For example, after 160 attacks it will be much easier to survey 5 edges than attack opponents another 160 times (though attacking opponents gives other desirable benefits as well).

The other way to earn points is by controlling areas which gives as many points as the controlled areas are worth every time step cf. [1]. But before we have probed the vertices of the graph each vertex we control will only give 1 point per time step instead of its real value (which is in the interval $\{1, ..., 10\}$ in the competition). It seems like an obvious choice to let our two explorer agents probe a number of vertices in the beginning of a match before trying to have our agents control an area with high value. In the meantime the other agents can try to do as many achievements as possible. In the competition we used the first 80 time steps to get as many achievements as possible and thereafter we would try to control an area with as high value as possible for the rest of the match. We will refer to the two strategies as the *achievement* strategy and the *area controlling* strategy respectively. The choice of the 80 time steps is based on our experience of how long it typically takes our agents to reach a reasonable number of achievement points while also discovering some "valuable" parts of the graph. This can clearly be refined and is not necessarily the best choice on bigger maps than what was typically used in the competition.

4.2   Achievement Strategy

The goal of this phase is to explore the graph to get information about the map structure while getting as many achievement points as quickly as possible. This naturally also involves probing as many nodes as possible which will prepare us for the *area controlling* phase.

To be versatile and obtain different kinds of achievements, most of the agents will perform the task that is unique to them given their role during this phase of the game. Explorers will probe vertices and typically reach 60-80 probes before the phase is over. Sentinels will survey and inspectors will inspect other agents and start surveying if all opponents are inspected before the phase ends. Saboteurs will attack non-disabled opponent agents, prioritizing repairers and saboteurs over other agent types. Repairers will survey if no team agents are disabled, otherwise they will repair team agents, prioritizing a disabled repairer over other agents. When choosing between multiple possibilities, i.e. different unprobed vertices, multiple disabled agents, etc. the agents will always choose the closest target where the distance is calculated using the pathfinding algorithm discussed in [10] taking path length, the number of vertices on the path and the agents' recharge rates into account.

4.3   Area Controlling Strategy

As the vertices with high values are typically placed close to each other in the maps of the competition, both teams will usually not have any choice but to try to get control of as much of this area as possible. We will call this area the *good* area. Because if we try to control areas in other parts of the graph, the opponent team will get control of the good area, leading to us losing the match. In our area controlling strategy the saboteurs will still try to attack opponents and the repairers will also use the same strategy as in the achievement phase. If our opponents try to get control of the good area as well, our saboteurs and repairers will also be in the good area and indirectly help us to get control of as many vertices as possible in this area. The other six agents will place themselves on strategically important vertices given by the area controlling algorithm as discussed in [10] to give us control of as valuable an area as possible. If there is a part of the good area that has not been probed, our explorers will probe that part before helping to control the area so we will not miss out on any area points due to unprobed vertices. In addition, the agents capable of parrying attacks will do so, while they try to control vertices giving us achievement points and making the time spent by the opponent saboteurs for each successful attack longer.

4.4   Putting It All Together

In the above we have omitted the discussion of how the agents agree on who does what when conflicts can occur. The assignment problem is simply solved using the strategy described in section 2.1. In this way each agent will specify his benefit for the different goals according to his beliefs about the world and then the agents will in a distributed manner negotiate an assignment that gives as large benefit for the whole team as possible. Also, the assignment algorithm guarantees that the disabled agents are divided among the repairers in a way such that they will not try to repair the same agent. The same concept applies to agents with survey goals and any other type of goal which more than one agent is capable of accomplishing. We did not cover what our agents will do when the whole graph is surveyed before the 80 steps are over. In this case the agents will start using the area controlling strategy one by one. This makes the transition between the two strategies natural and our coordination algorithm will make sure this is done automatically.

Our solution came in as number two in the final ranking. Out of 24 matches we lost all three matches against the team taking the best ranking and only one other match. The total score of all teams was also compared and in this category our team came in as number one scoring almost 20% more than the second best which was the overall winner. Even though the total score didn't count in the final ranking, we still think that it is very important and that it suggests that our solution had very much potential. It is very hard to point out the exact reasons that we lost some matches. This is because matches cannot be directly compared due to the random map generation and because one action may have great side-effects in one match but not in another. However it seemed like the winning team only did better than us on some key points, especially in upgrading their saboteurs and that we were equally fit in most other areas. For some areas we even did better than the winning team, which is backed by the fact that our team got the highest overall score.

5   Conclusion

We have implemented an auction based agreement algorithm which turned out to be a very good solution for cooperation between the agents. We have found a close to optimal solution to the non-trivial problem of pathfinding in discrete time. Tweaking our solution with prioritized attacks and repairs have also proven very effective for the given scenario.

Even though the nature of the competition and the time limitation encourages very domain specific solutions, we have considered genuine multi-agent challenges such as agreement, cooperation and communication. Python has proved to be a suitable programming language for implementing a multi-agent system. We did not encounter any programming language specific problems or limitations and many features of Python helped us develop an effective yet very compact solution. We were mostly satisfied with the behavior of our agents, however there is still room for improvement. Our general approach and strategies turned out to be very effective, but because of the time limitation we could not implement all of our ideas. Especially our vertex expansion algorithm could have been further optimized and our buying strategy could have been dynamic so that it took the opposing team's strategy into account.

Acknowledgements. Thanks to Andreas Schmidt Jensen, John Bruntse Larsen and Niklas Christoffer Petersen for comments.

References

1. Behrens, T., Dix, J., Hübner, J., Köster, M., Schlesinger, F.: Multi-Agent Programming Contest — Scenario Description — 2011 edn. (2011), http://www.multiagentcontest.org/
2. Zavlanos, M.M., Spesivtsev, L., Pappas, G.J.: A Distributed Auction Algorithm for the Assignment Problem. In: Proceedings of the 47th IEEE Conference on Decision and Control, Cancun Mexico (2008)
3. Bertsekas, D.P., Castanon, D.A.: Parallel synchronous and asynchronous implementations of the auction algorithm. Parallel Computing 17, 707–732 (1991)
4. Boss, N.S., Jensen, A.S., Villadsen, J.: Building Multi-Agent Systems Using Jason. Annals of Mathematics and Artificial Intelligence 59, 373–388 (2010)
5. Vester, S., Boss, N.S., Jensen, A.S., Villadsen, J.: Improving Multi-Agent Systems Using Jason. Annals of Mathematics and Artificial Intelligence 61, 297–307 (2011)
6. Behrens, T., Dastani, M., Dix, J., Köster, M., Novák, P.: The Multi-Agent Programming Contest From 2005-2010: From Collecting Gold to Herding Cows. Annals of Mathematics and Artificial Intelligence 59, 277–311 (2010)
7. Bordini, R.H., Hübner, J.F., Wooldridge, M.: Programming Multi-Agent Systems in AgentSpeak Using Jason. Wiley (2007)

8. Hirsch, B., Konnerth, T., Hessler, A.: Merging Agents and Services — The JIAC Agent Platform. In: El Fallah Seghrouchni, A., Dix, J., Dastani, M., Bordini, R.H. (eds.) Multi-Agent Programming. Springer (2009)
9. Behrens, T., Dix, J., Hindriks, K.: The Environment Interface Standard for Agent-Oriented Programming — Platform Integration Guide and Interface Implementation Guide, Department of Informatics, Clausthal University of Technology, Technical Report IfI-09-10 (2009)
10. Ettienne, M.B., Vester, S., Villadsen, J.: Implementing a Multi-Agent System in Python. In: Multi-Agent Programming Contest, Technical Report (2011) (to appear)

Bogtrotters in Space

Dominic Carr, Sean Russell, Balazs Pete,
G.M.P. O'Hare, and Rem W. Collier

University College Dublin

Abstract. This is the fourth year in which a team from University College Dublin has participated in the Multi-Agent Programming Contest[1]. This paper describes the system that was created to participate in the contest, along with observations of the team's experiences in the contest. The system itself was built using the AF-TeleoReactive and AF-AgentSpeak agent programming languages running on the Agent Factory platform. Unlike in previous years where a hybrid control architecture was used, this year the system was implemented using only agent code and associated actions, sensors, modules and platform services.

1 Introduction

This years entry to the 2011 Multi-Agent Programming Contest was designed and built using the Agent Factory framework, which provides support for the development and deployment of agent-based applications using a variety of Agent-Oriented Programming (AOP) languages [5]. As with the previous years entry, our approach was centered around the use of two specific AOP languages: *AF-AgentSpeak*, an AgentSpeak variant that is based on Jason [4] and *AF-TeleoReactive*, an implementation of Nilssons Teleo-Reactive programming language [8]. Both of these langages were implemented using the Common Language Framework [11], a set of reusable components that aims to simplify the prototyping of AOP languages.

This is the fourth year in which a team from University College Dublin has participated in the contest. Last year [1] the team performed well in the herding scenario coming in third in the contest, that entry building on the work of the two preceding years [7,6]. This years team included four members from the previous year: Rem Collier (lecturer), Sean Russell (Ph.D. Student), Dominic Carr (Ph.D. Student) and Gregory O'Hare (professor). Rem and Gregory are active researchers in the area of Multi-Agent Systems and AOP languages, Sean and Dominic are working in the area of agent-enabled Wireless Sensor Networks. The final member of the team was Balazs Pete, a 2nd year undergraduate student who worked on the contest as part of a summer internship.

Our primary motivation to compete in the contest was to test and debug AgentFactory, and further refine and direct its development trajectory. As in in previous years we were strongly motivated to provide new researchers with practical exposure to AOP using Agent Factory. The contest fits this need, well

---

[1] http://www.multiagentcontest.org/2011

L.A. Dennis, O. Boissier, and R.H. Bordini (Eds.): ProMAS 2011, LNCS 7217, pp. 197–207, 2012.
© Springer-Verlag Berlin Heidelberg 2012

providing an interesting problem to solve. We also wanted to drive language development within AgentFactory.

To this end, one of our goals was to remove our dependency on a behaviour-based architecture that had previously been used to implement core behaviours of the system. Instead, we aimed to increase our utilization of AOP languages, and to replace the behavioural layer with Teleo-Reactive functions. Additionally, we sought to use the Environment Interface Standard (EIS)[3] integration provided with the contest server instead of building a custom solution. Further details of our approach can be found in section 3.

2   System Analysis and Design

The development model used was based on a team programming approach to system development that was adopted for the previous contest [1]. At any point in time, one team member was actively engaged with coding and the other team members provided strategy analysis, debugging assistance etc. Whenever the team identified a possible strategy, a "champion" was assigned to seperate from the main group and to flesh out the idea. Once finished, the "champion" then presented the idea to the rest of the group. If accepted by the group, the idea was prioritised and added to the to do list.

The overall approach adopted was decided upon at the start of our involvement in the project. In essence, our objective was to maintain the centralised task allocation model used in the previous architecture, but to replace the low level behaviours with teleo-reactive functions and EIS integration. All of our analysis and design work was targeted at solutions which were compatible with this general architecture. We did not consider any of the software engineering methodologies outlined in the literature. Where necessary, Agent UML Protocol Diagrams were used to illustrate interaction protocols and pseudo code, adapted to our planning language, was used to outline plans. For the AF-TeleoReactive programs, a function hierarchy diagram was used to outline designs.

In our architecture coordination of information is carried out through the use of a number of platform services, which represent shared platform wide resources for the agents. The primary service is the map service, in simplest terms this service could be viewed as a whiteboard where agents could post relevant information to be made available to other agents, secondly it also allowed some analysis of the data to be performed e.g. identifying the highest value zones or routing between two vertices in the graph. Team coordination was achieved through the use of another platform service, the group service, which was used by the leader agent to assign tasks to the individual agents.

The attributes of *autonomy*, *pro-activeness* and *reactiveness* were implemented by making use of two AOP languages and more specifically through the structure of the *AF-TeleoReactive* programs which can allow the agents to bypass their assigned task in favour one of their own goals.

Our system is a true multi-agent system with centralised coordination. The choice of centralised coordination was made in an effort to allow the rapid prototyping of different task allocation strategies during development while abstracting from communication issues. In order to facilitate this centralised coordination, a leader agent was specified to complement the in-situ ATPV agents. This strategist agent performs some rudimentary analysis of the graph to determine the cluster of vertices with the highest value, then based on the structure of the graph a number of vertices are selected on which to position agents, which are then associated with individual agents.

During the course of the contest or prior to this we did not discuss our strategies with any other teams, this was primarily in an effort to remain competitive as our experience from participation in last years contest highlighted the importance of effective strategies. To this end we only participated in a single test match which we used to ensure we could successfully connect to the server and perform actions in a reasonable time.

The implementation of the system took approximately 600 hours, the majority of this time can be attributed to an internship undertaken by Balazs Pete over a 12 week period from June until the end of August. The remainder of the time can be accounted for when the rest of the team picked up the development two weeks before the contest.

3   Software Architecture

As in previous years, our system utilised Agent Factory (AF) [5] as our underlying agent technology. AF is an open-source Java-based framework that provides support for the development and deployment of agent-oriented applications. Specifically, it provides a generic Run-Time Environment (RTE) for deploying agent-based systems that is based on the FIPA standards [9] together with a set of *development kits* that facilitate the implementation of diverse agent types, ranging from custom agent architectures to agent programming languages.

The RTE consists of a set of configurable agent platforms that contain the machinery necessary to deploy these agent types together with support for the deployment of platform-level resources, known as platform services, that are shared amongst the agents residing on the platform. Other support includes a range of monitoring and inspection tools that aid the developer in debugging their implementations.

The development kits provide the core agent interpreter/architecture together with appropriate customisations for the AF tool support. This will typically include a set of plugins for the AF Debugging Tool and an Eclipse plugin for the AF IDE (which is a set of plugins for Eclipse). For the purposes of this competition, we made use of two of the AOP language development kits packaged with AF, which are introduced next.

3.1   AF-TeleoReactive

AF-TeleoReactive is based on Nils Nilsson's Teleo-Reactive agent paradigm [8] which was designed to react to a changing environment (hence reactive) whilst still performing actions which take it to it's goal (hence teleo, meaning goal oriented). The functional components of AF-TR agents are represented by an ordered list of production rules.

An example of a production rule would be $K \rightarrow A$, where the element K represent conditions on the input from the sensors or the model of the environment, and the element A represent an action on the environment. When a sequence is being interpreted it is scanned from the top until it comes across a rule whose condition is satisfied. The corresponding action is then performed and the interpreter is then restarted from the top of the list.

Information about the current state of the environment is gathered via a set of *Sensors*: Java classes that convert raw sensor data into beliefs that are added to the agents belief set. To handle the potentially dynamic nature of the environment that the agent is sensing, beliefs stored in the AF-TR belief base do not persist by default. Instead they are wiped at the start of each iteration of the agent interpreter. To cater for beliefs that should persist, consideration must be given to this when creating the sensor, which allows the programmer to define which types of beliefs should persist. Whether a belief should persist or not depends on the nature of the item being observed. For instance, in the context of the agent contest, it would safe to adopt a temporal belief regarding the position of a edge within the map (which by its very nature cannot move) whereas a belief about the location of a enemy agent will change over time.

AF-TeleoReactive was developed based on the notion of blind commitment, is so far as the agent will continue performing an action until its actions have modified the environment sufficiently to cause another condition to fire. As such it is assumed that the continuous execution of an action will cause such a change in the environment.

3.2   AF-AgentSpeak

AF-AgentSpeak is based on Jason [4], a purpose-built agent-oriented programming language that implements an extended and improved version of Rao's AgentSpeak(L) language [10]. The language consists of a set of plan rules, examples of which are shown in Fig. 1. Each plan rule consists of a triggering event, a context and a plan containing a number of actions that should be adopted if the plan rule is selected.

The deliberation cycle of AF-AgentSpeak is an adaptation of the algorithm used in Jason that is compliant with the AF common language framework.

1. An event is selected from the set of internal and external events.
2. All plan rules triggered by this event are then selected.
3. The list of rules is reduced to those whose context evaluates to true.
4. From this list a single plan rule is selected and added to a new or existing intention stack depending on whether it is a sub plan or new plan respectively.
5. The next step from each of the agents current intentions is executed in parallel by the agent.

As with Jason, AF-AgentSpeak offers an extended suite of functionality that is not available in the original version AgentSpeak(L). This includes support for inheritance, partial plans, abstract plans, and plan overriding as described in [2]; and an extended set of plan operators, including: *foreach* (plan expansion), *while* (loops), *if* (selection), *wait* and *when* (delayed execution), and = (assignment). This extended planning language is provided as part of the Common Language Framework [11].

```
#agent Leader

module groups -> com.agentfactory.mapc.GroupModule;
module map    -> com.agentfactory.mapc.MapModule;

@initialization
+initialized : true  <-
    groups.setup(groups, [
        team(home, [Repairer, Inspector, Sentinel, Sentinel, Explorer, Explorer, Inspector]),
        team(support, [Repairer]),
        team(away, [Saboteur, Saboteur])]),
    @setup;

+sim(end) : true <-
    groups.reset,
    map.resetService,
    .println("resetting"),
    @setup;

#partial @setup <-
    .abolishAll(strategy(?t, ?x)),
    groups.setShared([cash(0), stepNo(0)]);
...
```

Fig. 1. Example AF-AgentSpeak code from the Leader agent

Figure 1 contains part of the code for the Leader agent. As can be seen in this figure, the Leader agent accesses the Group and Map services through two purpose-built modules (these same modules are used by the AF-TeleoReactive agents). On creation, the leader sets up 3 groups: a *home* group, which is responsible for building and holding the zone; an *away* group, containing the Saboteurs, and which is charged with the task of attacking the enemy; and a *support* group which contains a single Repairer and is responsible for supporting the away group. Once the groups are setup, the *@setup* partial plan is invoked, which does additional configuration steps. A partial plan is used here because the code is common to both the initialization of the agent and the resetting of the agent when the current simulation ends.

3.3   Core Architecture

The core architecture of the system is shown in Figure 3, the agents communicate through the use of the two platform services *MapService* and *GroupService*. No agent communicates directly with another agent wether it represents an ATPV or the leader which has no embodiement in the simmulation. Receiving shared data is done without any requirment to request or subscribe to particular forms of data. All agents automatically pull all relevant information during the perception phase of their execution, allowing the agent to use the shared beliefs as if they were it's own percepts. An example of this is shown in the first rule in Figure 2, this is taken from the repair function, which is activated when a dissabled agent is on the same vertex as a Repairer. The first percept is one shared through the MapService and the second and third are shared through the GroupService. The second line of the example is taken from the *doAction* function where the *?action* variable is the first parameter of the function (in this case repair) and the *?param* variable is the second (the name of the agent to be repaired).

```
agentInfo(?name,?team,?ver,Saboteur,disabled) & memberOf(home) & groupOrder(away, ?name, primary)
        -> doAction(repair,?name, .nil)

step(?step) & (?action == repair) & ~doneActionForStep(?step, ?act) -> eis.perform(repair(?param))
```

Fig. 2. Example of role based action selection

Agent communication with the server is handled through the Agent Factory EIS layer and the eismassim jar, this is shown by the second rule in Figure 2 whereby the action and parameters are passed to the service in the form of a predicate.

The agents were not distributed across multiple machines, implementation of this would have required a modification to the platform service. this was not done due to time constraints.

4   Strategies, Details and Statistics

4.1   Strategy

The overall team strategy is the combination of a number of role dependent strategies and the over all zone creation strategy. As discussed in Section 3.3 agent coordination and information sharing is done through a number of white-board type services. Based on information shared through these services, the agents will perform different actions based on their role or assigned tasks.

4.2   Agent Mental State

In general the prevailing goals which drive the agents are to hold the positions assigned by the leader, but not all agents were assigned positions. Secondary to this goal some agents may override this goal with their own periodically. An example of this would be that *Inspectors* periodically decide to refresh the teams knowledge of the attributes of the enemy and as such move to inspect each one. Agents can change their behaviour based on a number of factors such as the conditions shown in Figure 4, or the exceptions is given in Table 1.

Saboteurs are not assigned tasks, they have a priority based attack system where the priority targets are Saboteurs then Repairers and then everyone else, when en-route to a target a Saboteur will attack any enemy agent the happens to be on the same vertex. Saboteurs also use a targeting separate targeting system when two friendly Saboteurs are on the same vertex ensuring that they both selected different targets.

Repairers are also not assigned tasks directly, rather they are associated with a Saboteur which they are charged to support. To mitigate the risk of repairers being disabled when traveling to repair a teammate, we elected to have the disabled agent travel to the Repairer. This decision also allowed us to keep the two repairers in relatively close proximity to their assigned Saboteur to minimise the risk of one of them being disabled.

The agents contain an explicit mental state composed of the percepts received from the server as well as all internally generated beliefs and those received from platform services.

There are both implicit and explicit hierarchies within the structure of the agents. Informally the Leader agent is responsible for assigning tasks to a sub group of the ATPV agents. Additionally the Repairers were tasked in a support role following the Saboteurs but did not answer to them explicitly.

Agent path planning was done using a form of breadth first search which can ignore edges above a certain weight, this algorithm was chosen as it seemed that the number of steps taken to travel the a distance was more important than the amount of energy expended.

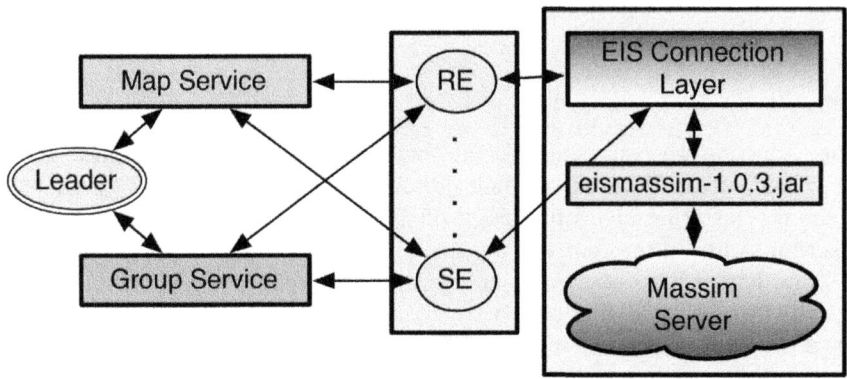

Fig. 3. Core Architecture

Table 1. Agent Autonomic Actions

Role	Condition	Action
Inspector	Enemy with data older than 100 steps	Inspect the enemy
All agents	Become disabled	Move to closest Repairer
Explorers	Map becomes dominated (all vertices owned)	Adopt goal to probe every vertex
All Agents (Except Saboteurers)	Enemy Saboteur on vertex	Parry presumed attack
Repairer	Disabled teammate on vertex	Repair teammate

4.3   Implementation Details

The topology of the map was not analysed in any great detail, basic clustering was performed to determine the best position to use as the centre of the captured zone, this is modelled on breadth first search where the cumulative value of the vertices is summed. When the value is not known it is assumed to be 1.

The agents use the eismassim package in order to communicate with the server, this is achieved through an existing integration of EIS with AgentFactory.

The role of an agent is captured during the initial percept and stored for reference within the code, in this way during the execution of the agent. An example of this is given in figure 4, the first line represents the goal that we should know the role of each of the enemy agents and the second rule states that we should refresh the information we hold on that agent if we haven't inspected them in the last 100 steps.

```
role(Inspector) & agentInfo(?name,?team,?vertex,?role,?s) & (?role == none) -> inspectAll
role(Inspector) & lastInspected(?n,?s)  & step(?step) & (?step > ?s+100) -> inspectEntity(?n)
```

Fig. 4. Example of role based action selection

4.4   Zones

Zone selection was very simplistic and was not concerned with the actual value we would attain if we we holding certain positions, instead we opted to use a simple clustering algorithm based on breadth first search to identify a good position to use as the centre of our zone.

Zone defense was designed around a well known concept in ship design whereby it is divided into a number compartments, the basic principle is that when agents are positioned two steps away from other agents, and sometimes the centre of the zone, this naturally creates a pattern where subzones exist within the zones. An example of this is shown in Figure 5(a), when an enemy attempts to break the frontier of the zone the compartment collapses but the rest of the zone remains, this is shown in Figure 5(b).

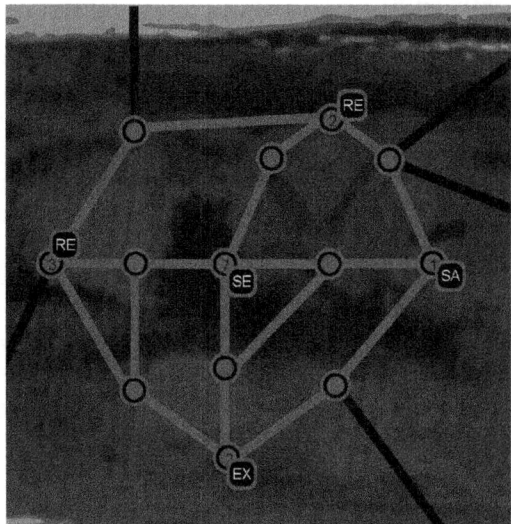

(a) Zone configuration

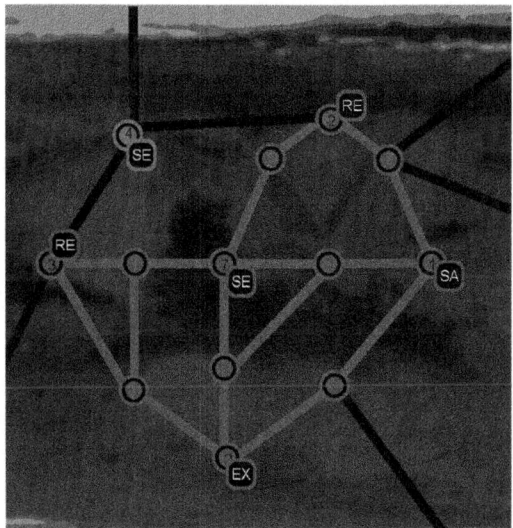

(b) Zone configuration under attack

Fig. 5. Subgraphs showing zone configuration

We did not specifically implement a team behavior for attacking enemy zones but this occasionally emerges out of aggressive Saboteur behavior, or frontiers may be broken by an Inspector approaching to inspect enemy agents.

4.5   Buying Algorithm

We used a complex recursive buying function designed to maximise the effectiveness of the our Saboteur agents, it was designed to react to the attributes of the enemy agents always ensuring that based on our current knowledge we could disable any of the enemies agents with one hit and survive one hit from the enemy saboteurs. The function was designed recursively such that when the cash was available a number of agents could purchase simultaneously based on a hard coded priority.

The achievement points were very important in our strategy as a number of our victories were based on the fact that our Saboteurs we able to dominate the enemy Saboteurs. Secondarily we relied on excess achievement points being spent on a very high visibility for one of the teams Sentinels in order to keep as much information on the enemy movements as current as possible.

As an aside during the final game when it was clear that we could not increase our standing in the league table we attempted a strategy whereby the team did not spend any of the achievement points. By the end of the simulation we had amassed 54 points resulting in a much more competitive and exciting simulation.

5   Conclusion

From our participation in the contest were were enable to evaluate and test the functionality of modifications made to the languages we were using. The contest proves every year to be an impetus for development of new features and thorough testing within the languages created using the Common Language Framework. It has further affirmed the stability of the chosen languages for their roles within the architecture of the system, In that Af-Agentspeak is suited for the organisational role of the leader and AF-TeleoReactive is suited for the more reactive and time dependent control of the ATPV units in the simulation.

The team overall performed well, the individual roles of the agents sometimes combining to work very well together, at an individual level the strategy of the agents worked quite well but on some occasions the team as a whole became uncoordinated. This resulted from a error in our approach to development, focusing too much on the low level individual strategies than the higher level coordination strategies.

As in our conclusion last year we believe that the results of the competition reflect the effectiveness of the team strategies. In both of the games with the top two teams we were outclassed in terms of strategy and as a result we were comprehensively beaten. Our closest match was with third placed TUB, despite losing all the simulations, it was much closer and much more exciting than any of the games with the lower ranked teams.

For next years contest some changes we would consider beneficial would be to introduce more static assignment of roles to agents, we believe that this could allow a greater diversity in capabilities and characteristics of the ATPVs.

References

1. Russell, S.E., Carr, D., Dragone, M., O'Hare, G.M.P., Collier, R.W.: From Bogtrotting to Herding: A UCD Perspective. Annals of Mathematics and Artificial Intelligence 61(4) (April 2011)
2. Jordan, H.R., Russell, S.E., O'Hare, G.M.P., Collier, R.W.: Reuse by Inheritance in Agent Programming Languages. In: Brazier, F.M.T., Nieuwenhuis, K., Pavlin, G., Warnier, M., Badica, C. (eds.) Intelligent Distributed Computing V. SCI, vol. 382, pp. 279–289. Springer, Heidelberg (2011)
3. Behrens, T., Hindriks, K., Dix, J.: Towards an environment interface standard for agent platforms. Annals of Mathematics and Artificial Intelligence 61, 3–38 (2011)
4. Bordini, R.H., Hübner, J.F., Wooldridge, M.: Programming multi-agent systems in AgentSpeak using Jason, vol. 8. Wiley-Interscience (2008)
5. Collier, R.W.: Agent Factory: A Framework for the Engineering of Agent-Oriented Applications. PhD thesis, School of Computer Science and Informatics (2002)
6. Dragone, M., Lillis, D., Muldoon, C., Tynan, R., Collier, R.W., O'Hare, G.M.P.: Dublin Bogtrotters: Agent Herders. In: Hindriks, K.V., Pokahr, A., Sardina, S. (eds.) ProMAS 2008. LNCS, vol. 5442, pp. 243–247. Springer, Heidelberg (2009)
7. Jordan, H., Treanor, J., Lillis, D., Dragone, M., Collier, R.W., O'Hare, G.M.P.: AFABLE in the multi agent contest. Annals of Mathematics and Artificial Intelligence, 1–21 (2009)
8. Nilsson, N.: Teleo-reactive programs for agent control. Arxiv preprint cs/9401101 (1994)
9. Poslad, S., Buckle, P., Hadingham, R.: The FIPA-OS agent platform: Open source for open standards. In: Proceedings of the 5th International Conference and Exhibition on the Practical Application of Intelligent Agents and Multi-Agents, pp. 355–368 (2000)
10. Rao, A.: AgentSpeak (L): BDI Agents Speak Out in a Logical Computable Language. In: Van de Velde, W., Perram, J.W. (eds.) MAAMAW 1996. LNCS, vol. 1038, pp. 42–55. Springer, Heidelberg (1996)
11. Russell, S., Jordan, H., O'Hare, G.M.P., Collier, R.W.: Agent Factory: A Framework for Prototyping Logic-Based AOP Languages. In: Klügl, F., Ossowski, S. (eds.) MATES 2011. LNCS, vol. 6973, pp. 125–136. Springer, Heidelberg (2011)

A Gaia-Driven Approach for Competitive Multi-Agent Systems

Sahar Mirzayi, Vahid Nateghi, and Fatemeh Eskandari

Department of Computer Engineering, Faculty of Engineering
Arak University – Arak 38156-8-8349, Iran
{sahar.mirzayi,vahid.nateghi,fatemeh.eskandari.69}@gmail.com

Abstract. This is a report on Simurgh team's participation in the 2011 multi-agent contest. The design and development process, architecture details, and team strategies for the multi-agent system have been discussed, along with experiences of the developers. Gaia methodology was used for the design and analysis of the Simurgh multi-agent system. The main strategy was obtaining a higher score through the support of agents with a better perceived strategic placement. Decision correction strategy was used to change the agent behavior, by taking the other conflicting team members' decisions, into account. Simurgh was implemented using Java language. Agents have the same degree of autonomy and the team is implemented in a completely decentralized fashion.

Keywords: Multi-Agent System, Gaia, Decentralized Coordination, Dynamic Role Assignment.

1 Introduction

The multi-agent programming contest (MAPC) is held every year in the pursuit of expanding researches and testing frameworks and development environments for the Multi-Agent Systems (MAS) [1]. In 2011, for the first time, Simurgh [1] team took part in the contest, in order to improve its knowledge of MAS. Taking part in MAPC was a project of "specialized studies in software engineering" course. Most of the material presented in the course was about analysis, design and development of MAS. The MAPC organizers introduced the "Mars" scenario for this year's competition, which was a complete redesign and different to the scenarios used in previous contests, especially in that the map was based on a graph this year. The Simurgh team decided to use Gaia methodology [2] for the analysis and design of the agents and use Java as the implementation language. The analysis phase started from Jan 2011 and because of multiple changes in the scenario, the development continued on until September.

---

[1] Simurgh is an old Persian myth, quite similar to the Phoenix, however, a Phoenix is believed to be quite small and to be reborn from its ashes, whereas a Simurgh is believed to be big, very wise, and can be called upon by burning one of its feathers.

L.A. Dennis, O. Boissier, and R.H. Bordini (Eds.): ProMAS 2011, LNCS 7217, pp. 208–216, 2012.

Simurgh is compromised of three members, Sahar Mirzayi, Vahid Nateghi and Fatemeh Eskandari. Mirzayi is a Graduate student at Arak University. Her interests are soft computing and distributed systems. Nateghi and Eskandari are under graduate students at Arak University, interested in the field of robotics.

2   System Analysis and Design

Our team used Gaia methodology for the analysis and design of Simurgh because of its high reactiveness property, accessibility of its notation and modeling and its flexibility. Even though Gaia has the same precision property in comparison with Tropos [3], clearness and understandability of Gaia were the main reasons for our choice. Furthermore Gaia is appropriate for developing systems with small number of agent types. It is a general methodology that supports analysis and design of both the individual agent structure and the agent society in the MAS development process. According to Gaia, MAS is viewed as a composition of a number of autonomous and interactive agents existing in a society, in which each agent plays one or more specific roles.

Gaia defines the structure of MAS in terms of role model [4], the model which identifies the roles that agents have to play within the MAS, and the interaction protocols between the different roles. The objective of the Gaia analysis process is the identification of the roles and modeling the interactions between them. the role model phase of Simurgh was analyzed using Gaia, the roles were identified as follows: the *Server Connector* role is responsible for connecting to the server, receiving perceptions and sending actions back. Agents should be capable of translating perceptions and extracting information within perceptions, this is the *Parser* role. The *Team Communicator* is another role which has to facilitate communication with other teammates and share perceptions and decisions with them. Moreover, the agents should explore the map and try to complete the world model; this is the operation for which the *World Explorer* role is responsible. The *Zone Holder* is a role which should try to create a zone or expand available zones. Some agents might be disabled by opponent's agents, the *Helper* role has to find these agents' positions and then approach and repair them. The *Water Well Explorer* role is responsible for finding water wells and increasing the team's score. Because in this year's scenario, opponents can attack each other the *Attacker* role is defined to blemish the nearest opponent's agents if there are any. The *Chaser* role is also defined for gathering position data on enemies' agents and to attack them. Because agents must have a plan to preserve themselves, the *Defender* role is also defined for parry. *Opponent Analyzer* role tries to inspect enemies in the maps' vertices. And there is also the *Savior* role, which helps teammates under opponent attack.

The roles are dynamically assigned to agents. The rules governing the dynamic role assignments are covered in section 4.

The requirements of the MAS were prioritized as goals. According to the scenario and our strategy, *supporting the best positioned agents, by other teammate, to obtain the highest score*, was our first priority. A very valuable goal is creating zones in the map by finding the nearest friend using the Dijkstra algorithm, but if there were already some zones, then the highest priority is assigned to the agents who can expand the most valuable available zone. Also, if there are some disabled agents, the important goal for the Repairer is to help these disabled teammates. So the priorities of goals for each role are different. The goals are as following:

- Move to a node for creating a zone
- Move to a node for expanding the zone
- Stand in a certain place to keep the zone
- Repair a disabled agent
- Move to a node for repairing a disabled agent
- Probe the node
- Move to a node for probing
- Parry
- Attack
- Move to a node for attacking opponents
- Move to a node for saving teammates
- Survey the map
- Buy

The most important goal is creating a zone. For each of the goals, a proper algorithm is designed and implemented according to team strategies, which will be discussed in section 4. All agents have the same degree of autonomy, which makes our implementation a true MAS.

Simurgh used a decentralized coordination and cooperation mechanism for implementing agents, which will be described in the following. In the beginning of each step, agents share their perception to other teammates via a shared channel and then update their perception according to the received perception messages from the channel. In each step, agents define some goals and inter-operate with other agents to make a final decision according to other agents' goals, autonomously. When agents share their goal with teammates, if there is a conflict between goals of two agents in the current step, one of them chooses to change its goal to prevent a conflict. It was decided that an agent with the lowest potential score for the team, changes its decision but according to deadline approach, this could not be implemented, therefore, in the final version, the agent which had to change its goal was chosen by its goal's priority. The agent should then replace its goal with the one that doesn't have any conflict with other teammates' goals. In conflicting situations, the agent with better energy proceeds and the other one changes its action. The conflicts found in agents' decisions are listed below:

- If two Explorers try to explore a same node one of them is doing a useless action. So there is a conflict between two explore actions.
- If two agents try to survey the same node, one of them can do another action because the resulting perceptions are shared at the beginning of each step. In this case, the agent who has a larger visibility range does the action and the other one should change its decision.

- Inspections done in the same node have the same result and therefore, redundant. One of the agents should change its decision.
- When an agent tries to create a zone with a teammate, this teammate should not move to other nodes for any reason except repairs.
- When an agent is trying to expand its zone, other agents in the zone, which have a maximum distance of 2 from it, shouldn't move to nodes which have a maximum distance of more than 2 from the agent's new position.

Doing 2 Go-to actions with the goal of repairing a same agent, must not generate a conflict, because one of the repairers may face an attack and not be able to get to the disabled agent. After taking these precautions, conflicts are still possible because a second level of chosen goal message sharing was not implemented.

According to the above, two types of communication were needed: shared perception messages and shared chosen goal messages. Shared perception messages are sent and received at the beginning of each step and the shared chosen goal messages are exchanged after all agents make a decision about their goal. Because each agent communicates with its teammates via a shared channel, communication complexity in each step will be $O(n)$, in which n is the number of agents. Gaia can transform the analysis models into a sufficiently low level of abstraction. The design phase of Gaia is agent model design [3]. The purpose of the agent model is to document the various types of agents that would be used in the system. Creating the agent model means aggregation of roles into agent types [5]. The agent model of Simurgh is shown in figure 1. Agent types in the system are defined in MAPC scenario as Explorer, Repairer, Saboteur, Sentinel, and Inspector. Each agent should implement the Server Connector, Parser, Team Communicator and World Explorer roles. As we described in section 4 explorers and saboteurs don't implement the Zone Holder role. One of the saboteurs has attacker role and the other has chaser role.

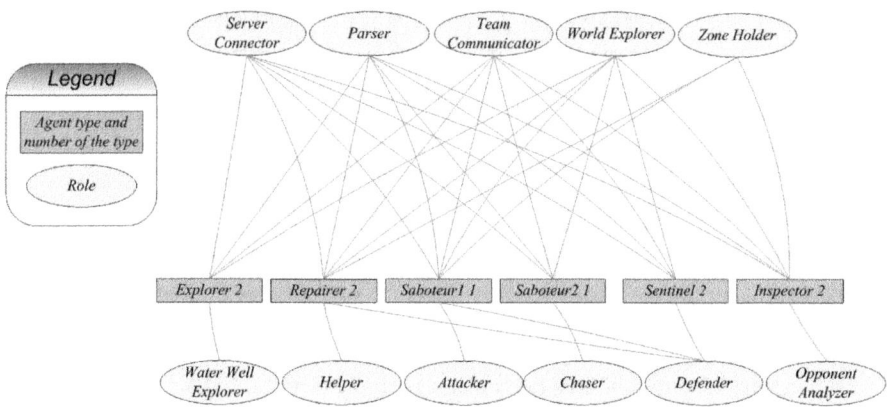

Fig. 1. Agent model diagram

3 Software Architecture

The difficulties faced during the implementation, mainly stem from goal choice. For example finding a good algorithm to create zones and keep them, required hundreds of test-runs. The communication complexity is not a major problem and doesn't force developers to use a specific runtime platform. Simurgh has been implemented using Java programming language and J2SE. The messaging between agents to share perceptions and decisions also uses apltk package features. As our team members were already familiar with Java, there was no learning curve for using the programming language.

The agent's architecture is shown in figure 2. Some of the ideas behind the design of agent architecture were adapted from [6]. The eis-massim package [7]

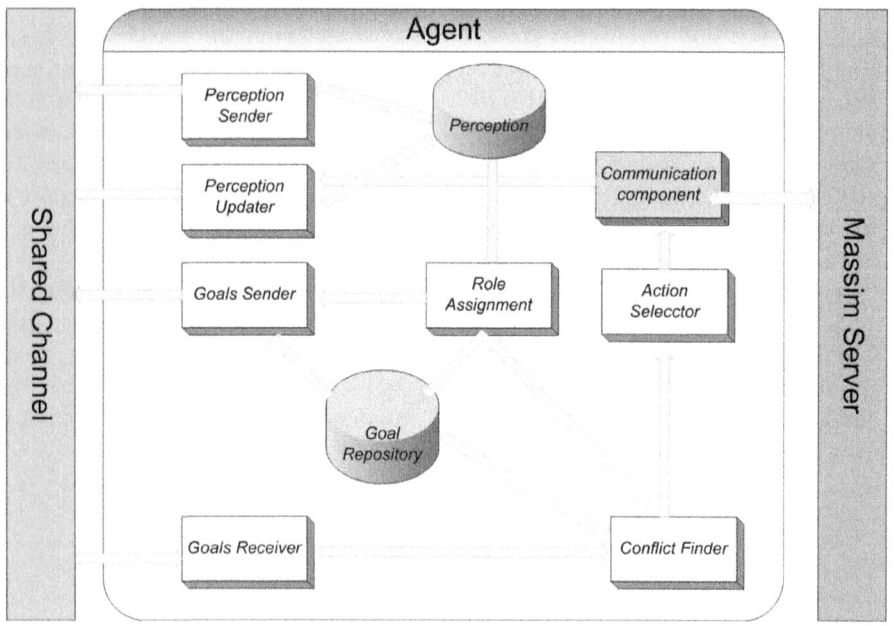

Fig. 2. The agent's architecture

was used as the component for communication with the server. Inspired from black board design pattern [8], the channel is a shared data structure where all agents can push and pull messages. The perception updater module extracts information from perceptions and saves it in an understandable format for agents. The perception sender shares perception with other teammates. The role assignment chooses a role for the agent according to the perceived strategic placement. Then the proper goal is selected from the goal repository. The goals are sent to teammates for decision correction. If there is a conflict between two agents' goals, the conflict finder exposes them. The new role assignment process will be done, thereafter. In the end, proper actions are selected and sent to the server.

Java doesn't provide a convenient message broadcast mechanism. Moreover, synchronization points cause bottlenecks because the independent code lines after the point can't execute and agents should stop decision process until others reach the point. Using an object-oriented programming language accelerates the design and implementation process. Furthermore, using eis-massim, encapsulates connection handling details. Therefore, the whole implementation is just a bit more than 4000 lines of code.

The synchronization takes less than 1 percent of each step's length. All agents execute on the same physical machine, as the computation cost of the agents is relatively low and as latency of connection to the server was one of our biggest barriers, distribution of agents did not appear to be a wise deployment decision.

4   Strategies, Details and Statistics

In order to get to know the environment and fill the agents' world model as soon as possible, in the first ten steps, all agents have the explorer role. They survey and go to new random vertices. After these steps, roles are assigned to agents iteratively during the rest of the tournament. Then each agent should follow a specific set of instructions according to its role.

Some criteria trigger agents to change their roles, such as: being disabled, being in a zone, being near a better zone, possibility of an attack, having a low level of energy and the existence of a disabled teammate.

If an agent is low on energy, it recharges itself. If an agent is disabled, it tries to approach a helper until it acquires energy. However a disabled repairer tries to repair other teammates first (helper role), and then tries to approach other repairers to acquire energy. The zone holder role (all agent types except explorers and saboteurs) first expands the zone by scattering away from teammate in the right manner. If the zone can not be expanded anymore and there is a bigger nearby zone, an agent may leave the zone and join the other. If a zone holder senses a nearby probed node, it will change its position, so that the score of the node is achieved in the current step. If a zone holder doesn't find a zone it tries to find the nearest zone holder agent and create a zone with it. The water well explorer tries to survey new nodes in a way that new non-probed vertices are visited. the World Explorer role uses a taboo list to fill the world model quickly. If a savior receives a help message from a nearby teammate which it has a maximum distance of two, it will decide to attack the opponent in the next two steps. A chaser gathers opponents' position information and chases them with the goal of an attack. When an agent knows that there is an attacker in its node, it chooses the defender role and parries itself. An inspector chooses the opponent analyzer role when an attack occur.

As described earlier, each agent shares its world model updates with team-mates and then sends their decisions and if there is a conflict, it will be changed in a way that the higher priority goal would be followed. At the end of each step, agents send their actions to the server using the eis-massim package.

The main strategy of Simurgh is Cooperation with teammates and supporting them to realize better goals. There is no central or hierarchal leadership and data doesn't route to any specific agent.

Each agent has a world model that contains every detail captured from per-ception messages. The most important element in the world model is the map, a weighted graph in which both edges and vertices are weighted. The other el-ements found in the world model are teammate positions, disabled teammates, repairer teammates, teammates who are in a zone, savior teammates, each zone's position and its score, explored water wells and enemies' positions. if agents don't have enough information about the world model (usually in the first steps of the tournament) they should move to nodes in a random fashion, in which case, a taboo list of visited nodes is kept to avoid visiting nodes twice for several steps to ensure that world exploring is done as soon as possible.

Each agent evaluates zones separately by the formula 1, as follow:

$$ZoneValue_{i,j} = \frac{\alpha * score_i}{\sum_k score_k} + \frac{\beta * distance_{ij}}{\sum_h distance_{hj}} \tag{1}$$

Where i is the zone's number, j is the agent's number, $score_k$ is the score of the kth zone, $distance_{h,j}$ is the distance of jth agent from nearest agent in the hth zone. α and β are constant values which are chosen by experimental tests as $\alpha = 3$ and $\beta = 2$. If an agent has the zone holder role, it tries to join the zone with better Zone Value.

Finding enemies' zones and conquering them was not a part of our strategy but agents can defend zones using the savior role. For finding the shortest path to an agent, an improved Dijkstra algorithm [9] is used.

To improve the attacking power of the team, attacker and savior roles are allowed to use achievements' points and buy items like a shield, a sensor and three sabotage devices, when the team is in the risk of a huge attack. Although Simurgh uses achievement points to make purchases, no specific plan was developed to increase achievement points.

Agents don't have a mental state and plan for one step and if the priority doesn't force them to change their goal, the last goal is maintained. This goal has to be realized by exactly one agent. Although Our Agents' behaviors are planned individually, an agent must know how to provide valuable information to a specific teammate, for example, while chasing down enemy agents, some feedback from nearby teammate agents might be needed.

5   Conclusion

Simurgh members were new to the field of multi-agent programming. In that regard, MAPC was a very unique and valuable experience in design and implementation of MAS. The first lesson learned during the implementation is that multi-agent development methodologies are very diverse, and to make a proper choice of methodology, thorough investigations are needed. There are many multi-agent programming languages and tools, some of which directly implement the multi agent theory, while others extend existing languages to suit the MAS paradigm. The second lesson learned from MAPC was that different communication strategies are needed for decision making and realizing goals between agents living in a same society. Different approaches were examined and tested and choices were made based on the best results. Central leadership, hierarchal leadership and group-based goal realization with multiple leaders were surveyed; however, it was ultimately decided to have a monolithic society in which all agents can choose a goal according to their capabilities and coordination.

Because of the lack of reliable high speed connection and high delay times, we missed half of the tournaments and finally achieved the 6th place. Some strength and weaknesses were found in the team design. For example, Simurgh could parry very well because if an agent inspects an attacker, it informs the team savior agents quickly. Choosing the helper role instead of zone holder has a higher priority for repairers, so sometimes our zone broke during the movement of our repairers. We did not put any emphasis on attacks in Simurgh, especially breaking enemies' zones, so other teams could gain score simply when competing against us. The zone expanding algorithm has some weaknesses that cause zone breaking. This is one of the problems we hope to resolve for the next year's contest. Furthermore, for the next MAPC we hope to improve our attacks and design an algorithm for finding opponent's zones'.

Gaia proved to be a good base methodology for Simurgh MAS development. It was flexible, clear and understandable. Moreover J2SE did not impose any worrying constraints on us.

In the scenario, coloring algorithms could be improved. For example, zones should be able to expand only in 3 or 4 levels of colored nodes, so that if most agents of a team are disabled, the opponent can't expand the zone to the whole map.

References

1. Behrens, T., et al.: The multi-agent programming contest from 2005-2010. Annals of Mathematics and Artificial Intelligence 59, 277–311 (2010)
2. Zambonelli, F., et al.: Developing multiagent systems: The Gaia methodology. ACM Transactions on Software Engineering and Methodology (TOSEM) 12, 317–370 (2003)
3. Castro, J., et al.: Towards requirements-driven information systems engineering: the Tropos project. Information systems 27, 365–389 (2002)

4. Juan, T., et al.: ROADMAP: extending the gaia methodology for complex open systems, pp. 3–10 (2002)
5. Wooldridge, M., et al.: The Gaia methodology for agent-oriented analysis and design. Autonomous Agents and Multi-Agent Systems 3, 285–312 (2000)
6. Rafe, V., et al.: Galoan: a multi-agent approach to herd cows. Annals of Mathematics and Artificial Intelligence, 1–16
7. Behrens, T., et al.: The Environment Interface Standard for Agent-Oriented Programming Platform Integration Guide and Interface Implementation Guide (2009)
8. Wang, B., et al.: Active Blackboard Design Pattern for Distributed Agents Coordination. Computer Engineering 9 (2004)
9. Horowitz, E., et al.: Fundamentals of data structures in C. Silicon Press (2007)

Author Index

GPSR Compliance

The European Union's (EU) General Product Safety Regulation (GPSR) is a set of rules that requires consumer products to be safe and our obligations to ensure this.

If you have any concerns about our products, you can contact us on ProductSafety@springernature.com

In case Publisher is established outside the EU, the EU authorized representative is:

Springer Nature Customer Service Center GmbH
Europaplatz 3
69115 Heidelberg, Germany

Batch number: 09490872

Printed by Printforce, the Netherlands